CALVIN
AND
CLASSICAL PHILOSOPHY

CALVIN AND CLASSICAL PHILOSOPHY

CHARLES PARTEE

WESTMINSTER
JOHN KNOX PRESS
LOUISVILLE · KENTUCKY

Published in 1977 by E. J. Brill, Leiden, Netherlands

Published by Westminster John Knox Press, Louisville, Kentucky

This book is printed on acid-free paper that meets the American National Standards Institute Z39.48 standard. ♾

PRINTED IN THE UNITED STATES OF AMERICA

05 06 07 08 09 10 11 12 13 14 — 10 9 8 7 6 5 4 3 2 1

Library of Congress Cataloging-in-Publication Data

A catalog record for this book is available from the Library of Congress.
ISBN 0-664-22915-8

TO MARGARET

CONTENTS

PART ONE

CALVIN AND CHRISTIAN PHILOSOPHY

PART TWO

CALVIN AND PHILOSOPHY

PART THREE

CALVIN AND THE PHILOSOPHERS

PREFACE

In designating his work as "Christian philosophy," John Calvin uses a term which, in the sixteenth century, refers to the theological program of the Christian humanists in general. This program is based not only on a reformation of the understanding of Scripture and a recovery of patristic thought, but it also includes an appreciation of the insights of classical philosophy.

This study is devoted to the relationship between Calvin and classical philosophy. After an introductory section dealing with Calvin's *conception* of Christian philosophy, we turn in Part Two to an *exposition* of Calvin's use of some of the insights of classical philosophy and in Part Three to an *evaluation* of Calvin's judgments of the classical philosophers in general and with special regard to the understanding of the doctrine of providence.

I would like to thank President Keith G. Briscoe and the Board of Trustees of Buena Vista College for financial support; also the Officers of the Schaller Presbyterian Church; the Auburn Presbyterian Church and the Bruns family.

I would also like to express my gratitude to the editor of this series; to Professors E. David Willis and Robert J. Tollefson who read the manuscript; to Sally Arends who typed it; to Evelyn Johnson who prepared the index; and most of all to my wife, Margaret McC. Partee to whom it is dedicated.

ABBREVIATIONS

ANF   *The Ante-Nicene Fathers*
CO   The *Calvini Opera* of the *Corpus Reformatorum*
CRZ   *Huldreich Zwinglis sämmtliche Werke* in the *Corpus Reformatorum*
EO   The *Opera Omnia* of Erasmus
LCC   Calvin's *Institutes* in the Library of Christian Classics edition
MPG   *Patrologiae cursus completus*, series Graeca, ed. by J. P. Migne
MPL   *Patrologiae cursus completus*, series Latina, ed. by J. P. Migne
OS   *Calvini Opera Selecta*, ed. by P. Barth and W. Niesel
WA   The Weimarer Ausgabe of Luther's works

PART ONE

CALVIN AND CHRISTIAN PHILOSOPHY

INTRODUCTION

The relation between philosophy and theology is a subject of perennial interest. One might hold that philosophy is the schoolmaster of the Greeks leading to God, as the law is the schoolmaster of the Hebrews. One might think that philosophy is the handmaiden of theology, or conversely that theology is a primitive and imaginative stage on the way to the development of philosophy. Again, they might be considered as differing disciplines with incompatible goals and methods.

In general, the sixteenth century reformers respect the integrity of philosophy, yet they find it useful as an intellectual preparation and as a source of complementary and contrasting insights which may be utilized in proclaiming the gospel. Thus some of the Christian humanists use the term "Christian philosophy" to indicate a program of reformation which includes a return to a purer version of Christianity, based on the Scripture and the patristic fathers, but also to a better use of the insights of classical philosophy.

In Chapter One we will sketch some aspects of the philosophical tradition of Christian humanism as a background and context for Calvin's thought. In Chapter Two we will be concerned with Calvin's description of Christian philosophy as based on the Scripture and guided by the Holy Spirit.

CHAPTER ONE

CHRISTIAN HUMANISM AND CHRISTIAN PHILOSOPHY

The life and work of John Calvin is approachable from many directions. Among other things, he is a political leader, a church reformer, a theologian, a biblical exegete, a French literary figure, and a Christian humanist. This study is devoted to one aspect of Calvin's humanism, that is, his relation to philosophy. The story of the relation between philosophy and Christian thought is long and complex. Almost from the beginning, Christian theology has defined itself in terms of, or in opposition to, certain philosophical positions. Augustine writes, "I beg you, do not let the philosophy of the Gentiles be more honest than our Christian philosophy, for its name means the quest or love of wisdom."[1] Our concern in this chapter is the use of the term "Christian philosophy" in the sixteenth century in so far as it indicates a positive appreciation of classical philosophy.

In recent times the term "Christian philosophy" is often employed to describe medieval thought. Etienne Gilson, one of the leading exponents of this usage, asserts that the Christian *religion* is based on grace, but holds that Christian *philosophy* depends on a certain view of nature. This means that "the essential result of Christian philosophy is a deeply considered affirmation of a reality and goodness intrinsic to nature."[2] Gilson's paradigm for Christian philosophy is the Thomistic view of the relative integrity of nature from grace and reason from revelation.[3] "Thus I call Christian, every philosophy

---

[1] Augustine, "Against Julian," trans. by Matthew A. Schumacher, 35 (New York: Fathers of the Church, Inc., 1957), 228-9 (MPL XLIV, 774). The term "Christian philosophy" was also employed by Alexander, Bishop of Lycopolis, MPG, XVIII, 411.

[2] Etienne Gilson, *The Spirit of Medieval Philosophy*, trans. by A. H. C. Downes (New York: Charles Scribner's Sons, 1936), p. 420.

[3] See Chapter three of Gilson's *Reason and Revelation in the Middle Ages* (New York: Charles Scribner's Sons, 1938), p. 69ff. Gilson does not cite the term "Christian philosophy" in Thomas. See the bibliography in the French edition of *L'Esprit de la philosophie médiévale*, pp. 413ff. This bibliography is omitted in the English edition. However the term was used in the Middle Ages as shown by J. Leclerq, "Pour l'histoire de l'expression Philosophie chrétienne," *Mélanges de sciences religieuses*, IX (1952), 221-6.

which, although keeping the two orders formally distinct, nevertheless considers the Christian revelation as an indispensable auxiliary to reason."[4]

In the sixteenth century, however, the term "Christian philosophy" is used in a different and important sense by some of the Christian humanists in referring to their program of reforming Christian thought by returning to the correct understanding of Holy Scripture and purer Christianity in opposition to what they consider to be the fruitless speculations and philosophical accretions of scholastic theology. These reformers seek not only a proper and faithful understanding of the Scriptures and patristic theology, but also a better and freer use of the wisdom of classical thought which does not jeopardize the revealed truth of God. For them revelation is not auxiliary to reason, rather reason is auxiliary to faith.[5] That is to say, they object to the speculative use of reason to seek out hidden things, but not to its humble application to the understanding of God's word. Christian philosophy in the sixteenth century does not attempt a synthesis of revealed and reasoned theology in the Thomistic manner, but is willing, and even eager, to use the insights of classical philosophy as an aid to the exposition of Christian theology and as an admirable example of the fact that God has not left himself entirely without witness even among the pagans. Thus the Christian humanists study the philosophers not in order to achieve a balance between the unaided and the enlightened mind, but to point out the approximations of Christian truth which may be seen by the light of nature and also the darkness into which the errors of the philosophers lead.

Of course, the entire Renaissance recovery of and enthusiasm for classical learning is involved in the knowledge and appreciation of classical thought and culture on the part of the humanists. Moreover, since many, if not most, of the humanists are Christians in some sense, it is difficult to distinguish the Christian humanists from other humanists with precision. Paul Kristeller suggests that the Christian humanists "are those scholars with a humanist classical and rhetorical

---

[4] Gilson, *The Spirit of Medieval Philosophy*, p. 37.

[5] Since Christian philosophy for Erasmus and Calvin is based on faith rather than reason, Gilson argues that theirs is not properly Christian philosophy at all but theology in his *Christianity and Philosophy*, trans. by Ralph MacDonald (New York: Sheed and Ward, 1939), pp. 14, 18.

training who explicitly discussed religious or theological problems in all or some of their writings."[6]

It is true that the rhetorical tradition is an important identifying mark. As the Christian humanists use rhetoric, its relation to dialectics is a matter of emphasis. That is to say, they do not deny the values of dialectic, but they are more interested in the persuasive clarity of the truth than the irrefragibility of logic. In Plato and Isocrates one sees a conflict between rhetoric and philosophy. Plato opposes rhetoric, the art of persuasion,[7] to dialectic, the art of correct division and generalization.[8] Plato thinks of persuasion as a matter of opinion based on probability; dialectic he regards as a matter of knowledge based on truth.[9] The discussion develops in Aristotle's seeking to rescue rhetoric from the obloquy of Sophistic flattery, by teaching that rhetoric is the counterpart of dialectic.[10] In Cicero, whose ideal is the combination of rhetoric and philosophy which he sees exemplified in both Plato and Aristotle, wisdom is to be combined with rhetoric.[11]

The same emphasis on the combination of rhetoric and dialectic is seen in Augustine. Augustine, who was trained as a rhetorician, insists that dialectics is of great service in understanding the Scripture.[12] In Book Four of his *Christian Doctrine* he makes the point that rhetoric is necessary for the Christian orator, but truth is more important than the style of expression. The youthful study of the rules of oratory is not to be despised, but the study of the sacred writers who combine eloquence and wisdom, is sufficient to teach the wise man both what and how to communicate.

[6] Paul Oskar Kristeller, *The Classics and Renaissance Thought* (Cambridge: Harvard University Press, 1953), p. 86.

[7] *Gorgias*, 453 a. The classical writers, unless otherwise noted, are cited in the English translations of the Loeb Classical Library, emended against the original texts.

[8] *Phaedrus*, 266 b.

[9] *Ibid.*, 272 d. Interestingly in the *Phaedrus*, 279 a Plato suggests that the young Isocrates has an element of philosophy in him and would not be content with rhetoric.

[10] *Rhetorica*, I. 1354 a. Cicero, *De Finibus*, V. 4. 10 says that logic includes the rules of rhetoric and dialectic.

[11] Cicero, *De Oratore*, III. 35. 141-3; III. 19. 73; and III. 31. 122. See also Jerrold E. Seigel, *Rhetoric and Philosophy in Renaissance Humanism* (Princeton: Princeton University Press, 1968), p. 7ff. Cicero, *De Officiis*, I. 1. 4 suggests that Plato could have been an orator if he had been willing to devote his attention to it.

[12] *On Christian Doctrine*, trans. by J. F. Shaw (Chicago: William Benton, 1952), II, 31 (MPL XXXIV, 57).

Likewise the Christian humanists are concerned with clarity in the service of truth rather than with syllogisms in the service of logic or embellishment in the service of persuasion. Since Melanchthon thinks that truth and clarity go together, he defends the clarity of rhetoric in opposition to the obscurity of some philosophy, but insists that dialectic and rhetoric are joined by nature.[13] The Christian humanists associate scholasticism with sophistry and dialectical pride which seeks to find God at the end of a series of logical distinctions rather than with the attempt to make the truth evident and therefore persuasive. Moreover, as Rice observes,

> The Scholastics answered the question "Is theology a science?" in the affirmative; the fathers answered it negatively. Theology is not a scientia, but a sapientia, not a systematically ordered body of true certain knowledge derived from the certain but undemonstrable principles of revelation, but a doctrina sacra derived from the pagina sacra of Scripture, a holy rhetoric in the humble service of the text, unprofaned by the syllogism of the *Posterior Analytics*.[14]

Calvin certainly appreciates the values of logic. He places medicine, jurisprudence, astronomy, geometry, and logic (dialectica) among the learned sciences which proceed from God.[15] Further, it is obvious that Calvin employs dialectics. As Imbart de la Tour observes, "This grand systematician is also an incomparable dialectician. The theologian who forbade reason in the search for divine truths will put all the resources of his reason to disengaging and defending them. He will masterfully manipulate the usual procedures of logic:

---

[13] See Melanchthon's Reply in Behalf of Ermolao, trans. by Quirinus Breen in *Christianity and Humanism* (Grand Rapids: William B. Eerdmans, 1968), pp. 56-7.

[14] Eugene F. Rice, Jr., "The Humanist Idea of Christianity: Lefèvre d'Étaples and His Circle," *Studies in the Renaissance*, 9 (1962). 132. See also his article, "John Colet and the Annihilation of the Natural," *Harvard Theological Review*, 45, 3 (July, 1952), 153. Lefèvre preferred Aristotle among the classics but also defended Plato. Cf. Imbart de la Tour, *Les Origines de la Réforme*, II (Paris: Librairie Hachette et Cie, 1909), 384ff. Hermann Dörries, "Calvin und Lefèvre," *Zeitschrift für Kirchengeschichte*, 44 (1925), 554-81 is a Streitschrift against Scheibe and deals very little with Calvin.

[15] Com. Is. 28. 29 (CO 36, 483). The English translations of Calvin's commentaries and sermons listed in the bibliography and emended against the original texts are cited by book, chapter, and verse. The references include the volume and page of the *Calvini Opera* (CO). Calvin also says that God has willed that we be aided by dialectics in II. 2. 16 (OS III, 259, 15). The *Institutes* in the Library of Christian Classics edition (LCC), edited by John T. McNeill and trans. by Ford Lewis Battles is cited by book, chapter and paragraph. The second part of the reference is to the volume, page, and lines of the *Opera Selecta* (OS).

analysis and reasoning."[16] On this basis Calvin is often pictured as a strict theo-logician. Even Philip Schaff, who is generally appreciative of Calvin and sympathetic to his cause, makes the typical exaggeration in seeing Calvin as a consummate logician and dialectician.[17] But Calvin was not intimidated by the Law of Contradiction when he felt that the truth of Scripture was at stake. For example, the attempt to drive men to despair who believe in God's providence and yet suffer calamities, Calvin calls "Satan's logic".[18]

As a Christian humanist Calvin may be usefully viewed in terms of the rhetorical tradition. According to Breen, Calvin "follows the principle of Cicero's 'reform', to wit, that wisdom must go hand in hand with eloquence."[19] This understanding does not denigrate the values of logic and philosophy, but adds to it the conviction that the truth is convincing. It is helpful to observe, as Willis points out, that there are two rhetorical traditions. In the negative sense (with which Plato was concerned) rhetoric is a matter of persuasion whether the case is true or false. "The other conception of rhetoric concentrates not on rendering the speaker effective but the truth effective."[20]

---

[16] Imbart de la Tour, *Les Origines de la Réforme*, IV, 181. See also Alexandre Ganoczy, *Le Jeune Calvin: Genèse et Évolution de sa Vocation Réformatrice* (Wiesbaden: Franz Steiner Verlag, 1966), pp. 196-200 (hereafter cited as *Le Jeune Calvin*) and the thoughtful review of Ganoczy's works by E. Davis Willis, "Notes on A. Ganoczy's *Calvin, Théologien de l'Église et du Ministère*," *Bibliothèque d'Humanisme et Renaissance*, XXX (1968), 185-198. Willis correctly criticizes Ganoczy's view of transcendence in Calvin which gives birth to a dialectical theology in which the divine and human system is put opposite each other to the exclusion of unity.

[17] Philip Schaff, "Calvin's Life and Labors," *Presbyterian Quarterly and Princeton Review*, 4 (April, 1875), 265.

[18] Com. Mt. 27. 43 (CO 45, 771).

[19] Breen, "John Calvin and the Rhetorical Tradition," *Christianity and Humanism*, pp. 112-3. Breen bases his case on finding the enthymeme rather than the syllogism in Calvin's writings (pp. 122-3). Breen, following Quintilian's distinction, defines the enthymeme as an incomplete syllogism with one premise suppressed. Quintilian thinks that the orator must study philosophy (*Institutio Oratoria*, XII. 2. 4). Thus Pericles knows Anaxagoras, Demosthenes knows Plato, and Cicero learns more from the walks of Academe than from schools of rhetoric (XII. 2. 22-3). Still Quintilian sees dialectics as a concise form of oratory (II. 21. 13). Therefore dialectics is useful but oratory is superior (XII. 2. 13). For Aristotle the enthymeme is a rhetorical syllogism (*Rhetorica*, I. 1356 b 5). He does not set them in the same opposition as Quintilian.

[20] E. David Willis, "Rhetoric and Responsibility in Calvin's Theology," *The Context of Contemporary Theology*, ed. by Alexander J. McKelway and E. David Willis (Atlanta: John Knox, 1974), p. 46.

In the negative sense Calvin opposes frivolous rhetoric.[21] He makes a distinction between the orator and the minister of the spirit. Paul declares that he does not possess and does not desire even the true eloquence "which consists in skilful choice of subjects, in clever arrangement, and fineness of style." Calvin does not condemn the arts because they are gifts of God. Indeed he quotes Augustine that "He who gave Peter, the fisherman, also gave Cyprian, the orator," but Calvin insists "that the cross of Christ is made void, not only by the wisdom of the world, but also by the brilliance of words."[22] Referring to the debate between philosophy and rhetoric in the French edition of 1560, Calvin indicates that the subtlety expended has not profited anyone.[23]

Calvin clearly opposes both rhetoric in the negative sense of embellishment and dialectics in its inordinate confidence in the prowess of reason. Nevertheless, in the positive sense of rhetoric, as Willis demonstrates, Calvin belongs to the rhetorical tradition. The humanistic rhetorical interest in the study of classical and patristic texts is also descriptive of Calvin as well as the conviction of the persuasive nature of God's truth.[24]

It is useful to return to another aspect of Kristeller's definition. The humanists not only have rhetorical training, but an interest in classical learning. However on the basis of classical learning alone, it would be difficult to exclude Martin Luther from the ranks of the Christian humanists. Luther claimed to know Aristotle better than his opponents[25] and obviously supported the efficacy of the revival of classical learning.[26] Thus while Heinrich Maier says flatly

---

[21] CO 54, 70.

[22] Com. I Cor. 1 17 (CO 49, 319f.).

[23] I. 8. 11.

[24] Willis, "Rhetoric and Responsibility in Calvin's Theology." p. 47ff. See also Robert D. Linder, "Calvinism and Humanism: The First Generation," *Church History*, 44, 2 (June, 1975), 167-181.

[25] Cited by B. A. Gerrish, *Grace and Reason* (Oxford: Clarendon Press, 1962), p. 39.

[26] Luther wrote in 1529, "Do not give way to your apprehension lest we Germans become more barbarous than ever we were by reason of the decline of letters through our theology. I am persuaded that, without a skilled training in literary studies, no true theology can establish and maintain itself, seeing that in times past it has invariably fallen miserably and lain prostrate with the decline of learning. On the other hand it is indubitable that there has never been a signal revelation of divine truth unless first the way has been prepared for it, as by a John the Baptist, by the revival and the pursuit of the study of languages and literature." Quoted in Lewis W. Spitz, *The Religious Renaissance of the German Humanists* (Cambridge: Harvard University Press, 1963), p. 243. Though Spitz

that Martin Luther was not a humanist,[27] Brian A. Gerrish raises "the possibility that perhaps Luther may be, indeed should be, classed with the so-called 'Biblical Humanists".[28] A sounder basis for excluding Luther, not from humanism in general, but from the notion of Christian philosophy in particular, is the fact that Luther insists that philosophy and theology should be carefully distinguished.[29] Luther sees philosophy as the theology of the heathen.[30] With this understanding Luther is less interested in studying philosophy with appreciative intent than others are.

In any case, for our purposes, Kristeller's definition may be modified so that the Christian humanists with whom we are concerned are defined as those scholars with theological training, however acquired, who discuss philosophical insights in their writings with a strong sense of appreciation. These scholars include Budé, Melanchthon, also Erasmus, and Calvin. The use of the term "Christian philosophy" is not taken to be definitive but indicative. That is to say, other Christian humanists such as Lefèvre and Zwingli stand in the same general context, but, so far as I know, do not employ the term. However, the use of the designation has a meaning in the sixteenth century and offers a background for an aspect of Calvin's humanism.

Guillaume Budé, the learned humanist, whom Erasmus styled "the marvel of France" was devoted to the classics and to religious reform. Although Budé did not break with the Catholic church, his wife went to Geneva after his death and openly professed Protestantism. Budé was a proponent of Christian philosophy.[31] Budé believed that profane and sacred studies were not incompatible, and indeed that philosophy led to religion.[32] According to Budé, classical philosophy is a propaedeutic for Christian philosophy.[33] It is evident

---

does not claim that Luther was a humanist, he shows how closely related Luther's thought was to humanism, pp. 237-266.

[27] Heinrich Maier, *An der Grenze der Philosophie* (Tübingen: J. C. B. Mohr (Paul Siebeck), 1909), p. 40.

[28] Gerrish, *Grace and Reason*, p. 152.

[29] *Luther's Works*, ed. by Jaroslaw Pelikan, 26 (St. Louis: Concordia Publishing House, 1964), 261 (WA, 40, I, 410).

[30] *Tischreden*, WA, 5, 5557.

[31] Gulielmi Budaei, *Omnia Opera*, I (Basel, 1557), 169.

[32] Eugène de Budé, *Vie de Guillaume Budé* (Paris: Librairie Academique Didies, 1884), p. 119.

[33] Josef Bohatec, *Budé und Calvin: Studien zur Gedankenwelt des französischen Frühhumanismus* (Graz: Hermann Bohlaus, 1950), p. 23ff. Hereafter cited as *Budé und Calvin*.

that Calvin learned from Budé, whom he calls "the first ornament and pillar of literature,"[34] and this relationship is carefully worked out in Bohatec's magisterial study of Budé and Calvin. Budé formulated the definition of philosophy as the knowledge of God and man from the Stoic doctrine: σοφία ἐστὶ κατάληψις θείων τε καὶ ἀνθρωπίνων.[35] This definition is reflected in Calvin's opening statement in the *Institutes*, "Nearly all the wisdom we possess, that is to say, true and sound wisdom, consists of two parts: the knowledge of God and of ourselves."[36]

Philip Melanchthon, the grandnephew of the celebrated Reuchlin, became an accomplished humanist at an early age. As a scholar of the classics, he was convinced that the scholastic understanding of Aristotle was erroneous. Melanchthon praised both Aristotle and Plato,[37] and wanted to continue Pico's attempt to harmonize them. Thus he cherished the notion of producing a new edition of Aristotle's works. After going to Wittenberg, he abandoned the project, and he seemed to have repudiated his concern with philosophy under the influence of Luther. However, his humanistic interests reasserted themselves. Melanchthon always remained a friend of Erasmus and of Calvin whom he called "the theologian". The recovery of ancient languages and classical literature was an aid to Christian piety. Like Budé, Melanchthon adopted the term "Christian philosophy". According to Neuser, "Philosophia Christi was the designation of Erasmus of Rotterdam for the humanistic moral doctrine. This expression Melanchthon took from him and used for the Pauline doctrine. Yet he prefers to speak of the Philosophia Pauli, since this expresses more accurately his own opinion. Or he speaks of a philosophia sacra or a philosophia christiana."[38]

Perhaps the leading proponent of the value of the classics and

---

[34] *Calvin's Commentary on Seneca's De Clementia.* ed. and trans. by Ford Lewis Battles and André Malan Hugo (Leiden: E. J. Brill, 1969), pp. 114-5.

[35] Bohatec, *Budé und Calvin,* pp. 30-1. Cf. Cicero, *De Officiis,* II. 2. 5 and *Tusculan Disputations,* IV. 26. 57. Also Seneca, *Epistulae Morales,* XIV. 15.

[36] I. 1. 1 (OS III, 31, 6-8).

[37] "De Platone," (1538), CR 11, 413-25.

[38] Wilhelm H. Neuser, *Der Ansatz der Theologie Philipp Melanchthons* (Neukirchen: Verlag der Buchhandlung des Erziehungsvereins, 1957), p. 43. The term "Christian philosophy" was also used in letters to Zwingli by Beatus Rhenanus (CRZ 7, 115, 10-14); Kaspar Hedio (CRZ 7, 281, 7); and Melchior Macrinus (CZR 7, 589, 3-4). Cf. also Arthur Rich, *Die Anfänge der Theologie Huldrych Zwinglis* (Zurich: Zwingli-Verlag, 1949) for the relation of Zwingli to the Erasmian reform.

Christian antiquity was Erasmus, "the prince of the humanists". Budé wrote of Erasmus that he had caused "sacred truth itself to emerge from the Cimmerian darkness" of scholastic theology.[39] As an editor and educator, Erasmus continued and developed the movement begun by Ficino, Pico, and Valla in Italy, Cusa and Reuchlin in Germany, Colet and More in England, and Lefèvre and Budé in France.

Erasmus' conviction of the value of Christian philosophy is unmistakable. In the preface to the *Enchiridion*, Erasmus insisted that while the Gospel and the Epistles contained the whole "philosophy of Christ"[40] still since all truth belongs to Christ, it was profitable to study pagan literature as a preparation for understanding Scripture.[41] In the preface to his Greek and Latin edition of the New Testament (1516), Erasmus complained that the Platonists, Pythagoreans, Academics, Stoics, Cynics, Peripatetics, and Epicureans know their doctrine, but the Christians did not.[42] Erasmus insisted that Christans should know the literature of Christ. Thus he encouraged the study of "Christian philosophy".[43] This "philosophy of Christ", he said is not a matter of syllogisms but of feeling.[44]

In defining Christian philosophy in terms of the Scripture, Erasmus did not mean to deny the efficacy of classical literature. Erasmus believed that Christian philosophy was perfectly taught by Christ, but in pagan literature, he thought, much could be found which agreed with Christ's teaching. In this way the values of philosophical insight are evident.[45] Indeed so captivated was Erasmus by the example of Socrates that he wrote, "An admirable spirit, surely, in one who had not known Christ and the Sacred Scripture. And so when I read such things of such men, I can hardly help exclaiming, 'Holy Socrates, pray for us'."[46]

---

[39] Cited by W. K. Ferguson, *The Renaissance in Historical Thought* (Boston: Houghton Mifflin Company, 1948), p. 32.

[40] EO, 3, 365. See also Spitz, *The Religious Renaissance of the German Humanists*, pp. 197-236 and Paul Wernle, *Die Renaissance des Christentums im 16. Jahrhundert* (Tübingen: J. C. B. Mohr (Paul Siebeck), 1904), pp. 24-5.

[41] Erasmus, *The Enchiridion of Erasmus*, ed. and trans. by Raymond Himelick (Bloomington: Indiana University Press, 1963), p. 50 (EO 5, 7 d).

[42] Erasmus, *Paraclesis id est adhortatio ad christianae philosophiae studium*, EO 5, 139 b-c.

[43] *Ibid.*, 137 e.

[44] *Ibid.*, 140 e, 141 c.

[45] *Ibid.*, 141 f.

[46] Erasmus, *Ten Colloquies of Erasmus*, trans. by Craig R. Thompson (New York: Liberal Arts Press, 1957), p. 158. Some portions of the preceding material,

The term "Christian philosophy" or "philosophy of Christ" was common currency among the Christian humanists, as we have seen. Used by Budé, Melanchthon, Erasmus, Nicholas Cop,[47] and others, it referred to the reform in which they were engaged, a reform which included a genuine appreciation of classical philosophy. Thus it is not strange that John Calvin adopted the term "Christian philosophy" to describe his work, and it is to this description that we turn.

used by permission, are found in my essay, "The Revitalization of the Concept of 'Christian Philosophy' in Renaissance Humanism," *Christian Scholar's Review*, III, 4 (1974), 360-9.

[47] Nicholas Cop, "Concio Academica, " OS I, 4-5. Eng. trans. and annotations by Dale Cooper and Ford Lewis Battles, *Hartford Quarterly*, 6 (1965), 76-85.

CHAPTER TWO

CALVIN'S DESCRIPTION OF CHRISTIAN PHILOSOPHY

That Calvin belongs to the ranks of the Christian humanists may now be taken as axiomatic.[1] Of course Calvin's humanism may be examined in a variety of ways, and a number of helpful studies are devoted to the subject.[2] Concerning parts of the humanistic heritage which are present in Calvin's theology, Ganoczy says, "We think above all of the method of exegesis, of the importance attached to the study of the fathers, of the acceptance of a certain 'Christian philosophy', of the respect for certain thinkers of pagan antiquity, and of the strongly moral character of Christian existence."[3] Calvin does indeed respect certain pagan thinkers, as we shall see. Calvin does not suffer a painful conscience about his classical interests after the manner of Jerome and Augustine because he believes that pagan wisdom too is from God. Calvin's conversion does not involve a repudiation of his classical learning, but a transformation of it.[4]

Our immediate concern in this chapter is Calvin's description of Christian philosophy, which is based on the *Scripture* under the

---

[1] Cf. A. M. Hunter, "The Erudition of John Calvin," *Evangelical Quarterly*, XVIII (1946), 200.

[2] The general topic of Calvin and humanism has been studied by Abel Lefranc, *La Jeunesse de Calvin* (Paris; Librairie Fischbacher, 1888), pp. 59-125; Johaness Neuenhaus, "Calvin als Humanist," *Calvinstudien, Festschrift zum 400 Geburtstage Johann Calvins*, ed. J. Bohatec (Leipzig: Rudolf Haupt, 1909), pp. 1-26; Jacques Pannier, *Recherches sur la formation intellectuelle de Calvin* (Paris: Librairie Alcan, 1931); Quirinus Breen, *John Calvin: A Study in French Humanism* (2nd ed.; Hamden, Conn.: Archon Books, 1968); E. Bourilly, "Humanisme et Réforme, La Formation de Calvin," *Calvin et la Réforme en France* (Aix-en-Provence: Faculté Libre de théologie Protestante, no date), pp. 2-22; Basil Hall, *John Calvin, Humanist and Theologian* (London: The Historical Association, 1956). For the background of the period, the standard work is Augustin Renaudet, *Préréforme et Humanisme à Paris pendant les premières guerres d'Italie* (2nd ed.; Paris: Librairie D'Argences, 1953); also Bohatec's *Budé und Calvin*. H. A. Enno van Gelder, *The Two Reformations in the Sixteenth Century; A Study of the Religious Aspects and Consequences of Renaissance and Humanism*, trans. by J. F. Finlay (Martinus Nijhoff: The Hague, 1961), pp. 267-73 interprets Calvin as an adversary of humanism, but cites only secondary sources.

[3] Ganoczy, *Le Jeune Calvin*, p. 195.

[4] Ford Lewis Battles, "The Sources of Calvin's Seneca Commentary," *Courtenay Studies in Reformation Theology, I John Calvin*, ed. G. E. Duffield (Appleford: The Sutton Courtenay Press, 1966), p. 57.

guidance of the *Holy Spirit*. For Calvin word and Spirit are two complementary parts of the doctrine of God's revelation. Since the Reformers of the sixteenth century were under attack more from radical spiritualists than Biblical fundamentalists, Calvin devotes a good deal of attention to establishing the authority of Scripture. However, word and Spirit are two aspects of the doctrine of God's revelation. Calvin opposes the appeal to Scripture apart from the Spirit, which results in untoward literalism, and the appeal to the Spirit apart from the word, which results in unwonted fanaticism.

It is not insignificant that Calvin uses the humanistic term "Christian philosophy" to describe his work. According to Wilhelm Niesel, "Christian philosophy" means for Calvin the exposition of the contents of Scripture "which he has perceived through the illumination of the Holy Spirit as true and godly doctrine and has experienced in his own heart."[5] No doubt this definition is essentially correct. Calvin is indeed a Biblical theologian who declares that his purpose in writing the *Institutes* is to instruct candidates in sacred theology.[6] Calvin insists that the Scripture contains the perfect doctrine, but he believes that a guide is helpful to instruct simple people in the doctrine of salvation. This guide, Calvin calls "Christian philosophy" which is basically a key to correct understanding of the Scripture, "a sum of Christian doctrine."[7]

However, Calvin should not be understood as entirely excluding the appreciation of the insights of classical philosophy. A positive evaluation of classical insights is not only found in Lefèvre, Budé, Erasmus, Melanchthon, and Zwingli, but also in Calvin. Calvin does not think that the pagan philosophers are completely blind as he makes clear in the following quotations. He writes,

> I call "earthly things" those which do not pertain to God or his Kingdom, to true justice, or to the blessedness of the future life; but which have their significance and relationship with regard to the present life and are, in a sense, confined within its bounds. I call

---

[5] Wilhelm Niesel, *Die Theologie Calvins* (2nd ed.; Munich: Chr. Kaiser Verlag, 1957), p. 25.

[6] " John Calvin to the Reader," LCC, p. 4 (OS III, 6, 18-9).

[7] "Subject Matter of the Present Work," LCC, pp. 6-8 (OS III, 7, 25-32; 8, 18-9). Margaret Mann, *Érasme et les Débuts de la Réforme Française* (Paris: Honoré Champion, 1934) overemphasizes the differences between Erasmus and Calvin and concludes, "Il est difficile de trouver un point de vue plus éloigne de la Philosophia Christi" (p. 188). See also Martin Schulze, *Calvins Jenseitschristentum in seinem Verhältnisse zu religiösen Schriften des Erasmus* (Gorlitz: Rudolf Dulfer, 1902).

"heavenly things" the pure knowledge of God, the nature of true righteousness, and the mysteries of the Heavenly Kingdom. The first class includes government, household management, all mechanical skills, [Fr. ed. 1541 and following adds "philosophy"] and the liberal arts. In the second are the knowledge of God and of his will, and the rule by which we conform our lives to it.[8]

Human efforts, then, are valuable, especially when they concern earthly things. Calvin also affirms that the pagans teach things which are true and helpful to know. The "admirable light of truth shining in [the secular writers teaches] us that the mind of man, though fallen and perverted from its wholeness, is nevertheless clothed and ornamented with God's excellent gifts. If we regard the Spirit of God as the sole fountain of truth, we shall neither reject the truth itself, nor despise it wherever it shall appear unless we wish to dishonor the Spirit of God."[9] Thus in spite of the pervasive influence of the sin of man, there remains a kind of glory which belongs to the mind of man, and, since all truth is from God, it should not be denied.

Calvin recognizes both truth and error in the thought of the classical philosophers. He thinks that the Christian can safely pass over some of their teachings as unhelpful,[10] because the philosophers' views are vitiated by their ignorance of the corruption of nature which originates from the fall of man.[11] Although something of the understanding and judgment remains in man after the fall, the mind is not whole and sound but weak and dark.[12] Therefore, in expounding his Christian philosophy, Calvin accepts some of their views and rejects others. Calvin's use and evaluation of the classical philosophers is instructive not only as an illustration of his Christian humanism but as an important part of his theology.[13]

Calvin makes a sharp distinction between philosophy in general and Christian philosophy. Human philosophy is based solely on reason, but Christian philosophy is based on Scripture and the

---

[8] II. 2. 13 (OS III, 256, 23-31).

[9] II. 2. 15 (OS III, 258, 10-14). See LCC, p. 274, note 58. Seneca, *Epistulae Morales*, I. 12. 11 writes, "Quod verum est, meum est." Cf. Augustine, *Christian Doctrine*, II. 18. (MPL XXXIV, 49-50).

[10] Cf. I. 15. 6 (OS III, 184, 2-4).

[11] I. 15. 7 (OS III, 184, 26-8).

[12] II. 2. 12 (OS III, 255, 8-10).

[13] This aspect of Christian philosophy is ignored by Bois and Calvetti who write under the title *The Philosophy of Calvin*. Henri Bois, *La Philosophie de Calvin* (Paris: Librairie Générale et Protestante, 1919); Carla Calvetti, *La filosofia di Giovanni Calvino* (Milan: Società editrice vita e pensiero, 1955).

guidance of the Holy Spirit. Calvin is aware of the philosophers' interest in religion,[14] but since they have no other standard than reason they soon go astray. When the heathen speak the truth, it seems to be accidentally on their part but providentially on the part of God who enlightens their minds. On the basis of the truth revealed in Scripture, Calvin has no patience with the philosophers' adherence to their speculations,[15] and their presumptive confidence in their wisdom concerning divine matters.[16] Since the Lord has honored his disciples by the revelation of his heavenly philosophy,[17] a philosophy revealed in Christ which cannot be elicited from syllogisms,[18] Calvin maintains that to mix human philosophy with Christ is a corruption.[19]

Calvin believes that all men have a certain conviction about the existence of God and "none are so barbarous as not to have some sense of piety."[20] Thus God is naturally known to the extent that all men are left inexcusable, but the *works* of God cannot be properly understood or appreciated apart from his *word*.[21] Even in the early chapters of the *Institutes* when Calvin discusses the knowledge of God the Creator as experienced in the nature of man's benefits and miseries, he insists that the clear knowledge of God is found only in the word,[22] which is the "school of God's children."[23] The Scripture teaches that God has created and governs the world. Thus the one true God should not be confused with false gods. It is fitting that men contemplate God's wonderful works since man "has been placed in this most glorious theater to be a spectator of them," but it is even more appropriate to contemplate God as he is revealed in his word.[24]

---

[14] IV. 20. 9 (OS V, 480, 1-2).

[15] I. 11. 1 (OS III, 88, 22).

[16] Com. Rom. 1. 22 (CO 49, 25).

[17] I. 11. 7 (OS III, 95, 24).

[18] III. 20. 1 (OS IV, 297, 6-7).

[19] Cf. I. 10. 3 (OS III, 88, 8-13); I. 13. 1 (OS III, 108, 23-5); I. 14. 1 (OS III, 152, 9-11); Com. Col. 2. 8 (CO 52, 103).

[20] Com. Hab. 1. 16 (CO 43, 561). Cf. I. 14. 1 (OS III, 40, 31-2). Also Com. Jn. 1. 9 (CO 47, 9); Com. Dan. 2. 46 (CO 40, 611); Com. Jon. 1. 5 (CO 43, 213): Experience teaches that there is naturally implanted in all some knowledge of God. Com. Zech. 14. 9 (CO 44, 374): All the philosophers teach that there is one God.

[21] Arg. Gen. (CO 23, 9).

[22] I. 10. 1 (OS III, 85, 9). Cf. Com. Gen. 18. 18 (CO 23, 257).

[23] I. 6. 4 (OS III, 64, 21). The Scripture is also called the school of the Holy Spirit. III. 21. 3 (OS IV, 372, 1).

[24] I. 6. 2 (OS III, 62: 18—63: 2).

Calvin believes that nature points to the presence of God, "but faith is not conceived by the bare observation of heaven and earth, but by the hearing of the word. It follows from this that men cannot be brought to the saving knowledge of God except by the direction of the word. Yet this does not prevent them being rendered inexcusable even without the word, for, even if they are naturally deprived of light, they are nevertheless blind through their own malice . . . ."[25] Some knowledge of God may be gathered from his works, at least a knowledge sufficient to make men without excuse for refusing to worship God. It is true that under the condition of sin, men are blind by nature, but Calvin places the responsibility for this blindness upon men. Saving knowledge or faith is not an inherent capacity but is received only on the basis of God's revelation in Scripture.

According to Calvin, Christian philosophy depends not solely on the Scripture but also upon the work of the Holy Spirit. For as "God alone is a fit witness of himself in his word, so also the word will not find acceptance in men's hearts before it is sealed by the inward testimony of the Spirit."[26] To indicate the authority of the Scripture, Calvin points to the grace of style, the grandeur of content, its great antiquity, its accuracy, its marvelous preservation and so on.[27] But in the final analysis, the authority of Scripture is established by the secret witness of the Holy Spirit. One essential function of the Holy Spirit is the exposition of the Scripture[28] by whose power Christ is conveyed to men.[29] This means that the Holy Spirit is not considered as creating new doctrines but as making the gospel efficacious in the hearts and minds of the faithful.

The rational faculty of man is not sufficient to apprehend God. Man can relate to God, not by reason, but only in faith. Therefore, Calvin writes. "[T]he Christian philosophy bids reason give way to, submit and subject itself to, the Holy Spirit so that man himself may no longer live but exhibit Christ living and reigning within him."[30] Calvin insists that the Christian faith does not derive from philosophical arguments but from the work of the Holy Spirit. Thus he says,

---

[25] Com. Acts 14. 17 (CO 48, 327-8).

[26] I. 7. 4 (OS III, 70, 2-5).

[27] I. 8. 1ff (OS III, 71f.)

[28] *Defensio sanae et orthodoxae doctrinae de servitute et liberatione humani arbitrii adversus calumnias Alberti Pighii, Campensis,* CO 6, 270.

[29] I. 9. 3 (OS III, 84, 6).

[30] III. 7. 1 (OS IV, 152, 2-4).

The true conviction which believers have of the Word of God, of their own salvation, and of all religion, does not spring from the feeling of the flesh, or from human and philosophical arguments, but from the sealing of the Spirit, who makes their consciences more certain and removes all doubt. The foundation of faith would be frail and unsteady if it rested on human wisdom; therefore, as preaching is the instrument of faith, so the Holy Spirit makes preaching efficacious.[31]

To the philosophers Calvin's invocation of the Holy Spirit is an attempt to solve a problem by pointing to a mystery. Yet Calvin is writing, not to commend his thought to philosophers, but for the edification of the company of the faithful who have experienced the relation between God's word and God's spirit, however inadequate their intellectual formulations of it might seem to discursive reason.

The relation between word and Spirit, Calvin summarizes by saying, "For by a kind of mutual bond the Lord has joined together the certainty of his word and of his Spirit so that the perfect religion of the word may abide in our minds when the Spirit, who causes us to contemplate God's face, shines: and that we in turn may embrace the Spirit with no fear of being deceived when we recognize him in his own image, namely, in the word."[32]

Calvin describes "Christian philosophy" as the discipline based on God's word and the guidance of God's Holy Spirit. The question then arises concerning the connection of this discipline to the field of philosophy. Calvin's relation to philosophy admits of two opposite tendencies. One is that Calvin really has *nothing* to do with philosophy because he is simply an exegete of Scripture. This view denies or ignores Calvin's use of philosophy. The alternative extreme holds that Calvin has *everything* to do with philosophy because he offers an insight which leads to the development of a total world view. This position ignores or denies Calvin's unsystematic use of philosophy and goes beyond Calvin's own example of a selective, rather than a comprehensive, association with philosophy. It is true that no Calvin scholar adopts either of these views in its entirety, but they are present as tendencies.

---

[31] Com. Eph. 1. 13 (CO 51, 153).

[32] I. 9. 3 (OS III, 84, 14-20). H. J. Forstmann, *Word and Spirit* (Stanford: Stanford University Press, 1962), p. 16 observes, "[Calvin] solves the problem of the reception of revelation in the same way he solved the problem of the recording of revelation, by introducing the agency of the Holy Spirit." See p. 18 and notes.

Those who deal with Calvin's understanding of Scripture and/or theological tradition may ignore his relation to philosophy, with perfect propriety, as outside the scope of concern. Yet it is sometimes difficult to tell whether these scholars are denying the force of this aspect of Calvin's thought or simply omitting it from consideration. Since Calvin's texts contain references to philosophy, it is difficult to dismiss Calvin's use of philosophy entirely except for certain specific purposes. Nevertheless the impression is sometimes left that Calvin's relation to philosophy is negligible.

On the other hand, what is often called "Calvinistic philosophy," or "Christian philosophy," or simply "traditional Calvinism" is a distortion of Calvin's thought in the direction of a philosophic system. Of course, traditions are evidently and necessarily modified by time. Yet it is not easy to distinguish authentic developments from aberrations. Nevertheless, a good deal of recent scholarship sees a clear difference between Calvin and these forms of "Calvinism". For example, Brian Armstrong writes,

> [T]he Calvinist thinkers of the late sixteenth and seventeenth centuries rarely even take the trouble to refer to Calvin himself . . . The question then arises whether these orthodox Calvinists can in fact be regarded as proper representatives of Calvin's thought . . . I believe . . . that a careful comparison of [Calvin's] writings with those of representative Calvinists of the seventeenth century reveals a radical change of emphasis . . . so pronounced that at many points the whole structure of Calvin's thought is seriously compromised.[33]

This situation is not radically different in the eighteenth and nineteenth centuries and is still present.

Representatives of this "traditional" Calvinism, such as A. Kuyper, Bavinck, and Warfield define Calvinism as "that characteristic view of life and the world as a whole, which was born from the powerful mind of the French reformer . . ." producing "a specific view of the world and life as a whole; so to speak a philosophy of its own."[34] According to their view, Calvin "made the principle of divine sover-

---

[33] Brian G. Armstrong, *Calvinism and the Amyraut Heresy: Protestant Scholasticism in Seventeenth Century France* (Madison: University of Wisconsin Press, 1969), p. xvii. Hereafter cited as *Calvinism and the Amyraut Heresy.*

[34] Hermann Bavinck, "The Future of Calvinism," trans. by G. Vos, *Presbyterian and Reformed Review*, V, 17 (Jan., 1894), 3, 5. For a contemporary "Calvinistic philosophy" see Herman Dooyeweerd, *In the Twilight of Western Thought* (Nutley, N. J.: The Craig Press, 1960). For an opposing view see Émile Bréhier, "Y a-t-il une philosophie chrétienne?" *Revue de metaphysique et de Moralle*, 38 (1931), 133-62.

eignty operative *for the Church*, and through the Church in the life of *states* and *nations*."[35] Thus "[t]he root principle of this Calvinism is the confession of God's absolute sovereignty."[36] Closely related is the conviction that the distinguishing mark of Calvinism is the doctrine of predestination.[37] It should be noted that these Calvinists claim only that Calvin *provides* the *principle* of this philosophy, *i.e.*, the sovereignty of God, from which the remainder, such as the corollary of predestination, may be logically deduced. Since Calvin believes in the sovereignty of God and universal providence and common grace, it cannot be denied that Calvin provides a *basis* for this position, but it is doubtful that it is his intention to do so. Calvin does not appeal to the sovereignty of God as the basic premise of a deductive system and therefore not to common grace and predestination as logically necessary consequences of it.

The result of Calvinistic orthodoxy is the production of (1) a theological *system* based on deductions from a first principle, (2) which is considered to be revealed or implicit in Scripture (regarded as infallible and amenable to propositional-truth formulations), and (3) exalting the reason of the redeemed person to almost equal standing with faith as trust in God, (4) so that speculative and metaphysical thought becomes a necessary component of Christian theology.[38] To the extent that this is an adequate characterization of

---

[35] A. Kuyper, "Calvinism and Confessional Revision," trans. by G. Vos, *Presbyterian and Reformed Review*, II, 7 (July, 1891), 377. Original emphasis. Yet see p. 381.

[36] Bavinck, "The Future of Calvinism," p. 3.

[37] As for example, Lyman H. Atwater, "Calvinism in Doctrine and Life," *The Presbyterian Quarterly and Princeton Review*, IV (Jan., 1875), 75. Also Benjamin B. Warfield, "Predestination in the Reformed Confessions," *Presbyterian and Reformed Review*, XII, (Jan., 1901) cites with approval the notion that the doctrine of predestination is the central doctrine of the Reformation (p. 49). Further, although he suggests that the doctrine is based on a soteriological-Biblical motive rather than an intellectualistic-speculative one, still he writes, "[Calvin's] systematic genius perceived from the first [predestination's] central importance to the system of truth on which the Reformation was based . . . ." (p. 61). Warfield regards double predestination with complacency as a systematic necessity rather than with Calvin as an awesome decree.

[38] This definition is a modification of the one suggested by Armstrong, *Calvinism and the Amyraut Heresy*, p. 32ff. Typical of the judgment of Calvin's "system" is the comment of Charles Beard, *The Reformation of the Sixteenth Century in its Relation to Modern Thought and Knowledge* (The Hibbert Lectures of 1883) (5th ed.; London: Williams and Norgate, 1907), pp. 295, 296: "I am only expressing the opinion of friend and foe alike, when I say that Christianity has

"Calvinism", it is legitimate to argue that Calvin's thought and intention is primarily Scriptural and confessional rather than systematic and rational.[39] That is to say, Calvin is concerned to expound the word of God with the Scripture as the source, the theological tradition as an instructor, and with some attention to philosophy as an aid.

Against the tendency to dismiss Calvin's relation to philosophy, the present study intends to demonstrate the importance of Calvin's comments on classical philosophy. Against the opposite tendency to exalt Calvin as a philosopher, we hope to show that his references to philosophy, while instructive, are too occasional to warrant the conclusion that Calvin proposes to introduce a substitute for philosophy. Calvin thinks that his theology is superior to philosophy, but he does not seek to displace philosophy in a higher synthesis in which all of philosophy's legitimate concerns are resolved. Calvin gives us marginal notes on philosophy which are suggestive rather than a philosophical program which is exhaustive.

In his exposition Calvin is quite aware that he is using philosophical insights on occasion to clarify his position. Thus Hunter's view that Calvin is unconscious of the influence of philosophy is to be rejected. According to Hunter, Calvin would have denied the influence of philosophy entirely, though, as Hunter points out, philosophical elements are clearly present. Calvin is doubtless influenced by doctrines which appear in classical, patristic, and medieval

---

never before or since been so completely cast into the mold of a system." Again Beard writes that Calvin believed that "Christianity can be presented in dialectical form [and] can be stated with scholastic accuracy and tied together by bonds of logic."

[39] On this subject see Gilbert Rist, "Modernité de la methode Théologique de Calvin," *Revue de Théologie et de Philosophie*, 3, 18 (1968), 19-33. The modernity of Calvin's theology consists in its being practical and Biblical rather than speculative and systematic. That is to say, theology is not a "science" but a proclamation. See also T. F. Torrance, "Knowledge of God and Speech about Him According to John Calvin," *Regards Contemporains sur Jean Calvin*: Actes du Colloque Calvin, Strassbourg, 1964 (Paris: Presses Universitaires de France, 1965), pp. 140-60 who points out that Calvin's followers fell back on Aristotle to interpret Calvin thus developing his thought in the direction which is known as "Calvinism". Cf. John Patrick Donnelly, "Italian Influences on the Development of Calvinist Scholasticism," *The Sixteenth Century Journal*, VII, 1 (April, 1976), 81-101 who argues that the Calvinistic scholastics often used philosophy in a way quite contrary to Calvin's own. See also his "Calvinist Thomism," *Viator*, 7 (1976), 441-445 and John S. Bray, *Theodore Beza's Doctrine of Predestination* (Nieuwkoop: De Graff, 1975).

thought.[40] While it is true, and important, that Calvin does not formally adopt one philosophy for the presentation of his thought, his utilization of various distinctions, with conscious approval or disapproval, makes an entirely unconscious influence impossible. Calvin evidently knows and quotes the sources of some of his insights.

Further Calvin is quite aware that in his writing he is doing more than simply organizing Scripture. For example, he writes, "But what prevents us from explaining in clearer words those matters in Scripture which perplex and hinder our understanding, yet which conscientiously and faithfully serve the truth of Scripture itself, and are made use of sparingly and modestly and on due occasion."[41] Therefore Calvin consciously uses theological tradition and even philosophic concepts, not as determinative, but when he feels they serve the truth of Scripture.

----

[40] A. Mitchell Hunter, *The Teaching of Calvin* (2nd ed.; London: James Clarke and Co., Ltd., 1950), p. 38. Emile Doumergue, *Jean Calvin, Les hommes et les choses de son temps*, IV (Lausanne: Georges Bridel, 1910), 21 cites Krücke to the effect that "Calvin 'everywhere betrays his philosophical training, but nowhere does he supply a philosophy'." Doumergue's work is hereafter cited as *Jean Calvin*.

[41] I. 13. 3 (OS III, 112, 11-5).

James Barr, *Old and New in Interpretation: A Study of the Two Testaments* (New York: Harper & Row, 1966) in a brief but helpful section, which I encountered after this book was written, remarks that there is no doubt that Calvin "evaluates the philosophers with agreement and disagreement from within a Christian position" (p. 43). But the Reformers' programme "did not involve the *necessity* of differing from what the Greeks had thought" (p. 42). Emphasis added.

CONCLUSION

As we have seen in Part One, the concern for a Christian philo-sophy is part of the sixteenth century milieu. Calvin adopts the term to describe his work which is based on the Scripture and the guidance of the Holy Spirit. It is true that Calvin's Christian *philosophy* does not differ significantly from Christian *theology* except that the desig-nation "Christian philosophy" places Calvin in the context of Chris-tian humanism and indicates a humanistic interest in classical thought. In the next section we will consider the results of Calvin's interest in classical thought in terms of his citations of philosophical insights, both in praise and blame, as he expounds elements of his thought.

PART TWO

CALVIN AND PHILOSOPHY

INTRODUCTION

As a Christian humanist, John Calvin appreciates classical philosophy. Doubtless, Calvin is influenced both directly and indirectly by classical philosophy, but the method of studying *his direct citations* of philosophical insights provides a sounder basis for considering his relation to them than the search for "affinities" between Calvin and philosophy which offers such a large scope for the interpreter's ingenuity at finding "common themes". Calvin does not attempt to synthesize classical philosophy and Christian doctrine, but he does devote attention to certain doctrines of Plato, Aristotle, the Epicureans, and the Stoics. Some philosophical insights Calvin commends, others he condemns, and still others he simply ignores. The references to classical philosophy occupy an instrumental place in Calvin's thought, but his comments are made in passing as he develops various features of his "Christian philosophy".

Our purpose is to focus on what Calvin says about philosophical views and the alternative positions which he occupies in relation to them. Thus in Part Two, as illustrative of Calvin's use of philosophy, we will deal with Calvin's judgments of philosophical insights under the philosophical categories of epistemology (Chapter Three), ontology (Chapter Four), anthropology (Chapter Five), and ethics (Chapter Six). Of course Calvin does not organize his thought on the basis of these divisions, and he does not provide exact equivalents of them. Calvin is not a philosopher in the modern sense.[1] Calvin does not develop a technical epistemology but rather a doctrine of the knowledge of God. Calvin does not produce a philosophical ontology but a doctrine of God the Creator and Redeemer. Calvin does not have a philosophical anthropology but a doctrine of man's relation to God. Calvin's ethics is primarily concerned with

---

[1] John P. Le Coq, "Was Calvin a Philosopher?" *The Personalist*, 29 (July, 1948), 253 writes, "Learning alone, that is, the mere acquisition of facts, does not make a philosopher; it is a certain spirit of open-mindedness and systematic thoroughness of work, a search for causes, that gives meaning to philosophy, a quality Calvin was lacking." However, Calvin does not claim to be doing philosophy but Christian philosophy which is based on faith and revelation, the very items which Le Coq argues exclude Calvin from the ranks of the philosophers.

the obedience of man in terms of the revealed will of God.[2] Nevertheless, Calvin's thought is amenable to this construction as a heuristic device and instructive in the light of it.

---

[2] Georgia Harkness, *John Calvin: The Man and His Ethics* (New York: Henry Holt and Company, 1931), p. 63 says, "Calvin did not have an ethical system in a philosophical sense." It is true that Calvin was concerned with Christian practice rather than philosophical theory. Yet he criticises philosophical ethics in II. 2. 26 (OS III, 269, 3-8).

CHAPTER THREE

REASON AND EXPERIENCE IN EPISTEMOLOGY

Epistemology in itself is an empty science since knowledge cannot be isolated from its content. Knowledge depends on what is thought capable of being known. Therefore Calvin's "epistemology" can be considered apart from his "ontology" only for convenience in exposition. Calvin's opposition to rational speculation[1] does not preclude the necessity of ontological affirmations, but he is more concerned with the *knowledge* of God than the *being* of God. That is, Calvin is not interested in speculating about God-in-himself, but in God-as-revealed in his word.[2] Calvin is concerned with God-for-us.[3] Thus to know God is to know his relationship to us as it is revealed and to refuse to search for a hidden God.[4] Of course, God-revealed-in-us implies God-sovereign-in-himself, but Calvin rejects the attempt to go behind or above God's self-revelation.[5] He advises that the faithful "not indulge in curiosity or in the investigation of unprofitable things. And because the Lord willed to instruct us, not in frivolous questions, but in solid piety, in the fear of his name, in true trust, and in the duties of holiness, let us be satisfied with this knowledge."[6]

In this chapter we will deal with the contrasting epistemological functions of reason and experience in Calvin and the classical philosophers. Calvin has a positive evaluation of reason within its proper bounds, but he criticizes what he considers to be an overweening confidence in it on the part of the philosophers. Calvin maintains that the knowledge of God is revealed in Jesus Christ, and accepted in faith, but rather than treating the relation of faith and reason directly, we will consider Calvin's suggestions about the role of experience for the Christian's epistemological stance.

---

[1] I. 14. 4 (OS III, 156, 24-7). See also Theodore Beza, "The Life of John Calvin," *Tracts Relating to the Reformation*, trans. by Henry Beveridge, I (Edinburgh: Calvin Translation Society, 1844), 1. (CO 21, 139). Hereafter cited as *Calvin's Tracts*.

[2] I. 10. 2 (OS III, 86, 17-8).

[3] Cf. I. 2. 2 (OS III, 35, 11f.).

[4] I. 5. 1 (OS III, 45, 4-5).

[5] I. 14. 4 (OS III, 156, 17f.).

[6] I. 14. 3 (OS III, 156, 3-5).

The classical philosophers do not ignore the divine aspect of knowledge. The Stoics see man as "a part of God",[7] "a part of the universe".[8] Calvin approves of the philosophers' understanding of man as a "microcosm" and agrees that man can find God by descending within himself.[9] For the classical philosophers and for Calvin the knowledge of man alone is not sufficient. Cicero writes, "Wisdom, moreover, as the word has been defined by the philosophers of old, is 'the knowledge of things human and divine and of the causes by which these things are controlled'."[10] Concerning the knowledge of things human and divine, Plato says that we know ourselves only by self-contemplation of Nous in the knowledge of God.[11] Cicero holds that self-knowledge is to know the powers of the body and mind. Calvin affirms the classical maxim "Know thyself", but he objects that it is too often considered in an exclusively human sense.[12] "Let us therefore remember, whenever each of us contemplates his own nature, that there is one God who so governs all natures, that he would have us look to him, direct our faith to him and worship and call upon him."[13]

Calvin accepts the philosophic view that the soul has faculties. Aristotle teaches that one element in the soul is irrational (ἄλογος) and one has a rational principle (λόγος). The irrational element he calls vegetative or nutritive which, causing growth, men share with the animals. The other element is appetitive which shares in reason to the extent that the desiring element obeys reason.[14] Aristotle also maintains that there are three things in the soul which control action and truth—sensation (αἴσθησις), reason (νοῦς), and desire

---

[7] Seneca, *Epistulae Morales*, XCII. 30.

[8] Cicero, *De Finibus*, III. 19. 64.

[9] I. 5. 3 (OS III, 46:33—47:8-9).

[10] *De Officiis*, II. 2. 15. Seneca, *Epistulae Morales*, LXXXIX. 4-6 commenting on this passage says that the last phrase is superfluous since the causes themselves are part of the divine system. His own distinction holds that wisdom is the perfect good and philosophy, the love of wisdom, is the endeavour to attain wisdom.

[11] *Alcibiades Major*, 132 e-133 c.

[12] II. 1. 1 (OS III, 228, 15-8).

[13] I. 15. 6 (OS III, 50 : 29—51 : 1).

[14] *Ethica Nicomachea*, I. 13. 1102 a 26f. Cf. Plutarch, *On Moral Virtue*, in *Moralia*, VI. Cicero, *De Officiis*, I. 28. 101 writes, "Now we find that the essential activity of the spirit is two-fold: one force is appetite (that is, ὁρμή in Greek), which impels a man this way and that; the other is reason, which teaches and explains what should be done and what should be left undone. The result is that reason commands, appetite obeys."

(ὄρεξις).[15] Referring to this position Calvin says, "I shall not strongly oppose anyone who wants to classify the powers of the soul in some other way; to call one appetitive, which, even though without reason, if directed elsewhere, yet obeys reason; to call the other intellective, which is through itself participant in reason. Nor would I refute the view that there are three principles of action: sense, understanding, appetite."[16] However, Calvin says that the philosophers do not take sin into account. Therefore, "Let not those minutiae of Aristotle delay us here, that the mind has no motion in itself but is moved by choice."[17] Calvin then states his own position that the human soul consists of understanding, which distinguishes between good and evil, and that the will chooses what the understanding finds good. "For this reason, Aristotle himself truly teaches the same: that shunning or seeking out in the appetite corresponds to affirming or denying in the mind."[18]

Calvin separates his discussion of the parts of the soul from that of the philosophers because they confuse the original and the present state of man, being ignorant of the fall.[19] Calvin insists that the faculties are not properly understood apart from the sin and fall of man and his redemption. Calvin refers to the fall of man throughout Book One of the *Institutes*, but its systematic development is found at the beginning of Book Two (chapters 1-5) as the prologue to redemption which is the "second creation".[20] The knowledge of ourselves involves not only a consideration of the creation but also of the misery of man's condition.

According to Calvin, Adam would not have opposed God unless he had first disbelieved God's word. Adam was not content with God's bounty, and this disobedience was the beginning of man's fall. It was unfaithfulness which caused the woman to be led away from God's word. "Unfaithfulness . . . was the root of the Fall."[21] God created Adam for a life of obedience, but sin caused his death. Thus sin "is an adventitious quality which comes upon man rather than a substantial property which has been implanted from the

---

[15] *Ethica Nicomachea*, VI. 2. 1139 a 17.
[16] I. 15. 6 (OS III, 184, 4-10).
[17] I. 15. 7 (OS III, 185, 6-8).
[18] I. 15. 7 (OS III, 185, 12-5).
[19] I. 15. 6 (OS III, 184, 4-10).
[20] II. 3. 6 (OS III, 280, 25).
[21] II. 1. 4 (OS III, 232, 6).

beginning."[22] God is not the author of death,[23] but Calvin admits that it was ordained by God that Adam should not only possess but lose the gifts which God had bestowed. Men were created good but mutable. Calvin refuses to speculate why man was not granted perseverence.[24]

Sin affects men to the extent that "no part is immune from sin and all that proceeds from him is to be imputed to sin."[25] In the fall Calvin believes that the supernatural gifts such as faith, love of God, and charity toward the neighbor are taken away. Further the natural gifts which remain are corrupted. The natural gift of reason which distinguishes men from the beasts is not destroyed but its light is darkened.[26] The will also did not perish because it is inseparable from man's nature, but it is now captive to evil desires. Man is not deprived of will altogether, but the will is no longer sound.[27] Therefore, "even though something of understanding and judgment remains as a residue along with the will, yet we shall not call a mind whole and sound that is both weak and plunged into deep darkness. And depravity of the will is all too well known."[28]

In discussing the faculties of soul, Calvin focused on the understanding (intellectus) and will (voluntas)[29] which he thinks sufficient for the edification of the pious. Calvin says that there are two faculties in the human soul, the understanding and the will. The understanding distinguishes between good and evil, and the office of the will is to choose what the understanding pronounces good. Calvin associates this distinction with Plato's myth of the charioteer and the winged horses.[30]

Calvin also accepts with Aristotle[31] and the Stoics that man as a

---

[22] II. 1. 11 (OS III, 240, 17-20). The distinction between substance and accident is, of course, Aristotelian.

[23] II. 1. 6 (OS III, 235, 28).

[24] II. 1. 10 (OS III, 239 : 31—240 : 1).

[25] II. 1. 9 (OS III, 239, 22).

[26] Com. Ps. 119. 73 (CO 32, 246).

[27] II. 3. 5 (OS III, 277, 10-2).

[28] II. 2. 12 (OS III, 255, 8-11).

[29] I. 15. 7 (OS III, 185, 2).

[30] I. 15. 7 (OS III, 185, 6). Cf. Plato, *Phaedrus*, 254 e. Hermann Barnikol, *Die Lehre Calvins vom unfreien Willen und ihr Verhältnis zur Lehre der übrigen Reformatoren und Augustins* (Heusersche Buchdruckerei (J. Meincke): Neuwied a. Rh., 1927), p. 107 says, "In union with Plato [Calvin] divides the soul into two faculties: intellectus and voluntas."

[31] *De Generatione Animalium*, 736 b 27-9.

rational animal is superior to the beasts.[32] Cicero teaches that reason makes men superior to the beasts,[33] and Seneca claims that "man is a reasoning animal".[34] The argument is supported by Cicero this way: "Nothing, he said, that is inanimate and irrational can give birth out of itself to an animate and rational being, but the world gives birth to animate and rational beings. Therefore the world is animate and rational."[35] "All living things either are gifted with reason like men and gods, or else are irrational, like beasts and cattle."[36] It is "by virtue of reason [that man] surpasses the animals, and is surpassed only by the gods. Perfect reason is therefore the good peculiar to man; all other qualities he shares in some degree with animals and plants."[37] The distinction between the power of reason in God and man is only that the gods are immortal while men are mortal.[38]

According to Calvin, God created the understanding and will in man and even after the fall they still exist but in a corrupted condition. Man was created with an enlightened understanding and his will was fixed in obedience to God. Now, however, man's nature is corrupted by sin. Calvin criticizes Plato's optimistic view of knowledge,[39] but agrees that there is a conflict between reason and will.[40] Man cannot be understood solely in terms of nature because "the Spirit is so contrasted with flesh that no intermediate thing is left.

---

[32] II. 2. 12 (OS III, 255, 18-9); II. 2. 17 (OS III, 259, 30-1). Cf. Augustine, On Christian Doctrine, I. 22. (MPL XXXIV, 26).

[33] De Officiis, I. 30. 107; De Finibus, II. 14. 15.

[34] Epistulae Morales, XLI, 8.

[35] De Natura Deorum, II. 8. 22.

[36] Seneca, Epistulae Morales, CXIII. 17.

[37] Ibid., LXXVII. 9.

[38] Ibid., CXXIV. 14.

[39] In a sense education occupied the same place in Greek thought which salvation occupies in Christian thought. In the Meno, 81 c, Plato says that all learning is wholly recollection (ἀνάμνησις). This implies a previous time in which men learn what they now recollect (Phaedo, 72 e). Thus the human being needs a recollection of those things which the soul once beheld while following God (Phaedrus, 249 e). Calvin objects to this view, II. 2. 14 (OS III, 257, 28-30). Plato thinks that men err from defect of knowledge (Protagoras, 357 de). He is convinced that knowledge will not allow one who knows the difference between good and evil to do anything contrary to knowledge (Ibid., 352 b f.). Thus the only real evil is to be deprived of knowledge since no one errs voluntarily or voluntarily does evil (Ibid., 345 b). Calvin insists that sin and ignorance are not the same, II. 2. 22 (OS III, 265, 13-4) and II. 2. 25 (OS III, 267, 20-1).

[40] In the Laws, I. 644 e, Plato writes that affections pull men in different and opposite ways and to opposite actions. Therefore they should hold onto reason. Calvin cites this passage, II. 2. 3 (OS III, 243, 15-20).

Accordingly whatever is not spiritual in man is by this reckoning
called 'carnal'. We have nothing of the Spirit, however, except
through regeneration. Whatever we have from nature, therefore,
is flesh."[41] The Spirit comes not from nature, but from regeneration.[42] Man's guilt is from nature, but sanctification from supernatural grace.[43]

The fact that there are, and have been, virtuous men guided only
by nature means, according to Calvin, that God's grace restrains
men even when it does not cleanse them. Therefore even the integrity
of the natural man is not a matter of nature but a special grace of
God.[44] David, affirming the experience of the godly, points out that
the measure of understanding with which men are endued by nature
is such that it shines in the darkness, but the darkness does not comprehend it. Man is enlightened only by a supernatural gift, and only
the godly understand that they derive their light from God.[45] For
this reason Isaiah testifies "that the light of God will arise in the
church alone; and leaves only shadows and blindness outside the
church."[46]

In summary, Calvin agrees with the philosophers that no one is
without the light of reason,[47] and that reason is proper to man's
nature.[48] But Calvin also says that reason is blind,[49] and urges that
reason be renounced.[50] The ability to reason is part of human nature,
but it is affected by sin and cannot grasp divine matters. According
to Calvin the philosophers "set up reason alone as the ruling principle in man, and think that it alone should be listened to, to it alone,
in short they entrust the conduct of life."[51] But human reason can
neither understand who God is nor his relation to man.[52]

-----

[41] II. 3. 1 (OS III, 272, 10-4).
[42] II. 2. 27 (OS III, 270, 14-5).
[43] II. 1. 7 (OS III, 236, 27-8).
[44] II. 3. 4 (OS III, 276, 11-2).
[45] Com. Ps. 36. 9 (CO 31, 363).
[46] II. 3. 1 (OS III, 272, 35-7).
[47] II. 2. 13 (OS III, 257, 18-20).
[48] II. 2. 17 (OS III, 259, 30).
[49] Com. Jn. 3. 31 (CO 47, 68). F. W. Kampschulte, *Johann Calvin*; *seine Kirche
und sein Staat in Genf*, I (Leipzig: Duncker und Humblot, 1869), 200, 260 says
that Calvin surpassed Luther in refusing all concession to human reason.
[50] "On the Necessity of Reforming the Church," *Calvin's Tracts*, I, 147 (CO
6, 474).
[51] III. 7. 1 (OS IV, 151 : 38—152 : 2).
[52] II. 2. 18 (OS III, 261, 13-5). Cf. T. F. Torrance, *Calvin's Doctrine of Man*
(London: Lutterworth Press, 1949), p. 116.

Because Calvin's thought is not based on reason, he does not achieve or even attempt a logically unassailable system as most scholars have recognized. For example, writing of Calvin's doctrine of justification, Willy Lüttge argues for tensions (Spannungen) or contradictions (Widerspruchen) in Calvin's theology.[53] Emile Doumergue answers Lüttge by saying that while there are philosophical contradictions in Calvin, his pensée and pieté are combined in experience. "The diversity, the clashes, the contrasts, the dualism, the defects of logic, the contradictions, if you like, the elements which entered into the composition of Calvinism, constitute precisely its originality, its richness, its force, in a word, its own peculiar life."[54] Doumergue points out that Calvin uses both the a priori and a posteriori methods which had been developed in philosophy and theology, but maintains that while there is a logic of concepts, there is also a logic of life, of reality.[55] Hermann Bauke sees in these comments by Lüttge and Doumergue the differing approaches of the German and French minds. That is, the Germans tend to examine Calvin in metaphysical terms and the French in terms of the rhetorical tradition. Bauke remarks that Calvin was indeed a French orator, and he finds a complexio oppositorum in Calvin's theology.[56] Thus with these studies in mind, one might conclude that certain elements in Calvin's thought stand in a contradictory relation (Lüttge), or in a complementary relation (Doumergue), or in some kind of dialectical tension (Bauke).

François Wendel gives a helpful list of the "dialectical opposites" which Calvin affirms including God's love and wrath, man's complete justification and his imperfect regeneration, the gratitude and contempt for earthly goods, the omnipotence of God and the responsibility of man, the goodness of God and the fact of evil. Wendel correctly concludes, "It would be better, we think, to confess that Calvin's is not a closed system elaborated around a central idea, but that it draws together, one after another, a whole series of Biblic-

---

[53] Willy Lüttge, *Die Rechtfertigungslehre Calvins* (Berlin: Reuther und Reichard, 1909), pp. 78ff.

[54] Doumergue, *Jean Calvin*, IV, 278.

[55] Doumergue, *Le Caractère de Calvin* (2nd ed.; Neuilly: La Cause, 1931), pp. 76-81.

[56] Hermann Bauke, *Die Probleme der Theologie Calvins* (Leipzig: J. C. Hinrich'-schen, 1922), pp. 27, 16-9.

cal ideas, some of which can only with difficulty be logically reconciled. . . ."[57]

Calvin is aware that the faithful exposition of the Scripture does not produce a rational synthesis, but he asserts, "It is becoming in us, then, not to be too inquisitive: only let us not dare to deny the truth of what Scripture teaches *and experience confirms*, or to keep nagging that it does not reach agreement in God."[58] According to Calvin there "is a conviction that requires no reasons; such a knowledge with which the best reason agrees—in which the mind truly reposes more securely and constantly than in any reasons; such, finally a feeling that can be born only of heavenly revelation. *I speak of nothing other than what each believer experiences within himself*—though my words fall far beneath a just explanation of the matter."[59]

There is no chapter in Calvin's writings which deals with experience by itself, but he often uses experience as a descriptive term in connection with Scripture and faith and even, as above, with reason. Thus the appeal to experience identifies an epistemological position which surpasses reason and in which Scripture and faith find confirmation. Calvin does not develop this insight in a technical way,[60] but it serves an important function in his thought.

Since faith is a gift of God, the experience of faith as sure and certain[61] is normative for Calvin, as has often been noted, but the description of faith also includes man's sinful uncertainty. Calvin recognizes that the Christian experiences both belief and disbelief, assurance and agitation, the 'dark night of the soul' and the feeling that God is absent. He writes that the two statements I believe and yet have unbelief "may appear to contradict each other, but there is none of us that does not experience both of them in himself. As our faith is never perfect, it follows that we are partly unbelievers; but God forgives us and exercises such forbearance towards us,

---

[57] François Wendel, *Calvin, the Origins and Development of his Religious Thought*, trans. by Phillip Mairet (New York: Harper and Row, 1963), pp. 358-9.

[58] *Concerning the Eternal Predestination of God*, trans. by J. K. S. Reid (London: James Clarke & Co., 1961), p. 185 (CO 8, 366). Hereafter cited as *Concerning Eternal Predestination*. Emphasis added.

[59] I. 7. 5 (OS III, 71, 8-14). Emphasis added. Cf. I. Thes. 2. 5 (CO 52, 147).

[60] For a contemporary statement, see the excellent studies of John E. Smith, *Experience and God* (London: Oxford University Press, 1968) and *The Analogy of Experience* (New York: Harper & Row, 1973). Also his "The Permanent Truth in the Idea of Natural Religion," *Harvard Theological Review*, 54, 1 (Jan., 1961), 1-19.

[61] Com. Eph. 1. 13 (CO 51, 153); III. 2. 7 (OS IV, 16, 33); Com. Jn. 16. 16 (CO 47, 365).

as to reckon us believers on account of a small portion of faith."[62] Calvin maintains, "The pious soul therefore perceives a division in itself, being partly affected with sweetness through a knowledge of the divine goodness, partly distressed with bitterness through a sense of its own calamity; partly relying on the promise of the gospel, partly trembling at the evidence of its own iniquity; partly exulting in the apprehension of life, partly terrified of death."[63] This conflict between assurance and agitation "is what every one of the faithful experiences in himself daily, for according to the carnal sense he thinks himself cast off and forsaken by God while yet he apprehends by faith the grace of God."[64]

The philosophers do not ignore experience, but the experience to which Calvin appeals is a specifically Christian experience. Hermann Bauke writes, "Calvin is from a material point of view entirely independent of philosophy, but formally he works with philosophy's rational-dialectic method. He is by no means a speculative philosopher or theologian, but he is throughout a theologian of experience (Erfahrungstheologe); at the same time he is a trained dialectician, a 'philosophically working' theologian."[65] Bauke has exaggerated the situation in saying that Calvin is "entirely independent of philosophy". Most of the "material" Calvin works with is Biblical, but some of it is also philosophical, as Calvin recognizes. Calvin knows Plato and Aristotle, Seneca and Cicero too well to be entirely independent of them. Their views neither constitute nor determine Calvin's, but they contribute to it. It is also erroneous to characterize Calvin's method as "rational-dialectic". Calvin's thought is based on exegesis rather than dialectics. However Bauke is correct in suggesting the importance of the category of experience in Calvin's thought. That is to say, Calvin appeals his exposition of Christian philosophy not primarily to logic and reason but to the experience of the faithful.

Indeed some attention has been devoted to the concept of experience in Calvin's thought. For example, Emile Doumergue points out that faith for Calvin is inseparable from experience.[66] H. Obendiek,

---

[62] Com Mk. 9. 24 (CO 45, 495).

[63] III. 2. 18 (OS IV, 29, 7-12).

[64] Com. Ps. 22. 2 (CO 31, 220). Cf. E. A. Dowey, Jr., *The Knowledge of God in Calvin's Theology* (2nd ed.; New York: Columbia University Press, 1965), pp. 192-7.

[65] Bauke, *Die Probleme der Theologie Calvins*, p. 43.

[66] Doumergue, *Jean Calvin*, IV, 437.

in dealing with the relation between experience and the word writes, "Certainly experience cannot affect the actuality of the word, but experience is the way in which the word demonstrates its convincingly present character."[67] Marcel Cadix treats faith and the inner illumination of the Holy Spirit.[68] However these three studies do not exhaust the meaning of experience for Calvin because Calvin's view of experience is not entirely subsumed under his doctrines of faith, Scripture, and the Holy Spirit. Calvin also appeals his doctrines of faith, Scripture, and the Holy Spirit *to experience*. In this sense experience is the arena of human life where events occur which properly understood show that man deals with God in everything. This conception of the experience of dealing with God in everything is a basic attitude of Calvin's which is more than a rational conclusion to be logically defended.

According to Calvin, David knew by his own experience that "No one will ever speak truly and seriously of heavenly doctrine, except he who has it deeply fixed in his own mind."[69] The knowledge of Christ "is a doctrine not of the tongue but of life. It is not apprehended by the understanding [intellectus] and memory alone, as other disciplines are, but it is received only when it possesses the whole soul, and finds a seat and resting place in the inmost affection of the heart."[70] "He who knows Christ in a proper manner holds him fast, embraces him with both arms, is totally occupied by him and desires nothing beyond him."[71] Thus Calvin believes that he can appeal to the experience of the faithful for the confirmation of his teaching.[72]

While Calvin bases his Christian philosophy on the Scripture,

---

[67] H. Obendiek, "Die Erfahrung in ihrem Verhältnis zum Wortes Gottes bei Calvin," *Aus Theologie und Geschichte der Reformierten Kirche: Festgabe für E. F. Karl Müller* (Neukirchen: Buchhandlung der Erziehungsvereins Neukirchen, 1933), p. 189.

[68] Marcel Cadix, "Le Calvinisme et l'expérience religieuse," *Études sur Calvin et le Calvinisme* (Paris: Exposition à la Bibliothèque Nationale à l'occasion du IVe Centenaire de *l'Institution chrétienne*, 1935), pp. 173-87. See also Ronald S. Wallace, *Calvin's Doctrine of the Christian Life* (Grand Rapids: Wm. B. Eerdmans Publishing Company, 1959), pp. 330-2.

[69] Com. Ps. 19. 11 (CO 31, 203).

[70] III. 6. 4 (OS IV, 149, 23-6).

[71] Com. Gal. 1. 4 (CO 50, 170).

[72] Paul Lobstein, "La Connaissance Religieuse d'après Calvin," *Revue de Théologie et de Philosophie* (Paris: Librairie Fischbacher, 1909), p. 20 remarks that the "direct appeal to the personal experience of the faithful is the corollary of his conception of the practical character of religious knowledge."

it is not *merely* the Scripture. The truth of Scripture is revealed to faith through the work of the Holy Spirit and confirmed in experience. Calvin writes in the *Catechism of the Church of Geneva*:

> Child: Scripture teaches that [faith] is the special gift of God, and experience confirms this.
> Minister: Tell me what experience you mean.
> Child: Our mind is too rude to be able to grasp the spiritual wisdom of God which is revealed to us through faith; and our hearts are too prone to distrust or to perverse confidence in ourselves or other creatures to rest of their own accord in God. But the Holy Spirit by his illumination makes us capable of understanding those things which would otherwise far exceed our grasp, and brings us to a sure persuasion by sealing the promises in our hearts.[73]

Calvin uses the concept of experience in a variety of ways. For example, in a negative vein, he says, "Faith cannot arise from a naked experience of things but must have its origin in the Word of God."[74] On a more positive note Calvin asserts that "with experience as our teacher we find God just as he declares himself in his word."[75] Also "daily experience teaches us that flesh is always uneasy until it has obtained a figment like itself in which it may fondly find solace as in an image of God."[76] Yet the Ephesians learn that they are partakers of salvation by experience.[77] Further the goodness of God cannot be placed beyond doubt "unless we really feel and experience its sweetness within ourselves."[78] "The teaching of the gospel will be beneficial to all the godly, because none offers himself as Christ's disciple who does not in return feel and experience him to be a faithful and true teacher."[79]

Thus Calvin sometimes uses Scripture and experience as opposites and sometimes as complementary. In the Commentary on Zechariah, Calvin states, "that there are two kinds of knowledge; one is of faith, which we derive from the word, though the thing itself does not appear; the other is of experience, when God adds accomplishment to the promise and proves that he has not spoken

---

[73] *Calvin: Theological Treatises*, trans. by J. K. S. Reid (Philadelphia: The Westminster Press, 1954), p. 105 (CO 6, 46). Hereafter cited as *Calvin's Treatises*.
[74] Com. Jn. 20. 29 (CO 47, 445).
[75] I. 10. 2 (OS III, 86, 29-30).
[76] I. 11. 8 (OS III, 97, 20-3).
[77] Com. Eph. 1. 13 (CO 51, 153).
[78] III. 2. 15 (OS IV, 26, 19-20).
[79] Com. Jn. 6. 37 (CO 47, 146).

in vain."[80] "And this is frequently the case that believers receive only a slight taste of the divine power from the word and are afterwards excited to admiration by experience."[81]

Experience also seems to have a future reference and in this sense is superior to faith. In his Commentary on Joel, Calvin writes,

> There is a two-fold knowledge [duplex cognitio]: the knowledge of faith which is received from the word alone and the knowledge of experience, as we say, which depends upon its effect. Therefore the faithful always acknowledge that salvation for them rests in God; but sometimes they stagger and suffer grievous torments in their minds, and are tossed here and there. However it may be, they certainly do not by effect feel God to be their Father. Therefore, the prophet now treats of real knowledge [notitia] when he says that they shall know that they have a God. How are they to know this? Of course by experience.[82]

Calvin also says that "it is proper to distinguish between the knowledge which springs from faith and the knowledge which springs from experience; for when the tokens of God's anger are visible all around, and when the judgment of the flesh leads us to believe that he is angry, his favor is concealed from us; but faith raises our hearts above this darkness, to behold God in heaven as reconciled towards us."[83] In this quotation the teaching of experience is corrigible and faith is preferred. The ideas in these two citations are combined in the Commentary on Zechariah.

> But it is to be observed, that there are two kinds of knowledge—the knowledge of faith [scientia fidei] and what they call experimental knowledge [scientia experimentalis]. The knowledge of faith is that by which the godly feel certain that God is true—that what he has promised is indubitable; and this knowledge at the same time penetrates beyond the world, and goes far beyond the heavens, that it may know hidden things; for our salvation is concealed; things seen, says the Apostle, are not hoped for (Romans 8.24). It is then no wonder that the Prophet says that the faithful shall know that Christ has been sent by the Father, that is in reality or by experience.[84]

---

[80] Com. Zech. 4. 9 (CO 44, 188-9).

[81] Com. Lk. 10. 17 (CO 45, 315).

[82] Com. Joel. 3. 17 (CO 42, 596).

[83] Com. Is. 14. 1 (CO 36, 273).

[84] Com. Zech. 2. 9 (CO 44, 162). Calvin uses the following words for knowledge: cognitio, notitia, agnitio, intelligentia, and scientia. See the LCC note to I. 1. 1, p. 35. For scientia see III. 2. 13-4 (OS IV, 23, 38; 24, 4; 25, 14). In Com. I Cor. 8. 2 (CO 49, 429) Calvin writes, "For the foundation of true knowledge [scientia] is personal knowledge of God [cognitio Dei] which makes us humble and obedient and far from putting us on a pedestal it wholly abases us."

Calvin understands man's experience in terms of dealing with God. He writes, "Therefore no one will weigh God's providence properly and profitably but he who considers that his business [negotium] is with his Maker and the Framer of the universe, and with becoming humility submits himself to fear and reverence."[85] Again he says, "Whoever is moderately versed in Scripture will understand by himself, without the admonition of another, that when we have to deal with God [ubi cum Deo negotium est] nothing is achieved unless we begin from the inner disposition of the heart [interiore cordis affectu incipimus]."[86] Also, "accordingly, the Christian must surely be so disposed and minded that he feels within himself that it is with God he has to deal throughout his life."[87] Calvin sees the hand of God in all the events of human life, in both adversity and prosperity. Thus in both good and evil, election and damnation, man is dealing with God. In the Genesis commentary Calvin says that God deals with man in a double way fighting *against* him with his *left* hand and for him with his *right* hand.[88] Calvin admits that man is also responsible in many areas of human life, but he refuses to try to measure out the credit or blame in any exact fashion. His point is that the experience of life is under God's control.

In summary, then, Calvin gives a positive evaluation to reason, not in its speculative endeavours, but in its humble search for connections. Reason may be used but not exalted. Reason is not able to penetrate heavenly things which are not first thought but rather experienced. And it is in the light of experience that they are to be considered. Scripture and faith, too, go beyond reason and Calvin, of course, appeals to both, but he also describes Christian experience as an important epistemological category which comprehends them.

---

[85] I. 17. 2 (OS III, 203, 18-21).

[86] III. 3. 16 (OS IV, 73, 4-6).

[87] III. 7. 2 (OS IV, 152, 15-7).

[88] Com. Gen. 32. 24 (CO 23, 438). Cf. Com. Hos. 6. 1 (CO 42, 319): God's "proper office is to heal after he has torn, to bind the wounds he has inflicted." Some of the preceding material on experience has appeared in my essay "Calvin and Experience," *Scottish Journal of Theology*, 26, 2 (May, 1973), 169-81. Used by permission of the editors and publisher.

CHAPTER FOUR

NATURE AND GOD IN ONTOLOGY

In general until the modern period philosophy was primarily concerned with ontology and therefore with epistemology as the way in which being or reality was perceived. Thus the themes of this chapter cannot be sharply separated from those of the preceding one. However the concern with the reality of God and the correct knowledge of him differs somewhat in emphasis from the prior consideration. With Locke, Hume and Kant the primary focus shifts to the nature and limitations of the human mind. Calvin begins with the knowledge of God not so much because he intends to develop a complete theory of knowledge, but because he opposes what he considers to be fruitless speculation on the part of philosophers and some theologians about the being of God in himself. Although we have indicated the caution with which philosophical categories may be applied to Calvin's thought, it is evident that his affirmations concerning the nature of reality include the existence of God and his creation of the world of nature. The classical philosophers know something of the existence of God and have some valuable insights about nature, but in their ignorance of God's nature as Triune and his creation of the world and the devastating effects of sin, their views are seriously defective. Thus in this chapter we will consider the relation between Calvin and the classical philosophers concerning nature and the being and work of God.

That the philosophers believe in the existence of God (or gods) is clear, though they affirm the nature of divine reality in their several ways. Plato goes to great length to demonstrate the existence of the eternal realm as part of his doctrine of the forms. Thus while Plato locates God with soul in the mediate region between forms and matter, it is not difficult to see parallels between the Christian God and Plato's idea of the good which is above all being. Then Plato's theory of forms can be utilized as the furniture of the mind of God.

Cicero begins Book Two of *De Natura Deorum* with the Stoic theological outline proving: (1) the existence of the gods, (2) the nature of the gods, (3) the government of the world, and (4) the care for mankind.[1] Cicero regards the existence of the gods as proved by the government of heaven, the agreement of men, and the appearance of the gods to men in such events as dreams. According to the Stoics, God is the pre-eminent Being[2] who is identified with the λόγος σπερματικός, the generative reason or cause of the world. The Stoic metaphysics, similar to that of Heraclitus, posits a rational principle in the universe which is referred to God or nature.

With qualified approval Calvin also comments, "One of the ancients seems aptly to have remarked, 'Whatever we see, and whatever we do not see, is God'."[3] However, Stoic theology inconsistently assigns will to God, as in theistic systems, but also identifies God with the necessary process of nature as in pantheism. The former tendency is illustrated in Cleanthes' "Hymn to Zeus" which speaks

---

[1] *De Natura Deorum*, II. 1. 3. In his helpful essay, "Calvin's Use of Cicero in the *Institutes* I : 1-5: A Case Study in Theological Method." *Archiv für Reformationsgeschichte*, 62 (1971), 5-37, Egil Grislis compares a number of statements by Cicero and Calvin dealing with the natural knowledge of God. It is true that Calvin knew Cicero well and was doubtless influenced by what he read, but the sense in which Calvin *used* Cicero is not entirely clear. Grislis is correct in "observing several close parallels between the insights of Cicero and Calvin" (p. 5). Further, concerning the natural knowledge of God, one may grant that "Calvin's perspective is remarkably similar [to Cicero's]" (p. 13), and even that "Calvin's argument is essentially a restatement of Cicero's insight" (p. 10) in the sense that parts of Calvin's view accord with Cicero's. However, in writing that "Calvin follows Cicero's argument very closely" (p. 16), Grislis draws a stronger conclusion than the evidence seems to warrant. Grislis thinks that Calvin has edited Cicero for his own purposes, but yet suggests that Calvin has selected and recorded Cicero's insights (p. 5). Thus Grislis believes that his "comparisons of Cicero have indicated both a literary dependence as well as a basic general agreement" (p. 14). Grislis modifies this position somewhat by noting that because of Cicero's eclecticism "the numerous parallels with Calvin do not necessarily argue for an exclusivistic dependence" (p. 14) which presumably means that the ideas which are similar in Cicero and Calvin may have other sources in Calvin. If then Grislis is maintaining that Calvin read Cicero, occasionally quoted him, and sometimes used similar vocabulary and ideas in his exposition, one may certainly agree, but if he is arguing that Calvin used Cicero's works as a source specifically and directly *in order to* develop his own position as the terms "literary dependence" and "general agreement" might suggest then one may demur. This is to say, as Grislis observes, Calvin's purpose for and evaluation of the natural knowledge of God is different from Cicero's and one can emphasize either similarities or differences. Grislis has marshalled some significant parallels between aspects of Cicero's and Calvin's view of the natural knowledge of God, but, granting their similarities *and differences*, it is not evident that Calvin used extensively, or depended on, Cicero's insights. The parallels are clear; the dependence is not.

[2] Seneca, *Epistulae Morales*, LVIII. 17.

[3] I. 13. 1 (OS III, 108, 25-6). Seneca, *Naturales Quaestiones*, I. 13: "Quid est Deus? Quod vides totum et quod non vides totum."

of God's omnipotence, his guidance, control, and purpose.[4] The latter view is represented by Chrysippus who wrote, "The [natural] law is king over everything, human and divine."[5]

Calvin asserts that there is "no nation so barbarous, no people so savage; that they have not a deep-seated conviction that there is a God."[6] The philosophers know that God exists, but they do not understand his character. These two assertions involving the relation between the natural knowledge of God and the revealed knowledge of God, form part of the controversy between Karl Barth and Emil Brunner concerning nature and grace.[7] Barth, emphasizing the importance of God's revelation, denies the reality of natural knowledge. Brunner, in asserting the primacy of revelation, does not want to deny the validity of natural knowledge entirely.

The specifically Calvin studies on this theme of Peter Barth[8] and Pierre Maury[9] are more amenable to Karl Barth's position and Günter Gloede[10] to Brunner's. Edward A. Dowey, Jr. moves the discussion beyond the either-or with his insight into the dialectical correlation between the knowledge of God as Creator and Redeemer.[11] T. H. L. Parker also writing on Calvin's view of the knowledge of God added an appendix in the American edition of his book criticizing Dowey's division of the *Institutes* into a duplex cognitio Domini as Creator and Redeemer (a division which Parker also uses), but overlooking the fact that Dowey explicitly states that other divisions of the *Institutes* are possible and proper as a way of treating other subjects.[12] The main difference seems to be that while both Dowey

---

[4] Trans. by James Adam in R. D. Hicks, *Stoic and Epicurean* (New York: Russell & Russell, 1910, reprinted 1962), pp. 14-9.

[5] H. von Arnim, *Stoicorum Veterum Fragmenta*, III (Leipzig: Teubner, 1903), 314, p. 77.

[6] I. 3. 1 (OS III, 38, 1-3).

[7] Emil Brunner, *Nature and Grace*, and Karl Barth, *No! Answer to Emil Brunner*, in *Natural Theology*, trans. by Peter Fraenkel (London: The Centenary Press, 1946). For a summary of the discussion see Edward A. Dowey, Jr., *The Knowledge of God in Calvin's Theology*, pp. 247-9.

[8] Peter Barth, *Das Problem der Natürliche Theologie bei Calvin, Theologische Existenz Heute*, No. 18 (Munich: Kaiser Verlag, 1935).

[9] Pierre Maury, "La Théologie Naturelle d'après Calvin," *Études sur Calvin et le Calvinisme* (Paris: Exposition à la Bibliothèque Nationale à l'occasion du IVe Centenaire de *l'Institution chrétienne*, 1935), pp. 257-69.

[10] Günter Gloede, *Theologia Naturalis bei Calvin* (Stuttgart: Kohlhammer, 1935).

[11] Dowey, *The Knowledge of God in Calvin's Theology*, p. 41 and *passim*. Cf. Wilhelm Lütgert, "Calvins Lehre vom Schöpfer," *Zeitschrift für systematische Theologie*, 9 (1932), 421-40.

[12] T. H. L. Parker, *Calvin's Doctrine of the Knowledge of God* (Grand Rapids:

and Parker affirm that the general revelation in creation can only be *properly* understood from the standpoint of special revelation and otherwise serves only a negative function, Parker emphasizes the aspect of negativity[13] while Dowey emphasizes the *reality* of the negative function. Thus Dowey writes, "While it is true that a negative sign stands over the whole revelation in creation in Calvin's theology, we must not allow this sign to erase from our minds the magnitude of the sum thus negatived."[14]

More recently, Werner Krusche[15] and E. David Willis[16] have suggested a fuller Trinitarian setting for this discussion in terms of Calvin's Pneumatology and Christology respectively. In seeking to go beyond the Barth-Brunner framework, Willis says that the question is no longer whether Calvin teaches a natural revelation, but rather in what senses does he teach natural revelation. "For it is clear that Calvin teaches a natural revelation in a certain sense, and it is equally clear that in another sense he teaches that our knowledge of God is limited to what we have through Christ."[17] "The bold either-or rests on the assumption that the cognitio redemptoris is a knowledge of the Redeemer which does not presuppose and include a knowledge of the Father and the Spirit."[18] Thus Willis and Krusche emphasize the unity rather than the dipolarity of the knowledge of God in the relation between the Eternal Son and the Incarnate Christ and the sustaining and reconciling work of the Holy Spirit.

It is true that Calvin accepted the doctrine of the Trinity,[19] which, as all theologians recognize, is an inexplicable mystery. Thus one may correctly emphasize the proper unity (ὁμοουσία, περιχώρησις, consubstantialitas, or coessentialitis) with Willis or the proper distinction (οἰκονομία, ἰδιοποίησις, persona, or discrimen) with Dowey. Both are found in Calvin.

Wm. B. Eerdmans Publishing Company, 1959), pp. 117-25. Dowey, *The Knowledge of God in Calvin's Theology*, p. 42 note 4.

[13] Parker, *Calvin's Doctrine of the Knowledge of God*, p. 123.

[14] Dowey, *The Knowledge of God in Calvin's Theology*, p. 72. For a helpful summary of the discussion to this point see John Newton Thomas, "The Place of Natural Theology in the Thought of John Calvin," *Journal of Religious Thought* (1958), 107-36.

[15] Werner Krusche, *Das Wirken des Heiligen Geistes nach Calvin* (Göttingen: Vandenhoeck & Ruprecht, 1957).

[16] E. David Willis, *Calvin's Catholic Christology* (Leiden: E. J. Brill, 1966).

[17] *Ibid.*, p. 104.

[18] *Ibid.*, p. 121.

[19] Cf. Jan Koopmans, *Das altkirchliche Dogma in der Reformation*, trans. by H. Quistorp (Munich: C. Kaiser, 1938, tr. 1955).

In terms of the present study it is important to notice that the tension between unity and distinction is a basic characteristic of Calvin's thought. Thus he makes distinctions between universal and particular providence and between general and special election, but he does not make a clear distinction between universal providence and general election or between particular providence and special election because these divisions do not affect the unity of man's dealing with God in everything.

However Calvin does not discuss the philosophers in terms of the two-nature Christological doctrine. Luther asserts that the philosophers know something about providence, but not about the Son.[20] For Calvin the knowledge of the Son includes knowledge of the Father and the Spirit, but it is not clear that the philosophers' vague knowledge of God includes even a dim recognition of the Eternal Son. The Stoic logos doctrine may be regarded as a kind of anticipation of the Christian doctrine, but its efficacy depends on the Christian ex post facto identification of the logos with Christ rather than being its logical or historical prerequisite. That is, Christology may claim the Stoic logos doctrine as an adumbration, but Christology is not a product of the Stoic understanding. Since, then, the philosophers affirm God's existence without knowing his proper nature, even their recognition of his existence, while commendable, is not dependable. Calvin says that it is a frigid speculation to discuss the proposition, "Quid sit Deus" when the real inquiry is "Qualis sit Deus."[21] The question is not whether there is a God, but what God is like. The classical philosophers are not totally ignorant concerning the existence of God, but without the light of Scripture, their insight is confused.

Further, the philosophers do not understand God's work in creation. The philosophers' metaphysical quest is determined by their analysis of nature and being. While recent Plato scholarship sees a shift in the later Platonic dialogues from the early and middle periods emphasis on a strong dualism between the ideas and things in the direction of what appears in Aristotle as the unity of form and matter in substance, neither philosopher has a doctrine of creation. Even the demiurge in the *Timaeus* works with a pre-existing stuff. The Epicureans, who appropriate the atomism of Democritus, see the universe as a result of chance, and the Stoic view of necessity

---

[20] *Luther's Works*, 2, 42-3 (WA 42, 292).
[21] I. 2. 2 (OS III, 35, 11-4).

sees God as a maker, but not as creator. The philosophy of Aristotle and the Epicureans denies that God is related to the world as creator. The Stoics identify God and nature. Thus they argue the immanence and concern of God in opposition to the Epicurean view of the gods' transcendence and unconcern.

Calvin asserts that the philosophers are correct in praising nature, but stupid "in failing to recognize God as the Lord and Governor of nature, who according to his will uses all the elements to serve his glory."[22] With Lactantius,[23] Calvin criticizes the Aristotelian and Stoic identification of nature and God. Calvin agrees with the Platonists[24] that the universe is founded as a theater or spectacle of God's glory.[25] However Calvin criticizes the Platonic view that God is the architect rather than the creator of the world.[26] Plato thinks that things made by nature are the work of divine art (θεῖα τέχνη).[27] In much the same sense as Plato the Stoics speak of God as the maker of the universe, but mean that God fashions the universe rather than creating it out of nothing.

On the basis of revelation Calvin affirms "that God by the power of his Word and Spirit created heaven and earth out of nothing [ex nihilo]."[28] God has "revealed himself and daily discloses himself in the whole workmanship of the universe."[29] According to Calvin the works of God are a "bright mirror of his wisdom".[30] The universe is a "mirror" in which men may contemplate God.[31] And from the contemplation of the universe every man receives, not a saving knowledge of God, but "a slight taste of the divine" [modicus divinitatis gustus].[32] It is clear that Calvin has a positive view of

---

[22] IV. 14. 18 (OS V, 276, 25-7).

[23] Lactantius, *Divine Institutes*, II. 5 ANF VII, 47 (MPL VI, 276 c f.).

[24] Plutarch, "On Tranquillity," *Moralia*, VI. 477 c.

[25] I. 5. 5 (OS III, 50, 6).

[26] Com. Jn. 1. 3 (CO 47, 4).

[27] *Sophist*, 265 e.

[28] I. 14. 20 (OS III, 170:29-171:13).

[29] I. 5. 1 (OS III, 45, 1-2).

[30] Com. I Cor. 1. 21 (CO 49, 326).

[31] I. 5. 11 (OS III, 55, 4). Calvin uses the term "mirror" of Moses' history, I. 14. 1 (OS III, 153, 12); of the law, II. 7. 7 (OS III, 332, 33); of Christ, III. 24. 5 (OS IV, 416, 3) and Serm. on Eph. 1. 3-4 (CO 51, 269); of man, Com. Col. 3. 10 (CO 52, 121); and in Com. Rom. 1. 20 (CO 49, 23) he calls the world a "mirror or theater" (speculum seu spectaculum).

[32] I. 5. 15 (OS III, 60, 2). Com. Jon. 1. 5 (CO 43, 212) says that there is a sense of divinity engraved on the heart so that everyone is conscious that there is some divine majesty (numen).

God's revelation in nature. Since God reveals himself in creation, all men have a natural non-redemptive knowledge of God to the extent that they are left without excuse for refusing to worship him. This knowledge is partial and insufficient, but nonetheless real. God the Creator has left his imprint on his works so that even some of the pagan philosophers were not entirely ignorant of God's providence in the world. For example Seneca calls God "the Father of us all".[33]

Calvin uses the word "nature" in two different senses.[34] In the first place nature means the perfection in things as they are created by God. In the second place nature refers to the present state of things fallen from perfection. Corruption is an adventitious quality rather than a substantial property implanted in man from the beginning. In the first sense Calvin maintains that the natural order was a school in which men might learn piety.[35] In the Commentary on Romans he says that the whole nature of things tends towards perfection,[36] and in the Psalms commentary he writes that the order of creation manifests the wonderful providence of God.[37] The sense of nature is so strong that it teaches unbelievers things that the faithful can scarcely believe from revelation.[38] For these reasons the believer should delight in nature and in contemplating the work of God should see his goodness. "For there are as many miracles of divine power, as many tokens of goodness, and as many proofs of wisdom, as there are kinds of things in the universe, indeed, as there are things either great or small."[39]

However, this created perfection was changed by the fall of man of which the philosophers are ignorant. The whole order of nature is subverted by the sin of man.[40] Now the condemnation of the human race is seen on the heavens, the earth, and the creatures.[41] Animals, young children, and even the elements are involved in this guilt.[42]

[33] *Epistulae Morales*, CX. 10.
[34] Cf. Augustine, *The City of God*, 15. 1 (MPL 41, 437); 18. 11 (MPL 41, 568); 21. 15 (MPL 41, 729) on the spiritual and natural.
[35] II. 6. 1 (OS III, 320, 13-4).
[36] Com. Rom. 8. 20 (CO 49, 152).
[37] Com. Ps. 24. 2 (CO 31, 244).
[38] Com. Gen. 26. 28 (CO 23, 368). On the sensus divinitatis, see Dowey, *The Knowledge of God in Calvin's Theology*, pp. 50-6.
[39] I. 14. 21 (OS III, 172, 18-21). Plato, *Parmenides*, 130 c, is not sure whether paltry things have a corresponding idea or not.
[40] Com. Gen. 3. 19 (CO 23, 75).
[41] Com. Rom. 8. 21 (CO 49, 153).
[42] Com. Joel 2. 16 (CO 42, 551); and 2. 22 (CO 42, 558f.).

Still Calvin holds that the creation which was subjected to vanity after the fall of man, yet obeys God and looks to the promised future. According to Calvin, the faithful should not speculate about this future state of redeemed perfection but rest content in the promise that "God will restore the present fallen world to perfect condition at the same time as the human race."[43]

Calvin believes that God creates, restores, and sustains nature. Calvin agrees with the philosophical statement that the "world is God"[44] or "nature is God," but he thinks it is preferable to say that nature is the order established by God since it is harmful to confuse God with his works.[45] While God is not contained in any place, it is sometimes said as an accomodation to man's understanding that God is above the heavens.[46] But in any case, the invisible God "clothes himself, so to speak, with the image of the world, in which he would present himself to our contemplation. They who will not deign to behold him thus magnificently arrayed in the incomparable vesture of the heavens and the earth, afterwards suffer the just punishment of their proud contempt in their own ravings."[47] According to Calvin the providence of God is made clear to the philosophers in the order of the stars.[48]

Calvin is aware that the philosophers too are concerned with the nature and orders of invisible reality. Calvin, following the Scripture and the Nicene Creed, teaches that God created all things visible and invisible and objects that Dionysius had speculated too freely about the angels.[49] Likewise of Plato he writes:

> They are wicked and perverse therefore who imagine the angels possess anything of their own or who make them mediators between us and God, so as to obscure the Glory of God, as if it were far from us, when in fact it reveals its presence in them. We must beware of

---

[43] Com. Rom. 8. 21 (CO 49, 153).

[44] Cicero, *De Natura Deorum*, II. 8. 21.

[45] I. 5. 5 (OS III, 50, 24-8). LCC note 22 points out that this view of nature as god is credited to Seneca by Lactantius.

[46] Com. Am. 9. 6 (CO 43, 162).

[47] Arg. Gen. (CO 23, 8).

[48] Com. Ps. 19. 4 (CO 31, 196-7). Com. Is. 13. 10 (CO 36, 263) says that the sun, moon, and stars are proofs of God's kindness to man. For an indication of the scope of Calvin's view of the rule of God see Heiko A. Oberman, "The 'Extra' Dimension in the Theology of Calvin," *Journal of Ecclesiastical History*, 21, 1 (Jan., 1970), 43-64. The German version appeared in the *Festschrift* Hanns Rückert, Berlin, 1966, 323-56.

[49] Com. Dan. 12. 7 (CO 41, 296).

Plato's silly speculations [Ideo cavendae sunt delirae Platonis specu-
lationes] for the distance between us and God is too great for us to
go to the angels that they may procure grace for us. On the contrary,
we must come straight to Christ, that by his guidance, protection
and command we may have the angels as helpers and ministers of
our salvation.[50]

Calvin's view of the angels is Scriptural not speculative. There is
no trace of the theories of Plato and Aristotle concerning intermediaries or astral intelligences.

---

[50] Com. Jn. 5. 4 (CO 47, 105-6).

CHAPTER FIVE

SOUL AND BODY IN ANTHROPOLOGY

Calvin's view of man is perhaps more indebted to the insights of the philosophers than any other area of his thought. Many of the philosophers' insights concerning man in the state of nature had long been accepted in Christian theology, and Calvin identifies and discusses some of them. It is not surprising that Calvin, like almost every other Christian thinker, adopts the soul-body dualism and that he exalts the soul's relation to God. However, to think that Calvin's anthropology is basically philosophical ignores or dismisses his criticism of the philosophers and the totality of the position he occupies. Our focus in this chapter is the soul's relation to God and more especially the soul's relation to the body. The differences between Calvin and the philosophers are as striking as the similarities. Calvin makes a sharp distinction between the natural and redeemed man, and he teaches the resurrection of the body as well as the immortality of the soul.

In various ways the classical philosophers emphasize man's essential kinship with the gods, especially in terms of soul or mind. Plato believes that the soul is divine and hopes that proper "tendence of the soul" will result in a return to the gods after the death of the body. Aristotle suggests that the active reason is immortal,[1] and the Stoics maintain that human reason is derived from divine reason. Thus reason is a common attribute of gods and men.[2] Seneca wrote to Lucilius, "God is near you, he is with you, he is within you."[3] "Do you marvel that man goes to the gods? God comes to man; nay he comes nearer,—he comes into man. No mind that has not God is good."[4] Likewise Cicero insists that the wisest men believe that the mind has an element of the divine.[5] Therefore philosophy is the gift of the gods,[6] and promises equality with the gods to those who follow it.[7]

---

[1] *De Anima*, 430 a 23.
[2] Seneca, *Epistulae Morales*, XCII. 27.
[3] *Ibid.*, XLI. 1.
[4] *Ibid.*, LXXIII. 16.
[5] *De Finibus*, II. 34. 114.
[6] Seneca, *Epistulae Morales*, XC. 1.
[7] *Ibid.*, XLVIII. 11.

In considering anthropology, Calvin treats both man's created perfection and his sinful condition. God creates man in his own image.[8] Indeed God might have made men dogs and asses since Adam was taken from the earth as were the other animals. In terms of the body there is no difference between man and the other creatures. Thus, according to Calvin, men differ from the animals only because God was pleased to make them men.[9] In a sermon on Job, Calvin said, "Was not the elephant created with us? Are we made of any more precious material than he? Is there any quality in us that we should be more excellent? No, there is nothing that makes a difference between us but God."[10] Since man was created by God, the glory of God is manifest even in the body, but most especially in the soul. "And although the primary seat of the divine image was in the mind and heart, or in the soul and its powers, yet there was no part of man, not even the body itself, in which some sparks did not glow. It is sure that even in the several parts of the world some traces of God's glory shine. From this we may gather that when his image is placed in man a tacit antithesis is introduced which raises man above all other creatures and, as it were, separates him from the common mass."[11]

According to Calvin the image of God in man is an inner good of the soul, implanted by nature,[12] which consists in the reason which men possess and by which they distinguish between good and evil; the seed of religion which is implanted in them; the sense of shame which guilt arouses; and the governance of the laws.[13] However,

---

[8] T. F. Torrance in *Calvin's Doctrine of Man* devotes four chapters to the image of God. Torrance distinguishes a general usage of the imago Dei in which all creation images the glory of God from the special usage which refers specifically to man (35 f.). Since the image of God is dynamic rather than static (61 f.), Torrance focuses on man's relation to God. The exposition of the relational aspect of Calvin's doctrine of the image of God tends to underemphasize the natural, i.e. created, character of the image of God which Calvin also affirms. In a key passage, I. 15. 3 (OS III, 176, 35 f.) Calvin uses the terms, imago, similitudo, and effigies. Calvin generally reserves the imago Dei for Christ, the Word, and man, but he does not sharply distinguish these other usages.

[9] Com. Mal. 1. 2 (CO 44, 40).

[10] Sermon on Job 40. 20 (CO 33, 466).

[11] I. 15. 3 (OS III, 178, 30-37) *Opera Selecta*, III, 177, N. 1 cites Ovid, Cicero, and Lactantius on this idea. Cf. Cicero, *De Natura Deorum*, II. 56. 140: "Nature lifted us from the ground and caused us to stand tall and erect, that we might contemplate the firmament and thus come to know the gods."

[12] I. 15. 4 (OS III, 181, 3-4).

[13] Com. Ps. 8. 5 (CO 31, 92).

Calvin also insists that the image of God is a bonum adventitium lest men should foolishly boast of the excellency of their nature.[14] Commenting on II Peter 1.4 Calvin writes:

> The word nature does not designate substance but quality. The Manicheans used to dream that we took our roots from the stem of God and that when we have finished the course of our life we shall revert to our original state. Likewise today there are fanatics who imagine that we cross over into God's nature so that His nature absorbs ours. This is how they explain Paul's words in I Cor. 15. 18—"that God may be all in all". They take this passage in the same sense. This kind of madness never occurred to the minds of the holy apostles. They were simply concerned to say that when we have put off all the vices of the flesh we shall be partakers of divine immortality and the glory of blessedness, and thus we shall be in a way one with God so far as our capacity allows. This teaching was not unfamiliar to Plato, because he defines the highest human good in various passages as being completely conformed to God. But he was wrapped up in the fog of errors, and afterwards he slid away into his own invented ideas. We, however, must leave aside these empty speculations and be content with this one thing, that the image of God in holiness and righteousness is reborn in us on the condition of our sharing in eternal life and glory, so far as is necessary for complete blessedness.[15]

Calvin's polemic against Osiander and Servetus deals with just this point of the relation of creation and redemption. According to Calvin both Osiander and Servetus believe that the image of God is physical rather than essentially spiritual.[16]

For Calvin, unlike the philosophers, the image of God is not to be understood primarily in terms of nature but in terms of the restoration of corrupted nature.[17] Thus the image of God is also to be understood as part of redemption. Calvin maintains that what was primary in the renewing of God's image in man also held the highest place in creation itself. "Hence, we may learn both what is the end of our regeneration, (that is, that we may be made like God, and that his glory may shine in us) and also what is the image of God which Moses speaks of, that is the rectitude and integrity of the whole soul, so that man reflects as in a mirror the wisdom, righteousness, and

---

[14] Com. Gen. 2. 7 (CO 23, 35).

[15] Com. II Pet. 1. 4 (CO 55, 446-7).

[16] For Osiander see I. 15. 3ff. (OS III, 177, 8ff.). Also Wilhelm Niesel, "Calvin wider Osianders Rechtfertigungslehre," *Zeitschrift für Kirchengeschichte*, 46, 3 (1927), 410-30. For Servetus see I. 15. 5ff. (OS III, 181, 5 ff.).

[17] I. 15. 4 (OS III, 179, 6).

goodness of God."[18] Speaking of the relationship of creation and regeneration in the commentary on Ezekiel, Calvin writes

> Regeneration is like another creation, and if we compare it with the first creation, it far surpasses it. For it is much better for us to be made children of God, and reformed after his image within us, than to be created mortal; for we are born children of wrath, corrupt and degenerate (Eph. 2. 3), since all integrity was lost when God's image was removed. We see, then, the nature of our first creation; but when God refashions us, we are not only born sons of Adam, but we are the brothers of angels, and members of Christ, and this our second life consists in rectitude, justice, and the light of true intelligence.[19]

The image of God in Adam is known from the image of God in the second Adam. Christ is the most perfect image of God and if men are conformed to him, they are restored to God's image.[20] "Our happiness lies in having God's image, which was blotted out by sin, restored and reformed in us. Christ is not only, as the eternal Word of God, his lively image [imago], but even on his human nature, which he has in common with us, the imprint [effigies] of the Father's glory has been engraved, that he might transform his members to it."[21] The end of regeneration is to restore the image of God which is almost obliterated by Adam's transgression. The image of God is found not in a return to nature but in obedience to God. This restoration is not immediate but a matter of life-long effort, so that "the closer any man comes to the likeness of God, the more the image of God shines in him."[22]

The philosophers devote a good deal of attention to the doctrine of soul and its relation to divinity. Calvin does not question the accuracy of their basic analysis of man's essential spirituality, but he denies its adequacy. Cicero speaks of a likeness between God and man,[23] and so does Calvin, but Calvin insists that a distinction between man's created nature and his redeemed nature is necessary. The image of God in man is not to be understood solely in terms of nature as with the philosophers but from man's redeemed nature as revealed and received through Jesus Christ.

---

[18] Com. Col. 3. 10 (CO 52, 121).
[19] Com. Eze. 18. 32 (CO 40, 456).
[20] I. 15. 4 (OS III, 179, 11-13).
[21] Com. Jn. 17. 22 (CO 47, 388).
[22] III. 3. 9 (OS IV, 65, 8-9).
[23] De Legibus, I. 8. 25.

Concerning the relation of soul and body, the philosophic con-
sensus of a dualistic understanding had a profound influence on
subsequent Christian thought.[24] According to Werner Jaeger, "The
most important fact in the history of Christian doctrine was that
the father of Christian theology, Origen, was a Platonic philosopher
at the school of Alexandria. He built into Christian doctrine the whole
cosmic drama of the soul, which he took from Plato, and although
later Christian fathers decided that he took over too much, that
which they kept was still the essence of Plato's philosophy of the
soul."[25]

Friedrich Solmsen writes, "In the first and fundamental section
of *Laws* 10, Soul is clearly the basic principle of Plato's theology as
well as of his cosmology."[26] The Platonic doctrine of soul had a
powerful impact on all subsequent thinkers. Plotinus uses it and
Marsilio Ficino follows Plato by giving the soul a decisive place
in his *Platonic Theology*. The separation of soul and body, which
Plato teaches, had a profound impact on Christian theology and
only recently has the separation of soul and body been questioned
as unbiblical.[27] Calvin however praises Plato's belief in the immortality
of the soul,[28] and on the basis of that doctrine is often considered
"Platonic".

In an influential article entitled "The Doctrine of Man in Calvin
and Renaissance Platonism," Roy W. Battenhouse suggests that
there are important resemblances between Calvin and Renaissance
Platonism in the treatment of human nature. He claims that "both
the Neoplatonists and Calvin base their thinking about man on the
premise of a dualism between soul and body," which reveals "Calvin's
fundamental Platonism". Although Battenhouse calls his study
"frankly exploratory and tentative" and uses such phrases as

---

[24] For a fuller presentation see my essay, "The Soul in Plato, Platonism, and
Calvin," *Scottish Journal of Theology*, 22, 3 (Sept., 1969), 278-95, some parts of
which are used here and by permission.

[25] Werner Jaeger, "The Greek Ideas of Immortality," *Harvard Theological
Review*, 52. 3 (July, 1959), 146. Although Jaeger recognizes that the New Testament doctrine of the resurrection of the body is quite different from Plato's
idea of the immortality of the soul, he correctly points out that the soul and its
immortality is central to Plato's thought, and it was fused with Christian doctrine.

[26] Friedrich Solmsen, *Plato's Theology* (Ithaca: Cornell University Press, 1942),
p. 138.

[27] Cf. Oscar Cullmann, *Immortality of the Soul or Resurrection of the Dead* (London:
The Epworth Press, 1958).

[28] I. 15. 6 (OS III, 182, 17-22).

"may have been" and "seems to have" and "it can be argued", the evidence demonstrates to him "that Calvin's so-called biblical theology is not quite so biblical as its nuggets of quotation would like to impress upon us."[29] Heinrich Quistorp also thinks that the question remains whether in fact Calvin does not develop a doctrine of soul which is more philosophical than theological. Quistorp thinks that Luther was more aware of the contrast between biblical anthropology and philosophical dualism than Calvin was.[30] It is true that both Calvin and Plato teach a separation of body and soul, but while Calvin teaches the immortality of the soul, he also believes in the resurrection of the body, which Plato did not.

Since Calvin's doctrine of soul has been called "Platonic", it will be useful to consider what Plato's doctrine of soul was. Traditionally the Platonic dualism refers to the divison between the ideal world and the world of changing, sensible things as in *Parmenides* 130 b, and involves the separation of soul and body. This view is then distinguished from the Aristotelian position understood in the form that soul and body exist only in combination.[31] However, the so-called "Platonic dualism" of soul and body is not maintained in the same form throughout the *Dialogues*. Further the emphasis on similarities between Calvin and Plato is one-sided since there are also notable differences.

The *Dialogues* of Plato contain three major approaches to a doc-

---

[29] Roy W. Battenhouse, "The Doctrine of Man in Calvin and in Renaissance Platonism," *Journal of the History of Ideas*, IX (April, 1948), 468, 469.

[30] Heinrich Quistorp, *Calvin's Doctrine of the Last Things*, trans. by Harold Knight (Richmond: John Knox Press, 1955), p. 73, 101.

[31] In the French edition of the *Institutes* (1560) Calvin referred to Aristotle's view of the soul's endowment with organs or instruments, "De dire selon Aristote, comme ils font, que l'âme est douée d'organes ou instrumens." I. 5. 4 (OS III, 48, 3-5). Aristotle's position is that the soul is the first actuality (ἐντελέχεια) of a natural body possessed of organs. Thus soul relates to body as shape does to wax (*De Anima*, 412 a 4). Calvin, I. 5. 5 (OS III, 48, 22f.) criticizes Aristotle's doctrine of soul by commenting on those who argue that since the soul has organic functions, it cannot exist without body. It is true that Aristotle teaches that the soul is inseparable from the body (*Ibid.*, 413 a 4), and cannot exist without a body (*Ibid.*, 414 a 20). However Calvin does not mention that Aristotle also insists that the soul cannot *be* a body and is, at least theoretically, separable (*Ibid.*). W. D. Ross, *Aristotle* (5th ed.; New York: Barnes and Noble, 1959), p. 132 correctly summarizes, "Soul and body form a union which while it lasts is complete, and in which soul and body are merely aspects distinguishable by the philosophic eye." Still when this union is broken by the death of the body, the highest element of the soul, the active reason or mind, continues to exist because Aristotle regarded *it* as separable (*De Anima*, 430 a 17). Calvin does not deal with Aristotle's conception of the immortality of the active reason.

trine of soul. The early approach may be called religious and dualistic, but the second approach, as found in the middle dialogues, is basically political in orientation. Here the soul is tripartite. Plato's third approach, contained in the later dialogues, may be called metaphysical, and considers the philosophical aspects of soul as self-moving. The common aspect of each approach is that soul is seen as some kind of intermediary. In the early dialogues soul is an intermediary between the forms and things, but nearer the forms. In the middle dialogues soul is also an intermediary but is viewed from the standpoint of this world. In the later dialogues soul is an intermediary between the principles of rest and motion. This view of soul as an immortal intermediary, with additions taken from Aristotle, is developed in the Neoplatonism of Plotinus and Ficino, but not in Calvin. It is true that Calvin's doctrine of the immortality of the soul has some "points of contact" with the early, religious aspect of Plato's doctrine and its transmission in Neoplatonism, but even there the differences are more fundamental than the similarities.

"The supporters of the ideal theory" argue that for each thing there is an entity which has the same name and exists *apart* from the substances. These ideas or forms are regarded as ontological principles existing in themselves apart from the sensible world. They are models or archetypes laid up in heaven and imperfectly copied in the sensible world. Thus the famous "Platonic dualism" appears in the early and middle dialogues, but most interpreters extend this dualism to the entire philosophy.

Plato is aware that putting the unchanging ideas and the changing things into juxtaposition makes their relation a major problem and expounds a doctrine of participation to explain the relation of the ideas to things. It is true that Plato never solves this problem to his satisfaction, but he is led to a doctrine of intermediaries and especially to the notion of soul as an epistemological intermediary between the ideas and things.[32] This theory develops out of the soul's kinship with the forms in the early dialogues. Here one sees the "other-worldly" doctrines of the pre-existence and immortality of the soul. In the middle dialogues, soul develops against a "this-worldly" backdrop in the *Symposium* and in the *Republic*.

Plato recognizes, as early as the *Phaedo*, the existence of an entity

---

[32] Cf. Joseph Souilhé, *La Notion Platonicienne d'Intermédiaire dans la Philosophie des Dialogues* (Paris: Librairie Felix Alcan, 1919), p. 197.

which is neither an idea nor a sensible thing. Soul is *akin* to the ideas, but it is *not* an idea.[33] Soul is an intermediate or mediating existence which makes real knowledge possible.[34] In the *Phaedo* Plato sees a difference between body and soul. The body is human and mortal, multiform and dissoluble, and changeable. Soul can be dragged by body into the region of the changeable, but when soul returns to herself, she passes into the other world, the world of eternity and unchangeableness. Cebes sums up the discussion this way, "I think, Socrates, that, in the opinion of everyone who follows the argument, the soul will be infinitely more like the unchangeable."[35] Without soul, knowledge would be impossible. The realm of ideas and the realm of things would exist in splendid isolation. In his doctrine of soul Plato attempted to relate the two grades of reality: the pure grade which is unmixed with body, and the impure which is mixed with body. Since the soul stands halfway between the unity of being and the multiplicity of matter, real knowledge is possible.

In the middle dialogues Plato considers soul in relation to this world. Soul is not now a divine visitant but an inhabitant of this world. Soul is still an intermediary between the forms and things, but the viewpoint is more earthly. In the *Republic*, Plato addresses himself anew to the relation of soul and body because he needs a psychology which develops the doctrine of soul along with that of the state. Plato indicates that the tripartite soul theory was of fundamental importance in understanding the state.[36] The same principles which exist in the state exist also in the individual, and they are three in number.[37] The view that Plato is not serious about the threefold division of the soul is not plausible. J. L. Stocks writes, "It is not too much to say that the doctrine of the tripartite soul dominates Plato's thought in the ethical sphere."[38] This means that Plato's doctrine of soul is obviously developing. In the *Phaedo* the

---

[33] *Phaedo*, 79 e.
[34] Léon Robin, *Platon* (Paris: Felix Alcan, 1935), p. 176. Cf. Paul Friedländer, *Plato*, trans. by Hans Meyerhoff (New York: Pantheon Books, 1958), p. 43.
[35] *Phaedo*, 79 e.
[36] *Republic*, IV, 435 e.
[37] *Ibid.*, 441 c.
[38] J. L. Stocks, "Plato and the Tripartite Soul," *Mind*, new series, XXIX (1915), 218. Cf. F. M. Cornford, "The Division of the Soul," *The Hibbert Journal*, XXVIIII (October 1929-July 1930), 206-219.

philosopher's aim was to overcome passion. In the *Symposium* passion was accepted as a way to the forms. In the *Republic* passion has become part of the soul.

Calvin is aware of the discussion of the parts of the soul,[39] and prefers Aristotle to Plato. Calvin writes, "Plato, in some passages, talks nobly of the faculties of the soul; and Aristotle, in discoursing on it, has surpassed all in acuteness."[40] If one chooses to focus attention exclusively on this aspect of Calvin, he could maintain that Calvin was "fundamentally Aristotelian". However Calvin says that one can safely leave the discussion of faculties to the philosophers. Pious readers need not torture themselves in these trivial, useless and obscure matters.

In the early and middle dialogues Plato's basic concern is with the theory of unchanging, invisible forms and changing, visible things. Because they are opposites the epistemological problem arises: How can both forms and things be known? Plato develops the concept of soul as a principle of meditation, partaking of both realms, to make knowledge possible. However, the opposition of forms and things not only creates a problem in epistemology, but also in metaphysics. If there is a changing order and an unchanging order, the assumption of an intermediate principle of motion is a necessary consequence of the opposition between rest and motion. In the later dialogues Plato criticizes both the friends of the forms and the advocates of the flux.[41] Interestingly, every feature of the view of the friends of the forms may be illustrated from Plato's own early dialogues. This fact suggests that Plato is not, perhaps, an orthodox Platonist in the sense that he does not intend that the early and middle dialogues exhaust his philosophy. He may be criticizing the members of the Academy who took certain of his suggestions, such as the doctrine of forms as separate, more seriously than he intended. For our purpose it need not be decided whether Plato abandons the doctrine of forms *as separate* after the *Parmenides* or merely does not mention them (with the exception of the mythical account in *Timaeus*, 51 d).[42] But it is clear in his later period that

---

[39] I. 15 6 (OS III, 183, 9f.).

[40] "Psychopannychia," *Calvin's Tracts*, III, 420 (CO 5, 178).

[41] *Sophist*, 243 d.

[42] Werner Jaeger, *Paideia: The Ideals of Greek Culture*, trans. by Gilbert Highet, III (New York: Oxford University Press, 1944), 260 says that the theory of forms does not appear in the later dialogues, but if "we started by saying that the theory of Ideas does not appear in *The Laws* that should not be interpreted as agreement

Plato is far from making the separate ideas the central doctrine of his philosophy. He recognizes the necessity of causes and identifies the origin of change with soul.

In the later dialogues Plato examines a doctrine of motion.[43] Plato is concerned in the *Cratylus* with names and motion, in the *Parmenides* with becoming in time, in the *Theaetetus* with extravagant claims for motion, in *Sophist* with motion elevated to the level of rest, and in the *Timaeus* with divine motion. The theory of motion in the *Laws* is a philosophical development of the mythical account in the *Phaedrus*. This is Plato's attempt to use soul as an intermediate between the animate and the inanimate, the unchanging and the all changing. Solmsen says, "It seems clear that this whole set of dialogues, namely *Theaetetus*, the *Sophist*, the *Statesman*, *Parmenides*, and probably *Cratylus* too, originated from the tense conflict between the claims of the Philosophy of Being and the Ideas and the Philosophy of Becoming."[44] Plato's concern with process in the later dialogues leads to the motion of soul and finally to the self-motion of soul. However, the emphasis changes as the dialogues develop. The early doctrine of soul is other-worldly and religious, the middle dialogues are this-worldly and political, the later dialogues regard soul from a metaphysical point of view, but in each period the soul is an intermediary principle, and it is this aspect which is continued in Neoplatonism.

Plotinus and Ficino, unlike Calvin, use Plato as a source and are strongly influenced by Plato's doctrine of soul. Plotinus did not find Plato entirely consistent, but he admitted his debt to the account given in the *Timaeus*. Plotinus teaches that soul holds mid-rank (μέση τάξις) among the authentic existences, being divine but at

---

with the well known modern hypothesis that Plato abandoned it in his old age." F. M. Cornford, *Plato's Theory of Knowledge* (London: Routledge and Kegan Paul, 1935), p. 45 *et passim* advances the strange theory that Plato has not abandoned the doctrine of the forms although he admits that they do not figure directly in the *Theaetetus* and *Sophist*. Cornford thinks that Plato is making an attempt to get along without the doctrine of forms in order to make us feel the need of them!

[43] The use of ψυχή in another sense than for the soul of man recurs from Thales to Democritus. It stood for the principle of animation and in its earliest usage may have stood for the principle of motion. Walter Pater, *Plato and Platonism* (New York: Macmillan and Co., 1893), p. 61 reflects a common error when he says that for Plato the philosophy of motion is identified with the vicious tendency in things and thought. Cf. J. B. Skemp, *The Theory of Motion in Plato's Later Dialogues* (Cambridge: Cambridge University, 1942).

[44] Solmsen, *Plato's Theology*, p. 77.

the lowest extreme of the Intellectual and above sense-known nature.[45] Marsilio Ficino recognizes that for the Platonists, soul occupies an intermediary region between the eternal and the temporal.[46] Ficino pictures soul as an intermediary, a double-faced Janus placed on the borderline between time and eternity looking toward the corporeal and toward the incorporeal world.[47] Plotinus specifically denies the resurrection of the body,[48] but Ficino, under the influence of the Christian tradition, says that soul will resume body. He argues that the inclination which souls have for bodies remains even after souls have been separated. Hence at some time the souls will again receive their bodies for which a natural affection remains. Thus the body will be resurrected to become entirely immortal.[49]

If Battenhouse's charge of Calvin's "fundamental Platonism" can be sustained, one would expect to find Platonic insights supported by Platonic argumentation at decisive points in Calvin's exposition. It would be important if Calvin uses Plato or the Neoplatonists as sources. This would be a Platonic influence in the "strong" sense— an influence which might be called "philosophical Platonism". But it is not very remarkable that Calvin is indirectly influenced by the common "theological Platonism" of so much of the Christian thought from the Greek fathers through Augustine and the Renaissance Platonists or that aspects of Calvin's doctrines "resemble" Plato's. In this "weak" sense Calvin is not alone in being influenced by Platonism.[50] Battenhouse does not indicate what he considers the relation between Plato and Neoplatonism to be, and he does not try to assess the direct influence of Plato's *Dialogues* or Ficino's *Theologia Platonica* on Calvin's *Institutes*. What Battenhouse seems to have in mind is a Platonic influence on Calvin in the "weak" sense indicated above. He takes the fact that Calvin criticizes the Renaissance concept of man to mean that Calvin had a "subterranean dependence" upon it.[51] But this kind of dependence requires no

---

[45] Plotinus, *Opera*, ed. by Paul Henry and Hans-Rudolf Schwyzer, II (Paris: Desclée de Brouwer, 1959), p. 247. *Enneads*, 4. 8. 7.

[46] Marsilius Ficinus, *Opera Omnia* (Basel, 1561), p. 824.

[47] *Ibid.*, p. 375, 658.

[48] *Enneads* 3. 6. 6.

[49] Ficino, *Opera Omnia*, pp. 416-7.

[50] Cf. R. Arnou, "Le Platonisme des Pères," *Dictionnaire de Théologie Catholique*, XII, 2257-392.

[51] Battenhouse, "The Doctrine of Man in Calvin and in Renaissance Platonism," p. 470.

more than a knowledge of what one rejects. The "affinities" between Calvin and the Renaissance Platonists which Battenhouse adduces are found on many levels of seriousness and should make us suspicious of evaluating Calvin as Platonic in terms of them.[52]

The importance of the Greek concept of soul can scarcely be overestimated. Jaeger writes, "The Greeks . . . share with the Jews the honour of creating an intellectualized faith in God, but it was the Greeks alone who were to determine for several millennia the way in which civilized man would conceive the nature and destiny of the soul."[53] Plato brought the soul into the area of faith, and established the theological conception of personal immortality in the heart of philosophy. Plato's own brother, Glaucon, appears astonished to hear that the soul is immortal.[54] Calvin praises Plato for believing that the soul is immortal, but he commends only part of the Platonic view of soul rather than endorsing the entire tradition. Calvin does not use Plato's doctrine of soul as a source but only commends his belief in immortality as an example that some kind of "natural" understanding of the immortality of the soul could be found in Platonism. By defending the primacy of soul Plato sought to establish the priority of the spiritual over the material, but Calvin's commendation is severely qualified. Calvin writes, "I readily acknowledge that the philosophers, who were ignorant of the resurrection of the body, have many discussions about the immortal essence of the soul, but they talk so foolishly about the state of the future life that their opinions have no weight. But since the Scriptures inform us that the spiritual life depends on the hope of the resurrection, and that souls, when separated from the bodies, look forward to it, whoever destroys the resurrection deprives souls also of their immortality."[55] Calvin obviously differs from Plato in believing that the immortality of the soul cannot be properly understood apart from the resurrection of the body.

Calvin teaches the union of body and soul, saying that the relation of union without confusion between soul and body is the closest human parallel to the two natures of Christ.[56] At the same time

---

[52] See my essay, "The Soul in Plato, Platonism, and Calvin," esp. pp. 287-9.

[53] Werner Jaeger, *The Theology of the Early Greek Philosophers*, trans. by Edward S. Robinson (Oxford: Clarendon Press, 1947), p. 3.

[54] *Republic*, X, 608 d.

[55] Com. Mt. 22. 23 (CO 45, 604-5).

[56] II. 14. 1 (OS III, 458, 24-8). B. B. Warfield, *Calvin and Calvinism* (New York: Oxford University Press, 1931), p. 337 calls Calvin a "dichotomist".

Calvin makes a distinction between soul and body,[57] but he thinks this distinction is Scriptural rather than philosophical. "Only a little teaching of the Gospel" is better than knowing all of Plato.[58] On the doctrine of soul the philosophers were unclear. Calvin writes, "Here let human wisdom give place; for though it thinks much about the soul it perceives no certainty with regard to it. Here, too, let Philosophers give place, since on almost all subjects their regular practice is to put neither end nor measure to their dissensions, while on this subject in particular they quarrel, so that you will scarcely find two of them agreed on any single point."[59] Whatever philosophical affinities there may be to Plato's view of immortality and the relation of body and soul, Calvin's doctrine is basically Christian.

According to Calvin, there would have been no separation of soul and body if there had not been sin. Without sin the body itself would have been immortal.[60] But now that sin has entered the world, "Death, it is true, ordinarily is the separation of the soul from the body."[61] Calvin says, "So, on the other hand, the word *body* signifies the more solid mass as yet unpurified by the Spirit of God from earthly defilements, which delight only in what is gross. It would be absurd otherwise to ascribe to the body the blame for sin. Again, the soul is so far from being life, that is does not even of itself have life."[62]

Calvin regards soul as an immortal yet created essence. Soul is the nobler part of man.[63] However the soul, while immortal, is not eternal because without God the soul dies.[64] When we say that the spirit of man is immortal, we do not mean that it is able to subsist apart from the power of God.[65] As Torrance puts it, "The soul is as much a creature as the body. Both depend on the grace of God . . . The soul survives the death of the body only at the mercy of God, and has no durability in itself."[66] Immortality, then, for Calvin is

---

[57] I. 5. 5 (OS III, 48, 29-30); I. 15. 2 (OS III, 176, 2).

[58] Com. Jn. 16. 29 (CO 47, 372).

[59] "Psychopannychia," *Calvin's Tracts*, III, 443 (CO 5, 196).

[60] Com. Gen. 3. 19 (CO 23, 77) and 2. 17 (CO 23, 45).

[61] Com. I. Thes. 4. 16 (CO 52, 167).

[62] Com. Rom. 8. 10 (CO 49, 145). Com. Ps. 31. 5 (CO 31, 303-4): Calvin recognizes that soul once signified life.

[63] I. 15. 2 (OS III, 174, 27-8).

[64] Cf. Wilhelm Niesel, *Die Theologie Calvins*, p. 64.

[65] "Psychopannychia," *Calvin's Tracts*, III, 478 (CO 5, 222).

[66] Torrance, *Calvin's Doctrine of Man*, p. 26.

not a natural characteristic as it is with Plato. If God withdraws his grace, then the soul becomes a passing breath just as the body is dust.[67]

Calvin, whose body was constantly wracked with pain, does call the body, that is the body under the condition of sin, a "reformatory" (ergastulum),[68] and "prison" (carcer).[69] At the same time he knew that men are called to present their bodies as a living sacrifice to God. The body is the temple of God.[70] The fourth petition of the Lord's Prayer shows that God does not disdain to take the body under his providence.[71]

It might be argued that Calvin "had a spiritualizing tendency" and that Luther was more sensitive to the Biblical antithesis of flesh and spirit as distinct from body and soul,[72] but this is a criticism of emphasis rather than ignorance. Perhaps Calvin over-reacts to the Anabaptists, Osiander, Servetus, and Socinus, but he firmly believes that both soul and body are from God.[73] Emile Doumergue comments, "Oh, no doubt the body is a *tent*, a *prison* and worse still in the vehement language of our preacher. But, at the same time, 'there is no part of the body in which some spark of the divine image is not to be found shining.' It is the 'temple of the Holy Spirit', 'the altar' on which God would be adored . . . And it is in a sort of canticle that Calvin celebrates its resurrection."[74]

Unlike Plato, Calvin teaches the resurrection of the body. He is aware that "It is difficult [for natural reason] to believe that bodies, when consumed with rottenness, will at length be raised up in their season. Therefore although many of the philosophers declared souls immortal, few approved the resurrection of the flesh."[75] Calvin confesses the resurrection not of the soul but of the body.[76] Calvin believes in the resurrection of the body in the first place because the resurrec-

---

[67] "Psychopannychia," *Calvin's Tracts*, III, 478 (CO 5, 222).

[68] I. 15. 2 (OS III, 175, 5). Warfield, *Calvin and Calvinism*, p. 339. thinks that "this is doubtless merely a classical manner of speech, adhered to without intentional implication of its corollaries."

[69] III. 9. 4 (OS IV, 174, 12).

[70] *Excuse de Iehan Calvin à Messieurs les Nicodemites*, CO 6, 611.

[71] III. 20. 44 (OS IV, 356, 24-5).

[72] Quistorp, *Calvin's Doctrine of the Last Things*, pp. 62, 58.

[73] III. 25. 7 (OS IV, 446, 16).

[74] Emile Doumergue, "Calvin, Le Prédicateur de Genève," address delivered at the 400th anniversary of Calvin's birth (July 2, 1909), p. 21. Original emphasis.

[75] III. 25. 3 (OS IV, 434, 33-7).

[76] "Psychopannychia," *Calvin's Tracts*, III, 470 (CO 5, 216). Doumergue, *Jean Calvin*, IV, 309 criticizes Schulze for ignoring this fact.

tion of Christ was attested by authentic evidence, and men are not separated from Christ. In the second place, resurrection is not part of the course of nature, but an incalculable miracle of the omnipotence of God. God does not call forth new matter, but dead men, and restores their bodies.[77] Calvin does not want to philosophize too freely, but he suggests that while the quality of body would be different, men shall be raised again in the same flesh which they now bear. Since God rules all the elements, he will have no difficulty commanding the elements to restore what they seem to have consumed.[78]

One might say with Schulze that Calvin was not serious about the resurrection and added it on the authority of Scripture,[79] or that resurrection of the body was "ein Fremdkörper" in Calvin's thought.[80] But one can argue more plausibly that the discussions of immortality of soul and resurrection of the body in Calvin can no more be separated than the discussions of God the Creator and God the Redeemer. If the doctrine of the Trinity allows a distinction between the persons of Godhead without a division, then Calvin's anthropology could, and does contain a distinction between soul and body without the Platonic division.

The immortality of the soul in Plato, Plotinus, and Ficino has some resemblances to Calvin's doctrine but Calvin's Biblical concerns forbid an identification of his view as entirely philosophical. Contemporary theology sees a sharper distinction between the immortality of the soul and the resurrection of the body than Calvin perceives, but this fact does not make Calvin Platonic. Calvin looks at the subject of soul and body, immortality and resurrection through the "spectacles of Scripture". The lens of Calvin's spectacles were certainly tinted by Platonism here, but the source of Calvin's view of soul and body is the Scripture.

---

[77] III. 25. 7 (OS IV, 446: 37—447: 4).

[78] III. 25. 8 (OS IV, 450, 10). *Cf.* Com. Jn. 3. 7 (CO 47, 58-9).

[79] Martin Schulze, *Meditatio futuræ vitæ* (Leipzig: Dieterich'sche, 1901), p. 88. For a balanced criticism of Schulze see Quistorp, *Calvin's Doctrine of the Last Things*, pp. 51-4. See also Bohatec, *Budé und Calvin*, p. 415ff.

[80] As Walter Zimmerli in the introduction to his edition of the *Psychopannychia* (1932), p. 6.

CHAPTER SIX

RULES AND CONTEXTS IN ETHICS

Calvin's interest in ethics is theological. That is to say, his concern is man's obedience to the revealed will of God. Man for Calvin is not only ignorant but sinful; not only willful but disobedient. Nevertheless, Calvin devotes some attention to the ethical teachings of the classical philosophers. Bohatec, who deals with such common themes as freedom, tranquillity, self-denial, and duty, correctly observes that since the classical philosophers do not know the regenerate man, Calvin's use of their categories is filled with a different content.[1] Bohatec's reference to the ethical personality which, according to Kant, stands under the discipline of reason also applies to the classical philosophers, while, according to Calvin, the Christian man is under the discipline of faith.[2]

The contemporary ethical discussion concerning rules and contexts poses a false alternative if the role of rule and context is considered to be mutually exclusive, but, as a matter of emphasis, it is a helpful distinction. As such it applies to Calvin's thought in the sense that he sees the faithful man dealing with God and the world in the context of grace and obedience in opposition to the philosopher who deals with God and the world in the context of reason and duty. We need not attempt to ascertain the priority between rules and contexts for Calvin since they belong together in either case. Each rule has a context, and each context has an effect. Still it is clear that the man of reason and the man of faith stand in somewhat different positions and therefore the rules which the faithful obey, while they may be similar to the reasonable man's in expression, are different in motivation.

Among the more interesting ethical ideas of the philosophers which may be formulated as rules that Calvin treats are the notion of following nature which Calvin criticizes on the basis of the perversion of nature; the concept of treating all men as brothers which Calvin accepts with a criticism of the Stoic avoidance of pity; and the view that all sins are equal which Calvin rejects. According to

---

[1] Bohatec, *Budé und Calvin*, pp. 346-438.
[2] *Ibid.*, p. 387.

Calvin sins are not equal, but they are equally mortal. The most interesting contextual feature is the notion of man's union with God, which Calvin cites in Plato, but develops in terms of Christ. Philosophical ethics is a means-end system. The end is known but not yet reached. The philosophers teach that the reasonable man must obey rules as a means toward the end. Thus it is claimed that no one realizes a happy life until his death. Since Calvin believes that the goal of life is already present in Jesus Christ, he teaches that the faithful man must obey rules because he is within the context of salvation.

The Stoics are chiefly concerned about the application of theoretical reason to the field of ethics. Cicero regards all philosophy as fruitful, but especially the part which deals with moral duties.[3] Thus one Stoic rule is "live according to nature."[4] For the Stoics the chief good of living in harmony with nature means leading a morally good life with an understanding of the course of events which is in accordance with nature.[5] The Stoic principle of apathy (ἀπαθεία) involves a passive acceptance of external events over which man has no control. Thus they feel that the wise man can be happy even upon the rack.[6] Living according to nature is considered a voluntary attitude. The wise man escapes necessity by willing to do what necessity forces upon him.[7] It is apparently only in the acceptance of necessity that man exercises his freedom, although how this freedom is grounded the Stoics do not say. Thus the Stoic doctrine of virtue or the excellence (ἀρετή) of man depends to some extent on the free will of man. According to Marcus Aurelius, to follow necessity is imposed on all, but only to the rational animal is given the power to follow voluntarily what happens.[8]

For the Stoics man's freedom consisted in desiring what God wills. "Let great souls comply with God's wishes, and suffer unhesitatingly whatever fate the law of the universe ordains . . . ."[9] Epictetus says, "I have submitted my freedom of choice unto God. He wills that I shall have fever; it is my will too. He wills that I should desire something; it is my will too. He wills that I should get something;

---

[3] *De Officiis*, III. 2. 5. Cf. *De Finibus*, III. 2. 6.
[4] Seneca, *Epistulae Morales*, V. 4. Cf. Cicero, *De Officiis*, III. 3. 13.
[5] *Ibid.*, 9. 32. Cf. *De Finibus*, II. 11. 34.
[6] *Ibid.*, III. 13. 42. Cf. Aristotle, *Ethica Nicomachea*, VII. 13. 1153 b 19-21.
[7] Seneca, *Epistulae Morales*, LIV. 7.
[8] *Meditations*, X. 28. Cf. Lactantius, *Divine Institutes*, V. 7 (MPL VI, 570-1).
[9] Seneca, *Epistulae Morales*, LXXI. 16.

it is my wish too. He does not will it; I do not wish it. To die—then I wish it; to be tortured on a rack—then I wish it."[10] Seneca thinks that reason is required in order to endure prosperity and misfortune.[11]

Calvin's view is not totally dissimilar. His view of man's responsibility precludes apathy, but nevertheless everything that happens is governed by the will of God. Thus disease, war, poverty, and death occur, but even in these things, the believer remembers God's kindness. "In short, whatever happens, because he will know it ordained of God, he will undergo it with a peaceful and grateful mind so as not obstinately to resist the command of him into whose power he once for all surrendered himself and his every possession."[12] The difference is that Calvin believes the world is governed by a loving and all-seeing God rather than by blind fate. Thus the Christian response is patience rather than Stoic resignation.

The Stoic ethical philosophy does not entirely deny chance, "The enormous two-fold power of Fortune for weal and for woe."[13] Cicero writes that "the most powerful influence in the choice of a career is exerted by Nature [but] the next most powerful by Fortune [therefore] we must, of course, take account of them both in deciding upon our calling in life; but of the two, Nature claims the most attention."[14] Calvin rejects the Stoic ideal of living in accordance with nature (κατὰ φύσιν) because it does not take the perversion of nature or sin seriously enough.[15]

The Stoic philosophers also teach that all men should be treated as brothers because men are drawn together by nature into a community of reason. Aristotle teaches that man is a social animal[16] and develops a doctrine of friendship,[17] but the Stoics add a deeper dimension to the notion of a community of men in their strong emphasis on the brotherhood of man. Seneca teaches that "we are born to help each other."[18] Thus since men live in common the individual must live for his neighbor. Opposing the Epicurean egoism, Cicero asks, "How can one man be another man's friend, if he does not

---

[10] *Discourses*, IV. 1. 89.
[11] *Epistulae Morales*, LXVI. 50.
[12] III. 7. 10 (OS IV, 161, 3-6).
[13] Cicero, *De Officiis*, II. 6. 19.
[14] *Ibid.*, I. 33. 120.
[15] III. 6. 3 (OS IV, 148f.).
[16] Cf. *De Clementia*, pp. 84-5 in the Battles-Hugo edition where Calvin cites Plato, Aristotle, Cicero, and Seneca on this idea.
[17] *Ethica Nicomachea*, Books VIII, IX.
[18] *De Ira*, I. 5. 2.

love him in and for himself?"[19] He adds, "The Stoics hold, everything that the earth produces is created for man's use; and as men, too, are born for the sake of men, that they may be able mutually to help one another; in this direction we ought to follow Nature as our guide, to contribute to the general good by an interchange of acts of kindness, by giving and receiving, and thus by our skill and industry, and our talents to cement human society more closely together, man to man."[20] Further Cicero says:

> But in the whole moral sphere of which we are speaking there is nothing more glorious nor of wider range than the solidarity of mankind, that species of alliance and partnership of interests and that actual affection which exists between man and man, which, coming into existence immediately upon our birth, owing to the fact that children are loved by their parents and the family as a whole is bound together by the ties of marriage and parenthood gradually spreads its influence beyond the home, first by blood relationship, then by connections through marriage, later by friendships, afterwards by the bonds of neighborhood, then to fellow-citizens and political allies and friends, and lastly by embracing the whole of the human race.[21]

With these exalted sentiments Calvin agrees in part. God's providence is indeed seen in human society because man is by his creation a social animal who tends by nature to preserve society. Calvin too thinks that men are created to love one another[22] and that whoever remembers that he is a man will gladly cultivate the society of others.[23]

However the Stoic motivation for observance of the brotherhood of man differs from the Christian. The Stoic sage seeks above all to maintain his tranquillity and security. It is considered good to help others but not to participate in their sorrows. Seneca recognizes that men will suffer and admits that he was overcome by grief at the death of his friend Annaeus Serenus.[24] In his opinion there are certain emotions which reason cannot expel.[25] Thus even the wise man will

---

[19] *De Finibus*, II. 24. 78.

[20] *De Officiis*, I. 7. 22.

[21] *De Finibus*, V. 23. 65. Cf. Aristotle, *Ethica Nicomachea*, VIII, 12. 1161 b 11f.

[22] Com. Gen. 29. 31 (CO 23, 405). Cf. Cicero, *De Re Publica*, I. 25. 39.

[23] Com. Gen. 10. 8 (CO 23, 159). In Com. Is. 5. 8 (CO 36, 108) Calvin writes that God has linked men so that they require each other.

[24] *Epistulae Morales*, LXIII. 14.

[25] *Ibid.*, LVII. 14. An eminent Stoic explained his fear to Aulus Gellius by saying that certain things on first appearance cause fear because they are not subject to the will. *Noctes Atticae*, Vol. III; Book XIX, 1f.

tremble, feel pain, and turn pale.[26] However excessive tears should not be allowed.[27] Seneca feels that sorrow may be humored for a little while, but he upbraids Marullus whose grief over the death of his little son, Seneca regards as unseemly and extravagant.[28]

Lactantius thinks it sufficient refutation of the Stoics that they place pity among the vices.[29] Calvin, too, maintains that Christian sympathy not only involves pity, but also putting one's self in the place of the needy. He writes, "Now he who merely performs all the duties of love does not fulfill them, even though he overlooks none; but he, rather, fulfils them who does this from a sincere feeling of love."[30] Thus Calvin condemns the "new Stoics" who do not weep and who reject sadness as a part of life.[31] Calvin claims that "we have nothing to do with this iron philosophy which our Lord and Master has condemned not only by his word, but also by his example."[32]

Further, the Stoics teach that all sins are equal. The earlier Stoics maintain that a man is either ruled by reason and therefore is completely virtuous or not ruled by reason and therefore completely vicious. In the *Paradoxa Stoicorum* Cicero writes, "And if virtues are equal to one another, vices also must necessarily be equal to one another."[33] His example is that a drowning man is no more able to breathe near the surface of the water than at the bottom.[34] Hicks puts it this way: "If sin is transgression, how far the transgressor goes astray makes no difference to the guilt, which consists in transgressing bounds at all."[35] However this denial of degrees of virtue and vice, leaving no room for moral improvement, was soon modified by the notion that between good and evil there are things merely

---

[26] *Epistulae Morales*, LXXI. 29.

[27] *Ibid.*, LXIII. 1.

[28] *Ibid.*, XCIX.

[29] Lactantius, *Divine Institutes*, III. 23. ANF VII, 93 (MPL VI, 423 a).

[30] III. 7. 7 (OS IV, 157, 24-7).

[31] On the "new Stoics" see Bohatec, *Budé und Calvin*, pp. 408-11. Bohatec writes, "Calvin thinks here most likely of the humanist leader Budé, otherwise highly esteemed by him, who by his diligent occupation with the Stoic concept of life in his determination of aequanimitas consciously or unconsciously accepted this Stoic trait."

[32] III. 8. 9 (OS IV, 168, 11-3).

[33] *Paradoxa Stoicorum*, III. 21.

[34] *De Finibus*, III. 14. 48; IV. 24. 65f. Plato, *Republic*, V, 453 d, writes that when a man is out of his depth, he must swim whether he has fallen into a small pool or the ocean.

[35] Hicks, *Stoic and Epicurean*, pp. 117-8.

indifferent.[36] Cicero comments, "Yet although the Stoics deny that either virtue or vices can be increased in degree, they nevertheless believe that each of them can be in a sense expanded and widened in scope."[37] Moral worth is the chief good but appropriate actions as means to this end are good even if they are not *the* good.[38]

Calvin's refusal to distinguish between mortal and venial sins is the occasion for his opponents to charge him with the Stoic paradox of the equality of sins. However he maintains that all sins may be mortal without being equal.[39] That is to say, Calvin believes in man's growth in sanctification, but his emphasis concerning sin is that while all sins are not equal, they are equally mortal.[40] According to Calvin no man can derive comfort from the fact that there are some sins which he has not committed, since all sin offends the holiness of God and is subject to his judgment.

Calvin's focus is not as with the Stoics, on the perfection of man but the holiness of God. Each sin must be forgiven since all are deadly without being equal. Calvin's point is that man is entirely dependent on God's mercy and cannot claim even relative merit with any assurance. Thus Calvin points out his disagreement with Augustine who made a distinction between covetousness and sin. Calvin, on the other hand, makes no such distinction and deems "it sin when man is tickled by any desire at all against the law of God. Indeed we label 'sin' that very depravity which begets in us desires of this sort. We accordingly teach that in the saints, until they are divested of mortal bodies, there is always sin . . . ."[41] God removes the power of sin but not the occasion of sin. Therefore in the elect "sin ceases only to reign; it does not also cease to dwell in them."[42]

Calvin's understanding of the nature and range of sin precludes the realization of perfect innocence. It is quite true that all sins are

---

[36] Cicero, *De Finibus*, III. 16. 53. Cf. Aulus Gellius, *Noctes Atticae*, Vol. I, Book I. 2. 9.

[37] *De Finibus*, III. 15. 48.

[38] *Ibid.*, III. 3. 1f.

[39] III. 4. 28 (OS IV, 117, 25f.)

[40] In Com. Zech. 5. 4 (CO 44, 196) Calvin says that the Stoic doctrine of the equality of sins is foolish. In Com. I Jn. 3. 4 (CO 55, 333) he writes that John does not make all sins equal but that sin comes from contempt of God. "Hence John's concept has nothing in common with the crazy paradoxes of the Stoics." Luther, too, thinks that every sin is mortal. Cf. Lectures on Galatians, *Luther's Works*, 27, 76 (WA 40, II, 95).

[41] III. 3. 10 (OS IV, 66, 7-12).

[42] III. 3. 11 (OS IV, 66, 26-7).

not the same and obedience to the commands of God may be approx-
imated, but all men remain sinners and even their best efforts fall
short of the holiness that God demands and provides in Jesus Christ.
This fact means, for Calvin, that the faithful Christian will remain
humble, never being able to believe that his ethical achievements,
however praiseworthy they might seem, and even be, to men, furnish
any basis for pride before God.

Aristotle's ethics is developed in terms of a means-end category.
According to Aristotle men do not deliberate about the end, which,
as end must be final and self-sufficient. Thus the end of human nature
is agreed to be εὐδαιμονια[43] which is usually translated as "happiness"
but is better translated as "well-being" (with a good demon attending).
Men do, however, deliberate about the means to this end and "those
actions concerning means must be according to choice and voluntary."[44] "Therefore virtue also is in our power, and so too is vice."[45]
Aristotle supports his assertion by the fact that the law encourages
the good and punishes the wicked. "But no one is encouraged to
do things that are neither in our power nor voluntary . . . ."[46] Thus
Aristotle believes that the principle of action depends on man. This
voluntarism is also basic to the Epicurean and Stoic ethics.

According to Calvin, freedom of the will and the government of
God are often seen as alternatives.[47] Philosophers, like Plato, locate
the will midway between reason and sense and argue that the will
could incline either way. Thus they teach that virtue and vice are
within the ability of man. The church fathers recognize the power
of sin over reason and will, but Calvin thinks that they unduly defer
to the philosophers on this matter.[48] Calvin, citing the philosophers,

---

[43] *Ethica Nicomachea*, X. 6. 1176 a 32-3. Aristotle writes in the *Ethica Eudemia*,
1249 b 21 that the contemplation and service of God is the goal of the ethical
life.

[44] *Ethica Nicomachea*, III. 5. 1113 b 3-4.

[45] *Ibid.*, III. 5. 1113 b 6.

[46] *Ibid.*, III. 5. 1113 b 26-8.

[47] Com. Lk. 24. 45 (CO 45, 816).

[48] *De Scandalis*, CO 8, 19 (OS II, 175). Cf. Bohatec, *Budé und Calvin*, pp. 119-
239. Bohatec has done elaborate work on *De Scandalis* and *Excuse à Messieurs
les Nicodemites*. Barnikol, *Die Lehre Calvins vom unfreien Willen und ihr Verhältnis
zur Lehre der übrigen Reformatoren und Augustins*, deals with the unfree will in
Bucer, Luther, Melanchthon, and Augustine. He argues correctly that the basis
of Calvin's doctrine of the unfree will is not part of the doctrine of providence
or predestination but of original sin. He concludes that Calvin is, in the same
way as Augustine, a determinist in the ethico-religious sense and an indeterminist
in the psycho-logical sense (p. 100).

says that they "hold as certain that virtues and vices are in our power. They say: If to do this or that depends on our choice, so also does not to do it. Again, if not to do it, so also to do it. Now we seem to do what we do, and to shun what we shun, by free choice. Therefore, if we do any good thing when we please, we can also shun it."[49] Calvin refers to this view of Aristotle's again in criticising the fathers who teach that unless both virtues and vice come from the free will of man, reward and punishment would not be consistent.[50] Calvin believes that the sin of man has deprived him of free will. Luther writes, "I wish that the little word (Wortlin) 'free will' had never been invented. It is not found in the Scripture and should more justly be called 'self will' which is worthless."[51] Calvin associates himself with Luther's view.

According to Calvin the fathers realized that the free will is not sufficient for good works without the grace of God, but they do not make clear whether man is unable to do good or has some power of operation. To recognize that man is not free to choose between good and evil, but to insist that he is free to act wickedly and to call this kind of action "freedom of the will" is, says Calvin, to label a slight thing with "a proud name" (superbus titulus).[52] The difficulty with even this kind of restricted freedom of the will is that it gives to man a foolish assurance. Calvin admits that it is possible to speak of freedom of the will without misunderstanding, but he prefers not to use the idea,[53] because the doctrine of freedom of the will is always in danger of robbing God of his due honor.

In dealing with man's freedom Calvin insists that the Christian is free in regard to "outward things that are of themselves indifferent [ἀδιάφοροι]." Thus he writes,

> If a man begins to doubt whether he may use linen for sheets, shirts, handkerchiefs, and napkins, he will afterward be uncertain also about hemp; finally doubts will even arise over tow. For he will turn over in his mind whether he will sup without napkins, or go without a handkerchief. If any man should consider daintier food unlawful, in the end he will not be at peace before God, when he eats either black bread or common victuals, while it occurs to him that he could

---

[49] II. 2. 3 (OS III, 243: 27—244: 3).
[50] II. 5. 2 (OS III, 299, 3-4).
[51] WA. 7. 448. Calvin defends Luther's view of free will in *Responsio Contra Pighium*, CO 6, 233f.
[52] II. 2. 7 (OS III, 249, 12).
[53] II. 2. 8 (OS III, 251, 8-12).

sustain his body on even coarser foods. If he boggles at sweet wine, he will not with a clear conscience drink even flat wine, and finally he will not dare touch water if sweeter and cleaner than other water.[54]

Thus Calvin asserts man's freedom in indifferent things (which he identifies with external things) if they are received with thanksgiving and used in an indifferent way. Such things include lavish banquets, clothes, and buildings. "Surely ivory and gold and riches are good creations of God, permitted, indeed appointed, for men's use by God's providence. And we have never been forbidden to laugh, or to be filled, or to join new possessions to old or ancestral ones, or to delight in musical harmony, or to drink wine."[55] Still it is certainly conceivable that the money expended on food, clothing, and shelter, even when accepted as a gift of God and used with indifference, could be unrighteous stewardship.

In short, Calvin does not solve the problem of the relation between man's freedom and God's government. He merely thinks that "[t]here is no danger of man's depriving himself of too much so long as he learns that in God must be recouped what he himself lacks."[56] The point is "that we should not rely on any opinion of our own strength, however small it is, if we want God to be favorable toward us."[57] According to Calvin no one aspires to the highest good except through the power of the Holy Spirit.[58] Therefore he says, "Let us not contend against God concerning our right, as if what is attributed to him were withdrawn from our well-being."[59]

For Plato the standard of ethical conduct, in the last analysis, is the judgment of the wise man, for Aristotle the great-souled man, and for the Stoics, the Stoic sage. For Calvin the standard of ethical conduct is love and the edification of the neighbor on the part of the *pious man* who realizes "that free power in outward things has been given to him in order that he may be the more ready for all the duties of love."[60]

Calvin's understanding of man's context differs sharply from that of the philosophers. The philosophers, at least Plato and the Stoics, dimly perceive man's dependent status and aspire to realize perfect

---

[54] III. 19. 6 (OS IV, 286: 27—287: 12).
[55] III. 19. 9 (OS IV, 289, 2-7).
[56] II. 2. 10 (OS III, 252, 22-4).
[57] II. 2. 10 (OS III, 253, 14-6).
[58] II. 2. 26 (OS III, 269, 5ff.).
[59] II. 2. 11 (OS III, 254, 21-2).
[60] III. 19. 12 (OS IV, 292, 14-6).

freedom whether beyond or within nature. Even Aristotle, in his doctrine of the active mind, and the Epicureans seek a salvation of some kind. But Calvin's exposition of salvation is not merely a goal toward which ethical conduct aims as with the philosophers. Salvation is already present as the context within which man acts.

Calvin sets this salvation in a Trinitarian framework of which the philosophers are ignorant. Salvation is decreed by God the Father, revealed in God the Son, and effected by God the Holy Spirit. Of course God is one, and the three-fold distinction of the proper work of each person is controlled by its communal nature.

That the philosophers are serious in their attempts to discover the basis of the moral life, Calvin is well aware. He writes, "We know how carefully the philosophers conducted their inquiries respecting the supreme good."[61] Further the philosophers recognize that man's actions are to be related to God. Calvin cites Seneca on following God,[62] a concept which is also found in Plato,[63] Cicero,[64] Epictetus,[65] and Marcus Aurelius.[66] According to Calvin, while the ancient philosophers anxiously discussed the highest good (summum bonum) none except Plato sees that man's highest good is to be found in union with God (coniunctio cum Deo).[67] In another place Calvin more correctly cites Plato's view of the highest good as likeness to God (simulitudo Dei),[68] but in any case Plato's expression

---

[61] Com. Mt. 6. 21 (CO 45, 205).

[62] *De Vita Beata*, XV. 5; III. 8. 4 (OS IV, 164, 22-4).

[63] *Laws*, IV, 716 b; *Phaedrus*, 248 a.

[64] *De Finibus*, III. 22. 73.

[65] *Discourses*, I. 12. 5f.; I. 20. 15.

[66] *Meditations*, VII. 31.

[67] III. 25. 2 (OS IV, 433, 23-8). In *De Legibus*, I. 15. 43 Cicero writes, "sed ea coniunctione, quae est homini cum Deo conservandas puto." Plato often refers to this idea: God ought to be the measure of all things and the man who would be dear to God must be like him (*Laws* IV. 716 cd; *Theaetetus*, 176 ab). Those who desire to be righteous are to be likened to God as far as possible for man (*Republic* X. 613 ab. cf. *Philebus*, 39 e). Man alone is kindred to the gods (*Protagoras*, 322 a). Thus Homer speaks of the image and likeness of God (θεοειδής τε καὶ θεοείκελος) (*Republic* VI. 501 b. cf. *Phaedrus*, 248 a; 253 c; *Timaeus*, 29 e).

[68] CO I, 286; I. 3. 3 (OS III, 40, 18-22): "Non enim aliud est quod voluit Plato, dum saepius [in Phaedone et Theaeteto.] docuit, summum animae bonum Dei similitudinem esse, dum percepta eius vera contemplatione, in ipsum tota transformatur." Plato says that the soul is immortal or undying (ἀθάνατος) like the gods and after this life finds gods for companions and guides (*Phædo*, 107 c f.) Therefore men should fly away from earth to heaven as soon as possible for to fly is to become like God (ὁμοίωσις θεῷ) as far as this is possible and to become like God is to become righteous, holy, and wise (*Theaetetus*, 176 b). Culbert Gerow Rutenber, *The Doctrine of Imitation of God in Plato* (Morningside Heights, N. Y.: King's Crown Press, 1946) deals with this aspect of Plato's thought.

of man's relation to God finds approval in Calvin.[69] Nevertheless, the philosophers who see man only in the context of nature, and do not know nature as redeemed in Christ, err in trying to locate the relation between God and man's conduct.

According to Calvin the *basis* of salvation is God's eternal decree. That is, salvation for each person depends on divine election before creation. In itself this eternal ordination is a "deep abyss". While, in the light of Ephesians One and other passages, Calvin thinks that God's election before the foundation of the world should be believed and humbly confessed, it cannot be scrutinized.

Calvin's intention to locate salvation entirely in God is clear and commendable, but its development is finally incomprehensible, as Calvin recognizes. For example, Calvin's discussion of the eternal decrees in terms of the "hidden counsel of God"[70] is intended to magnify the sheer grace of God in election (without denying the justice of God in reprobation) and to create a proper humility in man. This humility involves acceptance in faith and gratitude for grace. It obviates fear, but it also presents difficulties for the understanding because it leads Calvin to assert what seems to be an arbitrary will in God. Calvin insists that God's will is not arbitrary since the reason is in himself, but it is hidden from man. Men are chosen for salvation in God's "eternal counsel before they were born for whatever use he pleased" choosing some and rejecting others equally guilty.[71] That is, God bestows grace on a few which could justly be denied to all.[72] Why this is so, or how it can be, Calvin is unable to say. "If you ask the reason why God corrects the vice in his elect, but deems the reprobate unworthy of the same remedy, it is hidden in himself."[73] Calvin admits that God *could* save all men, but he does not because he wills otherwise. "Why he wills otherwise rests with him."[74] Therefore Calvin rejects the attempt to under-

---

[69] Calvin quotes Plato on prayer: "Plato, quum hominum imperitiam videret in votis ad Deum perferendis, quibus concessis pessime illis saepius consultum fuerit: optimam precandi rationem hanc esse pronuntiat, e veteri poeta sumptam: Iupiter rex, optima nobis et voventibus et non voventibus tribue: mala autem poscentibus quoque abesse iube." CO I, 923; III. 20. 34 (OS IV, 344, 17-23). Calvin appears to be quoting directly from Ficino's Latin translation of this prayer by an unknown author. The reference in Plato is *Alcibiades* II, 143 a.

[70] *Concerning Eternal Predestination*, p. 78 (CO 8, 278).

[71] *Ibid.*, p. 89 (CO 8, 287).

[72] III. 24. 3 (OS IV, 413, 23, 29).

[73] *Concerning Eternal Predestination*, p. 116 (CO 8, 310).

[74] III. 24. 13 (OS IV, 424, 20f.). Cf. *Concerning Eternal Predestination*, p. 120 (CO 8, 312-3).

stand the incomprehensible will of God as speculative and presumptuous. Thus he denies the scholastic distinction between God's absolute and regulative will.[75]

It is understandable in terms of Calvin's position that he rejects secondary causation as a way of dealing with salvation. Calvin opposes the Epicurean deism which teaches that the gods are not directly concerned with the affairs of men, and he thus insists that God directly governs all things. Calvin admits that Aristotle reasons very shrewdly about secondary causes, but, according to Calvin, Aristotle omits the main thing which is that everything in the world depends on the will of God, and the whole course of nature is nothing other than the proper execution of his will.[76] Calvin says, "Philosophers think that they have not reasoned skillfully enough about inferior causes, unless they separate God very far from his works."[77] Calvin, on the other hand, teaches that God's purpose governs all these intermediate causes (has omnes medias causas gubernat Dei consilium).[78] Thus he writes, "It must always be remembered that the world does not properly stand by another power than that of the Word of God, and that secondary causes derive their power from him, and that they have different effects as they are directed."[79] Calvin's doxological summary holds that God's providence "is the determinative principle of all things in such a way that it sometimes works through an intermediary, sometimes without an intermediary, sometimes contrary to every intermediary."[80]

Calvin's conviction of the primacy of God's will means that "it is vain to pretend that every man's condition begins in himself."[81]

---

[75] Ibid., p. 117 (CO 8, 310); p. 179 (CO 8, 361).

[76] Com. Ps. 147. 15 (CO 32, 430-1).

[77] Com. Ps. 29. 5 (CO 31, 288-9).

[78] Com. Jon. 4. 6-8 (CO 43, 275).

[79] Com. II. Pet. 3. 5 (CO 55, 473). Krusche, Das Wirken des Heiligen Geistes nach Calvin, pp. 25-6 correctly observes, "It is the common opinion of Calvin researchers that Calvin in his doctrine of providence conceded a greater importance to secondary causes than Zwingli, who did not even want to allow the validity of their mention. And it is in fact not to be overlooked how often Calvin speaks of inferior means which God uses in his providential dealing. But so much less is it to overlook with what stress Calvin emphasized the fundamental freedom of God in opposition to intermediate causes."

[80] I. 17. 1 (OS III, 202, 9-11).

[81] III. 22. 4 (OS IV, 383, 23). The observation of Heiko A. Oberman, "Iustitia Christi' and 'Iustitia Dei': Luther and the Scholastic Doctrines of Justification," Harvard Theological Review, 59, 1 (Jan., 1961), 4 that the will of God is the rule of all justice should be regarded as epistemological rather than metaphysical also applies to Calvin's view.

Both his opponents Pighius and Georgias maintain that salvation depends in part on man. Calvin insists that God's foreknowledge of man's action does not include any merits which he did not bestow.[82] In short, with Augustine, Calvin says that "God's grace does not find but makes those fit to be chosen."[83] Thus Calvin rejects Thomas' attempt to include the efforts of men as part of salvation. Against the view that "God is said to predestine glory for man on account of merits, because he has decreed to bestow upon him grace by which to merit glory," Calvin says that "predestination to glory is the cause of predestination to grace, rather than the converse."[84]

According to Calvin, God's will is such that even those do God's will who act contrary to it.[85] "[God] so governs the natures created by him, as to determine all the counsels and actions of men to the end decreed by him."[86] Calvin asserts that this view is incomprehensible.

> In a wonderful and ineffable way, what was done contrary to his will was yet not done without his will, because it would not have been done at all unless he had allowed. So he permitted it not unwillingly but willingly. Thus in sinning, they did what God did not will in order that God through their evil will might do what he willed. If anyone object that this is beyond his comprehension, I confess it. But what wonder if the immense and incomprehensible majesty of God exceed the limits of our intellect? I am so far from undertaking the explanation of this sublime, hidden secret, that I wish what I said at the beginning to be remembered, that those who seek to know more than God has revealed are crazy.[87]

Calvin's exaltation of the comprehensive will of God leads him not only to deny secondary causation but also to affirm God's responsibility for reprobation. "If then, we cannot determine a reason why he vouchsafes mercy to his own, except that it so pleases him, neither shall we have any reason for rejecting others, other than his will. For when it is said that God hardens or shows mercy to whom he wills, men are warned by this to seek no cause outside his will."[88] Since one cannot assign a reason for salvation apart from the will

---

[82] *Concerning Eternal Predestination*, p. 155 (CO 8, 308).
[83] III. 22. 8 (OS IV, 389, 30).
[84] III. 22. 9 (OS IV, 390, 15-6)
[85] *Concerning Eternal Predestination*, p. 68 (CO 8, 270).
[86] *Ibid.*, p. 178 (CO 8, 360).
[87] *Ibid.*, p. 123 (CO 8, 315).
[88] III. 22. 11 (OS IV, 393, 28-33).

of God, he cannot assign a reason for reprobation. This position, as well as its various alternatives, presents difficulties.

Calvin believes that the gospel is offered to all men, but not all men are to be saved. It is evident that some men hear the gospel and others do not, even though the reason for this is hidden.[89] The fact is that "we see that all are not members of Christ."[90] That is not all men are united to Christ. Calvin seeks to account for this situation in his doctrine of reprobation. Calvin has already showed that men are not saved by their human will but by grace or predestination.[91] "No one who wishes to be thought religious dares simply deny predestination, by which God adopts some to hope of life and sentences others to eternal death." [92] This means that God created men for his glory and decrees before the fall of Adam what he will do with them. "God's unchangeable plan, by which he predestined for himself those whom he willed, was in fact intrinsically effectual unto salvation for [his] spiritual offspring alone."[93] Thus Calvin attempts to explain God's salvation in terms of election and reprobation.

Jacobs suggest that "the relation of salvation to election is analytic because the relation of salvation to justification and to Christ is analytic, and the relation of election to God is analytic. Salvation is in God's eternal decree. The relation of sin to reprobation is synthetic because the realization of sin lies in man not in a decree of reprobation. Thus reprobation is not parallel to election."[94] It is true that Calvin could say that reprobation is subordinate to election. "That we are reconciled to God is proper to the gospel; that unbelievers are adjudged to eternal death is accidental . . . it is proper to the gospel to invite all to salvation, but it . . . is accidental that it brings destruction on any."[95] Thus election and reprobation are not clear parallels since God is essentially related to the one and accidentally related to the other.

However, it must also be recognized that Calvin does not always speak in these terms. Reprobation, too, is an eternal decree of God.

---

[89] *Concerning Eternal Predestination*, p. 136 (CO 8, 326).

[90] III. 22. 2 (OS IV, 381, 30).

[91] *Concerning Eternal Predestination*, p. 64 (CO 8, 266).

[92] III. 21. 5 (OS IV, 373:33—374:1).

[93] III. 21. 7 (OS IV, 378, 27-8).

[94] Paul Jacobs, *Prädestination und Verantwortlichkeit bei Calvin* (Neukirchen Kr. Moers: Buchhandlung des Erziehungsvereins, 1937), p. 156.

[95] Com. Jn. 20. 23 (CO 47, 442).

Calvin insists that "men are predestined by the eternal counsel of God either to salvation or to destruction."[96] Paul teaches that out of the mass of perdition God elects and reprobates those whom he wills. Calvin, like Paul, does not attempt to explain this situation but confesses his awe before it. Nevertheless, God elects those whom he wills and reprobates those whom he wills.[97] Thus Calvin writes, "For first, there is certainly a *mutual relation* between the elect and the reprobate, so that the election spoken of here *cannot stand*, unless we confess that God separated out from others certain men as seemed good to him."[98] That is to say, "to the gratuitous love with which the elect are embraced there corresponds, on an *equal and common level* a just severity towards the reprobate."[99] In these comments salvation and reprobation seem to be parallel. It is also a theme of Calvin's that "election itself could not stand except as set over against reprobation."[100]

Calvin tries to mitigate his position by insisting that man is also responsible for the fall. Man is not responsible for his salvation, but he is somehow responsible for his damnation. Calvin believes that "man falls according as God's providence ordains, but he falls by his own fault."[101] Thus Calvin attempts to meet the objection that the sinner should be excused since he cannot do otherwise than sin by admitting that man falls by God's ordination but suggesting that it is also by his own fault. Calvin does not explain how this can be understood. Still it is clear that Calvin thinks "even though by God's eternal providence man has been created to undergo that calamity to which he is subject, it still takes occasion from man himself, not from God."[102] Thus "as salvation depends solely on the election of God, the reprobate necessarily perish, in whatever way this happens; not that they are innocent, and free from all blame, when God destroys

---

[96] *Concerning Eternal Predestination*, p. 143 (CO 8, 332).
[97] *Ibid.*, pp. 124-5 (CO 8, 316-7).
[98] *Ibid.*, p. 68 (CO 8, 270). Emphasis added.
[99] *Ibid.*, p. 90 (CO 8, 287). Emphasis added.
[100] III. 23. 1 (OS IV, 394, 2-3).
[101] III. 23. 8 (OS IV, 402:38—403:1). H. Strohl, "La Pensée de Calvin sur la Providence divine au temps où il était refugié à Strasbourg, " *Revue d'Histoire et de Philosophie Religieuses*, 22, 2-3 (1942), 159 points out that Calvin teaches that God is absolutely sovereign, but man is nevertheless responsible for his acts. This, he says, is an antinomy which is inherent to religious and moral thought. Henri Gerber's University of Neuchâtel thesis (1940) *La Doctrine Calvinienne de la Providence* (Etude des chapitres XVI à XVIII du Iier Livre de *l'Institution chrétienne*, pp. 1-97 does not contribute significantly to the discussion.
[102] III. 23. 9 (OS IV, 403, 31-4).

them, but because, by their own malice, they turn to their destruction all that is offered to them, however salutary it may be."[103] While the actualization of sin lies in man, Calvin also insists that it is absurd to say that God saves the elect and the reprobate damn themselves. This is certainly a paradox if not an outright contradiction. The cause of election and reprobation is not in man but in God. The cause of reprobation, though hidden, must be considered just.[104] Calvin says that the decree of reprobation cannot be scrutinized, but maintains that reprobation illustrates the special grace of God to the elect. Why God's election is not general but special is not for man to inquire.[105] That is, the wicked are created for the day of evil because God willed to illustrate his glory in them.[106] Nonetheless, "we teach that they act perversely who to seek out the source of their condemnation turn their gaze upon the hidden sanctuary of God's plan, and wink at the corruption of nature from which it really springs."[107] "Yet this remains an incontrovertible fact, that the reprobate are set aside in the counsel of God to the end that in them he might demonstrate his power."[108]

Calvin's insistence that reprobation is to be understood in terms of man who is the proximate and voluntary cause while God is the remote (and therefore real) cause[109] may have some psychological but no logical value. However Calvin recognizes this situation and associates himself with Paul. "When Paul has discussed the hidden counsels of God so far as is needful, he, as it were, puts out his hand to forbid further advance."[110] God's election is taught in the Scripture and Calvin thinks it was wrong to keep silent about the subject. Nevertheless, he confesses his awe before the decree,[111] and often interjects, with Paul, "Who are you O man to argue with God? Does the molded object say to its molder, 'Why have you fashioned me thus?' Or does the potter have no capacity to make from the same lump one vessel for honor, another for dishonor'?"[112]

---

[103] Com. Mt. 15. 13 (CO 45, 453).
[104] *Concerning Eternal Predestination*, p. 99 (CO 8, 295-6).
[105] III. 23. 5 (OS IV, 398, 32-4).
[106] *Concerning Eternal Predestination*, p. 97 (CO 8, 293).
[107] III. 23. 9 (OS IV, 403, 27-30).
[108] *Concerning Eternal Predestination*, p. 84 (CO 8, 283).
[109] *Ibid.*, p. 101 (CO 8, 297); p. 116 (CO 8, 309). This distinction may have been suggested by Aristotle, *Metaphysics*, XII. 4. 5.
[110] *Concerning Eternal Predestination*, p. 61 (CO 8, 264).
[111] III. 23. 7 (OS IV, 401, 28). See note, p. 955 in LCC.
[112] III. 23. 4 (OS IV, 397, 30-3).

It is certainly true that Calvin considers reprobation to be more than a possibility, an empty class, and on the basis of Scripture he asserts that Ishmael, Esau, Pharoah, Saul, and Judas belong to it.[113] Still he thinks that believers should not indulge in curious speculations about the vast numbers of the reprobate.[114] Faithful teachers should try to gather all to Christ since they cannot tell the difference between the sheep and the wild beasts,[115] and it is not a rare experience that even the sheep can be alienated for a time.[116] For that reason those whose godliness is not evident cannot be lightly assigned to the devil.[117] It is not proper, according to Calvin, to say to any man, "If you do not believe, it is because you are destined by God to destruction, [because] he would not only foster his own idleness, but also indulge his malice. If anyone again should extend his opinions into future time, saying that those who hear never will believe because they are reprobate, this would be imprecation rather than doctrine."[118] Therefore since no one knows who is elect and who is not, one must hope for the salvation of all. With Augustine Calvin agrees, "Since we do not know who belongs to the number of the predestined and who does not, it befits us so to feel as to wish that all be saved."[119] The elect should not despair of others being elect and should pray for all men.

Not only is Calvin's position difficult to explain, but some of what seem to be logical consequences he denies. For example, Calvin's assertion that the divine justice is unlike human justice,[120] does not solve the problem of how one is to understand justice in an eternal election or eternal reprobation of each man before he was created. Likewise Calvin maintains that God created man good but fallible and refuses to consider this created fallibility except as

---

[113] Com. Jn. 13. 18 (CO 47, 310) speaking of Judas and Saul, Calvin makes a distinction between temporal and eternal election.

[114] Com. Lk. 13. 23 (CO 45, 222).

[115] Com. Jn. 21. 16 (CO 47, 453).

[116] Com. Jn. 10. 8 (CO 47, 239). P. H. Reardon, "Calvin on Providence: The Development of an Insight," *Scottish Journal of Theology*, 28, 6 (1975), 517-33 gives a judicious treatment of the development of Calvin's doctrine in comparison with the Stoic and correctly concludes "that Calvin, in spite of certain similarities with the Stoic view of Providence, was moved by a different spirit and directed by another insight."

[117] Com. Rom. 11. 4 (CO 49, 213-4).

[118] *Concerning Eternal Predestination*, pp. 137-8 (CO 8, 327). Cf. III. 23. 14 (OS IV, 409, 9-11).

[119] *Concerning Eternal Predestination*, p. 138 (CO 8, 328).

[120] *Ibid.*, p. 87 (CO 8, 286).

part of the hidden will of God about which it is fruitless to speculate.[121] His insistence that God does not passively permit, but actively
wills whatever happens and in fact ordained the fall of man, yet
without becoming the author of evil, while constantly reiterated,
is finally inexplicable.[122] Further Calvin states that in Adam's fall all
mankind is lost because it is God's will. He admits that God could
save all men from the mass of perdition, but he elects only some to
salvation.[123]

Calvin teaches that the state of salvation depends on God's eternal
and hidden decrees as we have seen, but he insists that *it cannot be
known* on that basis. This extremely important fact is the pivot on
which Calvin's doctrine turns. Had Calvin gone no further than
maintaining the eternal decrees, his doctrine would indeed be close
to the Stoic. But he says that men cannot seek the certainty of salvation in the hidden counsels of God but only in the revelation
of Christ. That is to say, concerning salvation God begins with
himself, *but man must begin with Christ*.[124] The knowledge of salvation is properly sought not in the eternal decrees but in Christ.
Calvin holds, "If we desire anything more than to be reckoned among
God's sons and heirs, we have to rise above Christ. If this is our
ultimate goal, how insane are we to seek outside him what we have
already obtained in him, and can find in him alone."[125] Therefore
Calvin writes that "if we have been chosen in him, we shall not
find assurance of our election in ourselves; and *not even in God the
Father*, if we conceive him as severed from his Son. Christ, then, is
the mirror wherein we must . . . contemplate our own election."[126]
The centrality of Christ is seen in this statement:

> We see that our whole salvation and all its parts are comprehended
> in Christ. We should therefore take care not to derive the least portion
> of it from anywhere else. If we seek salvation, we are taught by the

---

[121] *Ibid.*, p. 65 (CO 8, 267-8).

[122] In the Arg. Ps. (CO 31, 29) Calvin writes, "Because I assert and maintain
that the world is conducted and governed by the secret providence of God,
a multitude of presumptuous men rise up against me, and allege that I represent
God as the author of sin." This is the charge made by Castellio. Cf. *Calvin's
Treatises*, p. 331 (CO 9, 257). In a letter to Bullinger (1552) (CO 14, 253) Calvin
remarks that Zwingli made God the author of evil.

[123] *Concerning Eternal Predestination*, p. 101 (CO 8, 297).

[124] *Ibid.*, p. 127 (CO 8, 318)

[125] III. 24. 5 (OS IV, 416, 21-4).

[126] III. 24. 5 (OS IV. 415:39—416:4). Emphasis added. Cf. *Concerning
Eternal Predestination*, p. 127 (CO 8, 318).

very name of Jesus that it is "of him". If we seek any other gifts of the Spirit, they will be found in his anointing. If we seek strength, it lies in his dominion, if purity in his conception; if gentleness, it appears in his birth. For by his birth he was made like us in all respects that he might learn to feel our pain. If we seek redemption, it lies in his passion; if acquital [absolutio], in his condemnation [damnatio], if remission of the curse, in his cross; if satisfaction, in his sacrifice; if purification, in his blood; if reconciliation, in his descent into hell; if mortification of the flesh, in his tomb; if newness of life, in his resurrection; if immortality, in the same; if inheritance of the heavenly kingdom, in his entrance into heaven; if protection, if security, if abundant supply of all blessings, in his kingdom; if untroubled expectation of judgment, in the power given to him to judge. In short, since every kind of goodness is from his treasury, let us draw our fill from that place and no other.[127]

Although the Barthian interpreters of Calvin have overstated the case, the centrality of Christology for Calvin's entire theology should certainly be affirmed. Without denying the importance of Calvin's doctrine of Christ for other parts of his thought, it is especially crucial to recognize its role in the doctrine of salvation. According to Calvin, what God has done *for* and *in* man is not to be understood apart from Christ. In Book Two of the *Institutes* Calvin deals with what God has already done *for* mankind in Christ in terms of the Law and Gospel, the Mediator and the Covenants and the Person and Work of Christ.[128]

Calvin maintains, as we have seen, that the cause of salvation is found in God, but man's confidence in salvation is found in Christ.[129] Thus he says, "I do not merely send men off to the secret election of God to await with gaping mouth salvation there. I bid them make their way directly to Christ in whom salvation is offered to us, which otherwise would have lain hid in God."[130] According to Calvin,

Scripture everywhere declares that God gives to his Son those who were his, calls those whom he elects, and begets again by his Spirit

---

[127] II. 16. 19 (OS III, 507 : 1—508 : 17). A helpful summary is found in Alfred Göhler, *Calvins Lehre von der Heiligung* (Munich: Chr. Kaiser Verlag, 1934).

[128] On Law and Gospel see Dowey, *The Knowledge of God in Calvin's Theology*, p. 221f. On the Covenants, Hans Heinrich Wolf, *Die Einheit des Bundes das Verhältnis von Altem und Neuen Testament bei Calvin* (Neukirchen: Kr. Moers, 1958). On the Person of Christ: E. David Willis, *Calvin's Catholic Christology*. On the Work of Christ: John Frederick Jansen, *Calvin's Doctrine of the Work of Christ* (London: James Clarke, 1956).

[129] *Concerning Eternal Predestination*, p. 56 (CO 8, 260).

[130] *Ibid.*, p. 133 (CO 8, 306-7).

those he had adopted as sons; and finally that those men whom he teaches inwardly and to whom his arm is revealed, believe. *Hence whoever holds faith to be the earnest and pledge of grace confesses that it flows from divine election as its eternal source. Yet knowledge of salvation is not to be demanded by us out of the secret counsel of God.* Life is set before us in Christ, who not only makes himself known in the gospel but also presents himself to be enjoyed. Let the eye of faith look fixedly in this mirror, and not try to penetrate where access is not open. Since this is the way, let the sons of God walk in it, lest, by flying higher than is right, they plunge themselves into a deeper labyrinth than they had wished. For the rest, as there is no other gate into the kingdom of heaven than faith in Christ contained in the promises of the gospel clearly set before us, it is the most crass stupidity not to acknowledge that the eyes of our mind are opened by God, since, before we were conceived in the womb, he chose us to be faithful.[131]

Calvin rules out the speculative impulse which seeks to penetrate the hidden decrees of God. The philosophers and speculative theologians go astray when they seek to know God apart from Christ.

Since God is incomprehensible, faith can never reach to Him, unless it has immediate regard to Christ. There are two reasons why faith cannot be in God unless Christ intervenes as a Mediator. First, the magnitude of the divine glory must be taken into account, and at the same time the littleness of our capacity. Our acuteness is very far from being capable of ascending so high as to comprehend God. Hence all thinking about God outside Christ [extra Christum] is a vast abyss which immediately swallows up all our thoughts. There is clear proof of this not only in the Turks and the Jews, who worship their own dreams under the name of God, but also in the Papists. It is a common axiom of the schools, "God is the object of faith". Thus they extensively and carefully philosophize about his hidden majesty, leaving out Christ, but with what success? They entangle themselves in astounding delusions, so that there is no end to their wanderings. They think that faith is nothing but imaginative speculation.[132]

This means that God who is otherwise invisible is revealed in the Son alone; "since all the fullness of the Deity dwells in Christ, there is no God apart from him [extra eum] ....They may flatter themselves as they wish in their speculations who philosophize about divine things apart from Christ. But it is certain that they are only playing the fool."[133] Again Calvin states, "The sum is, that God in

---

[131] *Ibid.*, p. 50 (CO 8, 254-5). Emphasis added.
[132] Com. I Pet. 1 20 (CO 55, 226).
[133] Com. I Jn. 2. 22 (CO 55, 325).

himself, that is, in his naked majesty is invisible; and that not only to physical eyes, but also to human understanding; and that he is revealed to us in Christ alone, where we may behold him as in a mirror. For in Christ he shows us his righteousness, goodness, wisdom, power—in short, his entire self. We must, therefore, take care not to seek him elsewhere, for outside Christ everything that claims to represent God will be an idol."[134]

It is true that election is a matter of God's will, but God's will is revealed in Jesus Christ. Thus Jacobs correctly observes that Calvin does not build the ordo salutis on predestination but on Christ.[135] Calvin summarizes his viewpoint this way:

> The way we obtain salvation is by obeying the gospel of Christ .... And if God's will is that those whom he has elected shall be saved by faith, and he confirms and executes his eternal decree in this way, whoever is not satisfied with Christ but inquires curiously about eternal predestination desires, as far as lies in him, to be saved contrary to God's purpose. The election of God in itself is hidden and secret. The Lord manifests it by the calling with which he honors us .... Therefore, they are insane who seek their own or another's salvation in the labyrinth of predestination not keeping the way of salvation which is exhibited to them. Nay more, by this foolish speculation they endeavor, to overturn the force and effect of predestination; for if God has elected us to the end that we may believe, take away faith and election will be imperfect .... Therefore every man's faith is an abundant witness to the eternal predestination of God, so that it is sacrilege to inquire further: and whoever refuses to assent to the simple testimony of the Holy Spirit does him a horrible injury.[136]

Again Calvin says,

> Many persons, as soon as they learn that none are heirs of eternal life except those whom God "chose before the foundation of the world." (Eph. 1, 4) begin to inquire anxiously how they may be assured of God's secret purpose, and thus plunge into a labyrinth, from which they will find no exit. Christ enjoins us to come directly to himself, in order to obtain certainty of salvation. The meaning therefore is, that life is exhibited to us in Christ himself, and that no man will participate in it except he who enters by the gate of faith. We now see that he connects faith with the eternal predestination of God, which men foolishly and wickedly hold to be inconsistent with each other. *Though our salvation was always hidden with God, yet Christ is the channel through which it flows to us,* and we receive it by faith, that it may be

---

[134] Com. Col. 1. 15 (CO 52, 85).
[135] Jacobs, *Prädestination und Verantwortlichkeit bei Calvin*, p. 54.
[136] Com. Jn. 6. 40 (CO 47, 147).

secure and ratified in our hearts. We are not at liberty then to turn away from Christ, unless we choose to reject the salvation which he offers to us.[137]

What Calvin seems to mean by the relation between theology proper and Christology may be formulated this way; the *ontic* basis of salvation is the hidden (though gracious and just) will of God. The *epistemic* basis of salvation is the revelation in Christ. In terms of the hidden and revealed will of God, this position holds that the ontological basis of salvation is hidden in the decrees of God. It must be acknowledged but not questioned. The epistemic basis of salvation is revealed in Jesus Christ and must be believed and obeyed. Calvin does not develop this difficult concept with an emphasis and clarity sufficient to obviate the misunderstandings of his position which arose both among his followers and opponents. To suggest a distinction between the ontological and epistemological understanding of salvation does not solve the problems surrounding the doctrine, but it is intended to account for Calvin's usage. At least it is evident that having confessed God's eternal decrees Calvin wishes to go no further but to look to Christ.

Calvin's doctrine of salvation is expounded in terms of his doctrine of God eschewing a contributory role on the part of man. This entirely passive role for man causes problems for anthropology, but an active role causes problems in theology. In discussing salvation in terms of the Trinity, Calvin comes closest to the philosophers in dealing with the sovereignty of God. The philosophers also dimly recognize the need for an intermediary, but their insight is uncertain and the direction of their aspiration vague. Thus Calvin goes beyond the philosophers' views not only in his Christology but also in his exposition of the work of the Holy Spirit.

Having dealt in the *Institutes* with what God has done *for* man in his creation and providence (Book One) and *for* man in Christ (Book Two), Calvin turns in Book Three to what God does *in* man. Thus he expounds the benefits which the Father bestows on Christ for man's enrichment. Calvin begins his discussion by emphasizing the work of the Holy Spirit in uniting men to Christ. What God has done *for* man is useless unless it is also done *in* man. Calvin's position is, "We must either deny Christ or confess that we become Christians through his Holy Spirit."[138] On the basis of (1) the union

---

[137] Com. Mt. 11. 27 (CO 45, 319). Emphasis added.
[138] Com. Rom. 8. 9 (CO 49, 145).

with Christ, Calvin treats (2) the nature of faith through which men are (3) regenerated and (4) justified, and concludes by stating his understanding of election with which we will be concerned in Chapter Nine of Part Three. It will be useful, then, to sketch briefly these four themes as an indication of the position Calvin maintains and from which he cites the philosophers.

According to Calvin, salvation is effected by union with Christ through faith, "the principal work of the Holy Spirit."[139] The Holy Spirit is the bond by which Christ effectually unites the faithful to himself. This union is more than consent to the gospel history or the belief in God as an object.[140] It is a true and substantial communion with Christ,[141] "for until [Christ] becomes ours we must necessarily be completely devoid of all the graces which are wholly contained in him."[141] Thus "[God] begins to love us when we are united to the body of his beloved son.... if we wish to be beheld in him, we must truly be his members."[142] Calvin says, "Christ is not outside us, but dwells within us. Not only does he cleave to us by an indivisible bond of fellowship, but with a wonderful communion day by day, he grows more and more into one body with us, until he becomes completely one with us."[143]

Calvin confesses that this union with Christ is more to be adored than understood. "I am overwhelmed by the depth of this mystery, and with Paul am not ashamed to acknowledge in wonder my ignorance. How much more satisfactory is this than to undervalue by my carnal sense what Paul declares to be a deep mystery! Reason itself teaches us this; for whatever is supernatural is clearly beyond the

---

[139] III. 1. 4 (OS IV, 5, 14). Cf. Dowey, *The Knowledge of God in Calvin's Theology*, pp. 197-204.

[140] III. 2. 1 (OS IV, 7, 17-9). See also III. 2. 9 (OS IV, 19, 18-28); Arg. Jn. CO 47, 7; Com. Rom. 10. 9 (CO 49, 201).

[141] Com. Gal. 2. 20 (CO 50, 199). According to Jacobs, *Prädestination und Verantwortlichkeit bei Calvin*, p. 128 the concept did not originate with Calvin but was used in the struggle with Osiander. Calvin rejects the term "essential righteousness" III. 11. 10 (OS IV, 192, 5), but in the French edition of the *Institutes* in 1545 and following he uses the phrase "une mesme substance" (III. 2. 24). Wendel, *Calvin, The Origins and Development of his Religious Thought.* p. 236 seems correct in the opinion that Calvin "did not perceive the danger or at least imprudence, of certain formulations until he had read some of Osiander's writings which appeared in 1550 or 1551."

[142] Com. Jn. 17. 26 (CO 47, 391). Kemper Fullerton, "Calvinism and Capitalism," *Harvard Theological Review*, 21, 3 (July, 1928), 177 says quite incorrectly that the idea of mystical union is alien to Calvinism because of its strong emphasis on the transcendence of God.

[143] III. 2. 24 (OS IV, 34:37—35:11).

grasp of our minds. Let us therefore labor more to feel Christ living in us, than to discover the nature of that communion."[144]

The union with Christ is effected through faith. That is, "Christ, when he illumines us into faith by the power [virtus] of his Spirit, at the same time so engrafts us into his body that we become partakers of every good."[145] Since faith is a gift of God rather than an achievement of man, "[B]elievers ascribe to God's grace the fact that, illumined by his Spirit, they enjoy through faith the contemplation of the heavenly life.[146] Calvin holds that when faith is present it is known not by the head but by the heart and is a firm confidence which is experienced rather than a bare idea which is entertained.[147]

On the basis of faith Calvin views the double grace of justification and sanctification. He says, "Christ was given to us by God's pure goodness, to be apprehended and appropriated by us in faith and that from our fellowship with him we principally receive a double grace: namely that being reconciled to God by Christ's sinlessness, we may have in heaven instead of a Judge a gracious Father; and secondly that sanctified by Christ's spirit we may cultivate blamelessness and purity of life."[148] These two benefits may be distinguished but "Christ contains both of them inseparably in himself."[149]

Calvin's view of the summum bonum as union with Christ is not indebted to the philosophers. That part, i.e., the sovereignty of God, which superficially resembles the Stoic teaching, is to be differently understood when seen as a whole in its Trinitarian setting. Calvin believes that his doctrine of salvation is entirely Scriptural and basically Augustinian. It cannot be judged completely successful (though it is difficult to suggest a superior alternative) since his emphasis falls on Trinitarian distinctions rather than on God's unity in the work of salvation. Still it is clear that the doctrine of salvation is the context *within which*, rather than primarily *toward which*, men act.

Calvin's emphasis on salvation as already accomplished does not remove the imperative or urgency of ethical action. Calvin is not hostile to good works, but he insists that "justification is withdrawn

---

[144] Com. Eph. 5. 32 (CO 51, 227).
[145] III. 2. 35 (OS IV, 46, 30-2).
[146] III. 2. 40 (OS IV, 50, 29-31).
[147] Com. Rom. 10. 10 (CO 49, 202).
[148] III. 11. 1 (OS IV, 182, 4-8). The French edition adds that these two aspects are complementary.
[149] III. 16. 1 (OS IV, 249, 14-23). Emphasis added.

from works, not that no good works may be done, or that what is done may be denied to be good, but that we may not rely upon them, glory in them, or ascribe salvation to them. For our assurance [fiducia], our glory, and the sole anchor of our salvation are that Christ the Son of God is ours, and we in turn are in him sons of God and heirs of the Kingdom of heaven, called to the hope of eternal blessedness by God's grace, not by our worth."[150] The point is that confidence in ethical behaviour causes men to look away from what Christ has done for and in them and to trust in what they can achieve themselves.

---

[150] III. 17. 1 (OS IV, 253, 16-24).

CONCLUSION

The relation of Calvin's thought to other parts of philosophy such as political thought and aesthetics would be instructive to explore. However the areas which have been considered should suffice to indicate the way in which Calvin deals with philosophical insights. Obviously Calvin's primary concern is the exposition of the Christian faith. At the same time, Calvin knows philosophy and quotes the classical philosophers on occasion as complementary or contradictory to Christian teaching. Calvin does not attempt a thorough review of all the instances where philosophy is a help or hindrance, but his citations give evidence of his knowledge and interest.

Even where Calvin is often thought to be making common cause with philosophy, we have seen that a more complete view reveals significant differences. Epistemologically, Calvin is not a rationalist. Rather he expounds the Christian experience of dealing with God in all things. Calvin's view of reality is based on the God revealed in Scripture rather than on conclusions drawn from the observation of nature. Calvin places more emphasis on the immortality of the soul than is proper according to later research, but the Christian theme of the resurrection of the body is not only present but decisive for his doctrine of man. Calvin admires and commends some of the ethical insights of the philosophers, but the context of man's life redeemed in Christ is quite different from the philosophical understanding of man in nature. Withal Calvin uses philosophy, not as a source for the truth, but as a learned adjunct to the explanation of the Christian faith.

PART THREE

CALVIN AND THE PHILOSOPHERS

INTRODUCTION

As we have seen, Calvin's use of insights from classical philosophy, while forming an important element in his thought, is eclectic and unsystematic. That is to say, his estimates of philosophical insights occur within the context of his exposition of the Christian faith and not in the form of sustained argumentation designed to deal with any philosophy in its totality. Thus, in Part Two, we dealt with Calvin's references to philosophical views and his judgments on them organized under certain philosophical categories.

We turn in Part Three to an evaluative summary of Calvin's relation to the classical philosophers in general with particular regard to their understanding of the doctrine of providence. In seeking to understand nature, man, and God, the philosophers are not only concerned about being and knowing but also about the direction of the world. The sharpest alternatives are expressed by the Epicurean and the Stoic philosophies. The Epicureans argue that the world is ruled by chance and the Stoics that it is governed by fate. The Epicurean view denies purpose, and the Stoic doctrine, in effect, denies freedom.

Calvin opposes both positions. Against the Epicureans he contends that everything is governed by God. Against the Stoics, who say that everything is governed by God, Calvin criticizes their ignorance of God's particular providence. The philosophers who conceive of providence at all, only perceive a universal providence. It is extremely important to recognize that Calvin does not promulgate a philosophical doctrine of universal providence to which God's particular providence is attached as an, albeit crucial and Christian, addendum. Rather Calvin's basic standpoint is God's special providence. This fact is especially evident in Calvin's account of predestination, which is an example of God's providence for the individual, but Calvin's doctrine of God's special care is also clearly adumbrated in his earlier discussions of providence in the *Institutes*. That is to say, Calvin does not begin with universal providence as a genus and move downward to particular providence as a species, rather he begins with particular providence and moves outward to the affirmation of universal providence. Thus Calvin's doctrine of providence is not a Christian supplement to the Stoic teaching but a different way of viewing the doctrine.

Calvin makes it clear that the denial of providence in Aristotle and the Epicureans is to be opposed (Chapter Seven). Calvin commends in part the affirmation of God's universal providence in Plato and the Stoics (Chapter Eight), but he insists that the philosophers are ignorant of the most important aspect of the doctrine which is God's particular providence (Chapter Nine).

CALVIN ON ARISTOTLE AND THE EPICUREANS

The classical philosophers devote a good deal of attention to the principles which govern the universe, as Calvin recognizes. As a Christian Calvin believes that the world is governed by God's providence, a fact which both Aristotle and the Epicureans deny. In this chapter we will consider Calvin's view of Aristotle and the Epicureans in the context of their repudiation of the doctrine of providence.

Doubtless, in an indirect way, Calvin is influenced by Aristotle's identification of God as Supreme Being,[1] by the distinction between form and matter in substance, the four causes,[2] and by Aristotle's contribution to a subject-predicate logic, and a substance-attribute metaphysics,[3] but Calvin does not deal with Aristotle's role in these developments. Although Aristotle calls theology the highest branch of contemplation,[4] his concept of God as rooted in his doctrine of motion (*Physica*, Book VIII) is more mechanical than personal. According to Aristotle the world is eternal and without beginning, and a first cause of motion is logically necessary to account for change.[5]

---

[1] Com. Zech. 14. 9 (CO 44, 374): The philosophers teach that there is one supreme deity so that there is no excuse for not honoring God.

[2] Louis Goumaz, *La Doctrine du Salut d'après les Commentaires de Jean Calvin sur Le Nouveau Testament* (Paris: Librairie Fischbacher, 1917), p. 129f. deals with Calvin's doctrine of salvation under the four causes. Calvin writes that the four causes of the philosophers do not help us to understand our salvation because the Scripture teaches us that the *efficient* cause of salvation is the mercy of the Father, the *material* cause is the obedience of Christ, the *formal* cause is faith, and the *final* cause is the glory of God. Calvin's point is that none of these causes is the work of man. III. 14. 17 (OS IV, 235, 20f) Goumaz identifies faith with the Holy Spirit and thus treats the doctrine of salvation with a Trinitarian organization. See also H. Paul Santmire, "Justification in Calvin's 1540 Romans Commentary," *Church History*, 33 (Sept., 1964), 294-313.

[3] It is likely that Aristotle's view of substance influences the discussion of the "substance" of the Eucharist. Cf. "Last Admonition to Joachim Westphal," *Calvin's Tracts*, II, 481 (CO 9, 241).

[4] *Metaphysica*, VI, 1026 a 19f.

[5] I. 16 3 (OS III, 190, 26-8): "For it would be senseless to interpret the words of the prophet after the manner of the philosophers, that God is the first agent because he is the beginning and cause of all motion . . . ."

Aristotle's conception of God as Unmoved Mover is not satisfactory from the Christian point of view since it, like the Epicurean, denies God's creation of the world and any concern with it. Indeed Aristotle argues that the world has a purpose, but it is not God's purpose. Aristotle's argument for design in the universe is not based on the will of God but rather on the permanence of types, and while Aristotle could write that "God and nature create nothing that does not fulfill a purpose",[6] his basic position is that nature has a purpose.[7] Perhaps the nearest Aristotle comes to a doctrine of providence is in this cautious statement:

> For if the gods have any care for human affairs as they are thought to have, it would be reasonable both that they should delight in that which was best and most akin to them (i.e. reason) and that they should reward those who love and honor this most, as caring for the things that are dear to them and acting both rightly and nobly. And that all these attributes belong most of all to the wise man is manifest. He, therefore, is the dearest to the gods. And he who is that will presumably be also the happiest; so that in this way too the wise man will be the happiest.[8]

Thus in Aristotle's extant works we have neither the reverent awe nor the spiritual aspiration which are such an appealing feature of Plato's thought.[9]

---

[6] *De Caelo*, 261 a 33.

[7] *De Anima*, 434 a 31; *Politica*, 1253 a 9.

[8] *Ethica Nicomachea*, X, 8, 1179 a 24-33.

[9] Cf. E. Zeller, *Aristole and the Earlier Peripatetics*, trans. by. B. F. C. Costelloe and J. H. Muirhead, II (London: Longmans, Green and Co., 1897), 326. Werner Jaeger, *Aristotle, Fundamentals of the History of his Development*, trans. by Richard Robinson (2nd. ed.; Oxford; Clarendon Press, 1948) thinks that Aristotle's earliest metaphysics was theological (p. 219). According to Jaeger, "Nobody in the ancient world ever spoke more beautifully or more profoundly about the personal and emotional side of all religious life than Aristotle during the years when religion was the central problem in his mind" (p. 159). In *On Philosophy* "Aristotle founded not merely Hellenistic theology, but also that sympathetic but at the same time objective study of the inner life for which antiquity had no name and no independent discipline apart from metaphysics. It did not vindicate its independence until the modern age gave it the name of 'philosophy of religion'." (p. 156). Aristotle in the lost dialogue *On Philosophy* suggests the *ontological* argument for the existence of God by arguing that "where there is a better there is also a best; now since among existing things one is better than another; therefore there is also a best which would be divine" (Aristoteles, *Fragmenta*, collected by Valentinus Rose (Leipzig: B. G. Teubner, 1886), fragment 16). Cf. Thomas' fourth proof for the existence of God, *Summa Theologica*, Ia, qu. 2, art. 3. In *On Philosophy* Aristotle also uses the *teleological* argument that men who see the beauty of the earth and seas and the order of the sky will think that there are gods (Fragment 12, the source is Cicero, *De Natura Deorum*, II. 27. 95). In Book XII of

Although Calvin admits the greatness of the philosophers, he insists that those who do not know the providence of God are fools. In this category he places Aristotle and the Epicureans as the following quotation demonstrates:

> [W]e find that some of the greatest of philosophers were so mischievous as to devote their talents to obscure and conceal the providence of God, and, entirely overlooking his agency, ascribed all to secondary causes. At the head of these was Aristotle, a man of genius and learning; but being a heathen, whose heart was perverse and depraved, it was his constant aim to entangle and perplex God's overruling providence by a variety of wild speculations; so much so, that it may with too much truth be said, that he employed his naturally acute powers of mind to extinguish all light. Besides, the prophet not only condemns the insensate Epicureans, whose sensibility was of the basest character, but he also informs us that a blindness, still greater and more detestable, was to be found among these great philosophers themselves.[10]

In view of Aristotle's importance in scholastic theology, it is perhaps surprising that Calvin only cites him ten times in the *Institutes*.[11] Still on the basis of these references and others, it appears that Calvin knows Aristotle rather well, but in general the citations are more literary than substantial. Thus the direct Aristotelian influence on Calvin is slight.

Epicureanism, like Stoicism, is a philosophy of salvation which seeks man's happiness in a serene and tranquil relation to the nature of things as they are. In considering the nature of things, Epicurus admits the existence of the gods who live in the empty spaces between the material worlds (intermundia), but insists that the gods are not involved in the creation of the world. In this he opposes the Platonic view of the Craftsman, the Stoic doctrine of providence, and even

---

his *Metaphysica* Aristotle argues *cosmologically* that the substances are the first of existing things. Thus if the substances are perishable then all things are perishable. However, since Aristotle regards motion and time as eternal, he maintains that eternal motion must be produced by eternal substance which as an Unmoved Mover must be purely actual being which causes motion by being the object of desire (1026 a 19f.). Plato attempts to prove the existence of the gods in *Laws*, X, 887 b f.

[10] Com. Ps. 107. 43 (CO 32, 145).

[11] I. 8. 9 (OS III, 77, 32); I. 8. 1 (OS III, 72, 33); IV. 17. 26 (OS V, 378, 16-18); II. 2. 3 (OS III, 243 : 27—244 : 1-3); II. 5. 2 (OS III, 299, 3-4); I. 15. 7 (OS III, 185, 6-8) and 15. 7 (OS III, 185, 12-15); II. 2. 3(OS III, 266, 1-9); I. 15. 6 (OS III, 184, 4-10); I. 5. 5 (OS III, 48, 22f.) Also the French ed. of 1560, I. 5. 4 (OS III, 48, 3-5).

the Peripatetic belief in nature's unconscious purpose.[12] Epicurus' materialism, based on the atomism of Democritus, is expressed in Lucretius' comment that "all nature therefore as it is in itself is made of two things; for there are bodies and there is void, in which these bodies are and through which they move this way and that."[13] According to the metaphysics of Democritus, the universe is a purposeless interaction of atoms. To this theory Epicurus adds the notion that the atoms have the capacity to swerve or spontaneously deviate from the straight line of fall. This assumption, for which there is no supporting evidence, once granted involves a radical contingency. Thus according to the Epicureans the nature of things is not made by divine power, and they believe that this understanding will remove the baseless dread of the gods and the yoke of religion.

Not only is the universe without divine cause, it is without design. Lucretius thinks that after his explanation of the fixed laws of winds and storms, only the foolish man could still consider nature to be the result of the gods' activity. Thus he maintains that the world is not made for man. The gods in living a life of perfect happiness are totally unconcerned about man. As Lucretius puts it, "[T]he very nature of divinity must necessarily enjoy immortal life in the deepest peace, far removed and separated from our troubles; for without any pain, without danger, itself mighty by its own resources, needing us not at all, it is neither propitiated with services nor touched by wrath."[14]

Man is entirely alone in the world without divine guidance. According to Epicurus some events happen by necessity which cannot be called into account, some happen by chance and these are unpredictable, but some are within our control and these are subject to no other master.[15] Men can do nothing about necessity and chance. They control only certain events, but in all they can seek happiness which the Epicureans find in pleasure defined as the absence of pain.

---

[12] Lactantius, *Divine Institutes*, II. 9. ANF VII, 55 (MPL VI, 302 c-303 a) says the chief philosophers, the Pythagoreans, the Stoics, and the Peripatetics, all except the "crazy Epicurus" believe in God's providence.

[13] *De Rerum Natura*, I. 419-22. Calvin calls Lucretius a "filthy dog". I. 5. 5 (OS III, 50, 19f).

[14] *Ibid.*, II. 646-51. This section is repeated in I. 44-9 which editors often omit.

[15] Epicurus, "Letter to Menoeceus," in *The Stoic and Epicurean Philosophers*, trans. by Cyril Bailey, ed. by Whitney J. Oates (New York: The Modern Library, 1940), p. 33. Cf. Bailey's *The Greek Atomists and Epicurus* (New York: Russell and Russell, 1964 (1928)) and A. J. Festugière, *Epicurus and His Gods*, trans. by C. W. Chilton (Cambridge: Harvard University Press, 1956).

This pleasure requires the use of reason for weighing pleasures against pains and vice versa, but the goal is individual pleasure apart from which there is no more ultimate cosmic meaning.[16]

Calvin could scarcely object more strenuously to these views of God, creation, and providence. He resolutely opposes the notion that God sits idly in heaven.[17] Calvin says, "What good is it to profess with Epicurus some sort of God who has cast aside the care of the world only to amuse himself in idleness? What help is it, in short, to know a God with whom we have nothing to do."[18] Further Calvin remarks, "I say nothing of the Epicureans (a pestilence that has always filled the world) who imagine that God is idle and in- dolent . . . ."[19]

According to Calvin, God is not only active in the creation of the world, but in its preservation. "Nobody seriously believes that the universe was made by God without being persuaded that he takes care of his works."[20] That is to say, "the world was not created by God once, in such a way that afterwards he abandoned his work, but that it endures by his power, and that the same One who was once its Creator is its perpetual ruler."[21] God not only created the world out of nothing but prevents it from dissolving. "Moreover, to make God a momentary Creator who once for all finished his work, would be cold and barren, and we must differ from profane men, especially in that we see the presence of divine power as much in the continuing state of the universe as in its inception."[22]

This preservation of the world which God creates means that the sun and seasons are governed by the special providence of God so that no drop of rain falls without his command,[23] and no wind arises or increases without his will.[24] Calvin insists that God does not merely give a general impulse to nature "but governs the world

---

[16] Cicero feels that if morality is to be defended the Epicurean position must be opposed. *De Officiis*, III. 33. 116.

[17] Calvin refers to this view in I. 4. 2 (OS III, 42, 2-3); Com. Dan. 4. 17 (CO 40, 663); Com. Hos. 7. 2 (CO 42, 339); Com. Zeph. 1. 12 (CO 44, 22-3); Com. Ps. 10. 4 (CO 31, 111); Com. Ps. 24. 1 (CO 31, 243).

[18] I. 2. 2 (OS III, 35, 14-7).

[19] I. 16. 4 (OS III, 193, 12-4).

[20] I. 16. 1 (OS III, 188, 15-6).

[21] Com. Acts 17. 28 (CO 48, 417). Cf. *Congrégation sur la divinité de Jésus Christ*, CO 47, 479.

[22] I. 16. 1 (OS III, 187, 10-4).

[23] I. 16. 5 (OS III, 195, 24-6).

[24] I. 16. 7 (OS III, 197, 21-2).

by his providence and power."[25] According to Calvin, the splendor of divine providence is so apparent that even infants hanging on their mother's breasts can refute these enemies of God.[26] Calvin thus opposes the Epicurean view that nature is neutral, rather it is the arena of God's activity toward man. God has not only created the world and preserves nature, but "God himself has shown by the order of creation that he created all things for man's sake."[27] God is not indifferent to man, but indeed the goal of creation is the provision of a place wherein man can glorify God. Calvin teaches that the order of creation reveals that God did not create man until he had amply provided for man's needs.[28] The whole order and governance of the world, including the creation and preservation of animals is established for the comfort of man.[29] Thus even after the fall of Adam when men were dispossessed of their station, yet because of God's providence the animals continue to serve men, to clothe them, and to feed them.[30]

Calvin has nothing but scorn for the Epicurean view of chance. While men may think that chance governs events, they are actually governed by the hand of God.[31] Thus Calvin objects, "Let Epicurus answer what concourse of atoms cooks food and drink, turns part of it into excrement, part into blood and begets such industry in the several members to carry out their tasks...."[32] Not only is it

---

[25] Com. Jon. 1. 6 (CO 43, 215).

[26] Com. Ps. 8. 2 (CO 31, 88-9).

[27] I. 14. 22 (OS III, 172, 27-8).

[28] I. 14. 2 (OS III, 154, 11-4).

[29] Com. Ps. 8. 8 (CO 31, 95). Cf. I. 14. 22 (OS III, 172, 27-8) and I. 16. 6 (OS III, 196, 5-7).

[30] Com. Ps. 8. 8 (CO 31, 95).

[31] Com. Am. 3. 5 (CO 43, 41). In the *Physica*, 196 b 5-7 Aristotle says that chance is a cause inscrutable to human intelligence. For Plato (*Timaeus*, 48 a) the idea of necessity is opposed to intelligence. A thing either happens according to plan and will or as the result of some blind force or chance. Thus Plato means by necessity here what Aristotle means by contingency.

[32] I. 5. 4 (OS III, 48, 17-21). In a similar vein, Epictetus, *Discourses*, I. 16. 7-8 writes, "One single gift of nature would suffice to make a man who is reverent and grateful perceive the providence of God ... Take the mere fact that milk is produced from grass, and cheese from milk, and that wool grows from skin— who is it that has made or devised these things? 'No one' somebody says. Oh, the depth of man's stupidity and shamelessness." In criticism of Epicurus, Lactantius, *Divine Institutes*, ANF III, 17. p. 87 (MPL, VI, 401b) writes, "Also, if there is no providence, how is it that the bodies of animals are arranged with such foresight, that the various members, being disposed in a wonderful manner, discharge their own offices severally?"

obvious that the world is governed by God, but in its governance is true consolation to be found. Thus Calvin writes,

> Especially let that foolish and most miserable consolation of the pagans be far away from the breast of the Christian man; to strengthen their minds against adversities, they charged these to fortune. Against fortune they considered it foolish to be angry because she was blind and unthinking with unseeing eyes wounding the deserving and undeserving at the same time. On the contrary, the rule of piety is that God's hand alone is the judge and governor of fortune, good and bad, and that it does not rush about with heedless force, but with most orderly justice deals out good as well as ill to us.[33]

Calvin concludes, with Basil the Great, that "fortune" and "chance" are pagan terms with whose significance the minds of the pious ought not to be occupied.[34]

While Calvin rejects the Epicurean doctrine of chance, in a strange way he is willing, with Augustine, to use the idea of "fortune" as long as it is not taken to exclude divine providence. Thus he makes this curious distinction:

> [H]owever all things may be ordained by God's purpose and sure distribution, for us they are fortuitous. Not that we think that fortune rules the world and men, tumbling all things at random up and down, for it is fitting that this folly be absent from the Christian breast! But since the order, reason, end and necessity of those things which happen for the most part lie hidden in God's purpose, and are not apprehended by human opinion, those things which it is certain take place by God's will, are in a sense fortuitous.[35]

This seems to mean that some events appear to be contingent on the surface and one may *act* as if they are, but one may not *believe* they are fortuitous because the man of faith will recognize that the necessity is hidden in God.

Calvin recognizes that the Epicureans have views of both chance *and* necessity, but he insists that they cannot excuse their actions by objecting they are constrained by the necessity of divine predestination.[36] It is not clear precisely what Calvin means in this comment. The Epicureans have a doctrine of divinity and of necessity, but divinity is unrelated to human behavior. Calvin does not seem to be dealing with Epicureanism on its own terms here, but insisting

---

[33] III. 7. 10 (OS IV, 161, 6-15).
[34] I. 16. 8 (OS III, 199, 6-7).
[35] I. 16. 9 (OS III, 200, 6-13).
[36] III. 23. 8 (OS IV, 402, 22-6).

on the basis of his own point of view that no one may abdicate his responsibility before God by claiming necessity. He sees the Epicureans as "crass despisers of piety."[37]

Calvin summarizes his objections to the Epicurean materialism, theology, ethics, psychology, and view of providence in the following comment:

> [The Epicurean] philosophy was to think that the sun is two feet wide, that the world was constructed out of atoms, and by trifling like that, to destroy the wonderful craftsmanship which is seen in the fabric of the world. If they were refuted a hundred times, they had no more sense than dogs. Although, briefly, they admitted that there were gods, yet they imagined them to be idle in heaven and to be applying to magnificence of living, and that their blessing consisted in idleness alone. As they used to deny that the world was divinely created, as I have just said, so they supposed human affairs are turned by chance, and are not governed by the providence of heaven. To them the greatest good was pleasure, not obscene and unbridled pleasure indeed, but yet such as by its attractions more and more ruined men already naturally inclined to the indulgence of the flesh. The immortality of souls was like a fairy tale to them, so that the result was that they freely allowed the indulgence of their bodies.[38]

Calvin opposes the Epicurean doctrine of God's unconcern, their view of necessity which denies responsibility, and their view of chance which denies causality. Calvin objects to the denial of God's providence on the part of both Aristotle and the Epicureans, but his relative neglect of Aristotle contrasts with his total and vigorous repudiation of the Epicureans. Indeed the closest Calvin comes to a positive comment on an idea resembling an Epicurean doctrine is his affirmation that God does not need our service.[39]

---

[37] I. 5. 12 (OS III, 56, 35).

[38] Com. Acts 17. 28 (CO 48, 405-6).

[39] While God does not need our service, Calvin insists that we render homage to God by serving others. Com. Job 1. 1 (CO 33, 39).

CHAPTER EIGHT

CALVIN ON PLATO AND THE STOICS

Some of the classical philosophers have a doctrine of providence. According to Justin Martyr, the philosophers think that God takes care of genera and species, but not of you and me.[1] That is, they teach an idea of providence in general but do not extend it to the care of each individual. In contrast to Aristotle and the Epicureans who deny the providence of God altogether, Plato and the Stoics affirm God's providence. Calvin's criticism is that, while holding a view of universal providence, Plato and the Stoics do not understand God's particular providence which is the chief thing. Thus while their insights are partial and inadequate, they are nonetheless commendable but only to a certain extent. Scholars, who assert that Calvin's doctrine of providence is basically philosophical, miss this point. In this chapter we will consider Calvin's judgment of Plato and the Stoics in general and in particular their view of providence.

Calvin and Plato

The philosophy of Plato is often thought to occupy a kind of middle ground between Christianity and pagan antiquity.[2] Indeed various aspects of his thought are considered congenial by Christian thinkers. For example the fathers thought an adumbration of the doctrine of the Trinity was to be found in Plato.[3] Also Plato could be cited in opposition to materialism and in favor of the immortal soul's quest for the divine and eternal realm which Plato pictures in terms of future rewards and punishments. Plato believes in the existence of God (Book Ten of the *Laws*)[4] and in man's duty to imitate God. Plato's *Timaeus* was understood as teaching a kind of

---

[1] Justin Martyr, "Dialogue with Trypho," ANF I, 194 (MPG VI, 473).

[2] Richard Kroner, *Speculation in Pre-Christian Philosophy* (Philadelphia: The Westminster Press, 1956), p. 71. See also Auguste Diès, *Platon* (Paris: Les Grandes Cœurs, 1930), pp. 216-20 and George Santayana, *Platonism and the Spiritual Life* (New York: Charles Scribner's Sons, 1927).

[3] Cf. Epistle II, 312 e.

[4] Com. Hos. 2. 17 (CO 42, 246): The heathen "allowed some Supreme Being . . . that this was for the most part the common doctrine may be easily learned from Plato."

creation of the world, and Plato affirms the providence of God.[5] Plato's belief in daemons could be taken as an insight into angelology and his criticism of pagan myths was eagerly adopted.[6] "Besides [as Gilson remarks], the whole doctrine of Plato was animated with such a love of truth and of those divine realities which every true philosopher strives to attain that one could hardly imagine a philosophy that would come nearer being a religion without actually becoming one."[7]

That Plato's religious philosophy exerts an immense influence on subsequent Christian thought is obvious.[8] Platonism is an im-

---

[5] Lactantius appeals not only to the prophets but to poets and philosophers, especially to Plato, "the wisest of all who plainly and openly maintains the rule of one God . . . ." *Divine Institutes*, I, 5. ANF VII, 14-5 (MPL VI. 135 a-136 b). In the *Summa Theologica*, Ia, qu. 103, art. 6 Thomas writes, "For Gregory of Nyssa reproves the opinion of Plato who divides providence into three parts. The first he ascribes to the supreme god, who watches over heavenly things and all universals; the second providence he attributes to the secondary deities, who go the round of the heavens to watch over things subject to generation and corruption; while he ascribes a third providence to certain spirits who are guardians on earth of human actions. Therefore it seems that all things are immediately governed by God." This three-fold providence is apparently drawn from the *Timæus*. Thomas replies: "Plato's opinion is to be rejected, because he held that God did not govern all things immediately, even in the principle of government; this is clear from the fact that he divided providence, which is the principle of government into three parts." In attributing to Gregory of Nyssa, Nemesius' *On the Nature of Man*, Thomas is reflecting the confusion of the middle ages. Cf. Etienne Gilson, *History of Christian Philosophy in the Middle Ages* (New York: Random House, 1955), pp. 60-4. As a Platonist, Plutarch attacks both the Epicureans and the Stoics on providence in his *Moralia*. Philo also discusses the Platonic view of creation and providence in his *De Providentia*, although his chief interest is in the divine providence for the Jewish nation as is seen in his *In Flaccum*.

[6] Paul Shorey, *Platonism, Ancient and Modern* (Berkeley: University of California Press, 1938), p. 79.

[7] Gilson, *History of Christian Philosophy in the Middle Ages*, p. 94.

[8] Aspects of Plato's thought, often compared with Christian theology, are discussed by Edward Caird, *The Evolution of Theology in the Greek Philosophers*, I (Glasgow: James MacLehose and Sons, 1904); James Adam, *The Religious Teachers of Greece* (Edinburgh: T. & T. Clark, 1908) which treats especially the *Republic*, *Symposium*, and *Timæus*: Clement C. J. Webb, *Studies in the History of Natural Theology* (Oxford: Clarendon Press, 1915), p. 84-186; William Temple, *Plato and Christianity* (London: Macmillan and Co. Ltd., 1916); Paul Elmer More, *The Religion of Plato* (Princeton: Princeton University Press, 1921); A. Diès, *Autour de Platon* (Paris: Gabriel Beauchesne, 1927), pp. 523-603; Alfred Edward Taylor, *Platonism and its Influence* (New York: Longmans, Green and Co., 1927), pp. 97-132; John S. Hoyland, *The Great Forerunner, Studies in the Inter-relation of Platonism and Christianity* (London: Constable & Co., 1928); Friedrich Solmsen, *Plato's Theology* (Ithaca: Cornell University Press, 1942); Olivier Reverdin, *La Religion de la Cité Platonicienne* (Paris: E. de Boccard, 1945);

portant factor in the religious thinking of Philo and Plotinus, Origen and Augustine.[9] Solmsen correctly observes, "It would be difficult to name a later theological system that is not in some way or other, directly or indirectly indebted to Plato."[10] In Plato's philosophy Christian thinkers, even those who are more strongly influenced by Aristotle (who could also be called a Platonist), find certain elements which they adapt and utilize, both consciously and unconsciously, in the presentation of their doctrines.

During the Renaissance Platonism was introduced into Europe by Pletho and as a result the Florentine Academy, devoted to Plato,

---

Victor Goldschmidt, *La Religion de Platon* (Paris: Presses Universitaires de France, 1949); W. K. C. Guthrie, *The Greeks and their Gods* (London: Methuen & Co., 1950); *Plato and the Christians*, selections by Adam Fox (London: SCM Press, 1957;) the differences between Plato and Christianity are emphasized by René Schaerer, *Dieu, L'homme et la vie d'après Platon* (Neuchâtel: Editions de la Baconnière, 1944), especially the chapter on "Platonisme et christianisme": pp. 171-213. Other studies include B. F. Cocker, *Christianity and Greek Philosophy* (New York: Harper & Brothers, 1872); Johannes Hessen, *Platonismus und Prophetismus* (Munich: Ernst Reinhardt Verlag, 1955); and A. H. Armstrong and R. A. Markus, *Christian Faith and Greek Philosophy* (London: Darton, Longman and Todd, 1960).

[9] Of Augustine, Anders Nygren concludes, "All his life he remains a Neoplatonic Christian, or, if you will, a Christian Platonist. He has no need to set Christianity and Neoplatonism in opposition; he thinks he can find a remarkably large measure of agreement between them. He is convinced that if Plato and his disciples could live their lives over again in his time they would accept Christianity; *the change of but a few words and phrases* would bring their views into entire harmony with it." *Agape and Eros*, trans. by Philip S. Watson (Philadelphia: The Westminister Press, 1953). p. 458. In the *Christian Doctrine* Augustine says that Christians should claim the truths of the philosophers, especially the Platonists as their own (II, 40; MPL XXXIV, 63), but he thinks that Plato was probably influenced by "our literature" (II, 28; MPL XXXIV, 56). See James K. Feibleman, *Religious Platonism* (London: George Allen & Unwin, Ltd., 1959); Ernst Hoffman, *Platonismus und Christliche Philosophie* (Zurich: Artemis-Verlag. 1960) and C. Bigg, *The Christian Platonists of Alexandria*, (2nd ed.; Oxford: Clarendon Press, 1913) and Endre V. Ivánka, *Plato Christianus* (Einsiedeln: Johannes Verlag, 1964).

[10] Solmsen, *Plato's Theology*, p. 177. Of the appeal to Plato, George Boas, *Rationalism in Greek Philosophy* (Baltimore: The Johns Hopkins Press, 1961), p. 130 drily remarks, "Both the ancients and early Christians looked to [Plato] as the source of their doctrines, as if their consistency with his dialogues would give added proof to their theories. This is the more curious among the early Fathers with their theory of a praeparatio evangelica . . . for one might think that the Source of all light would produce His revelation without the help of heathen thinkers. The revelation to Abraham seems to have been preceded by no teaching from the Sumerian or Egyptian sages, and there is nothing, as far as I know, in the Prophets which any Biblical scholar asserts to have been prepared by Philistine, Persian, or Indian literature. It is true that in Saint Paul there are two references to Greek writers, but Paul was far from using them as authority for beliefs which he had been taught through revelation."

was founded. In 1482 Marsilio Ficino translated the *Dialogues* into Latin and beginning in 1541 French translations appeared.[11] However, as James K. Feibleman observes, "The rediscovery of Plato's writings and their availability through translation did little to restore the truth about Plato's own thoughts but instead reinforced the Neoplatonic tradition and indeed gave it new impetus."[12] Only within the last 150 years have scholars attempted to distinguish between Plato and the diffuse Platonic tradition. As Leland Miles writes,

> The distinction between Platonism and Neoplatonism was not recognized until the 19th century (see the *Oxford English Dictionary*, 6:90); and the distinction between these two and Florentine Platonism is of even more recent origin. From Augustine through the Renaissance and beyond, figures like Plotinus, Dionysius, and the Florentines were successively but erroneously regarded as accurate interpreters of Plato. Thus Augustine referred to Plotinus and his school as "Platonists". Ficino followed suit by exalting Dionysius as "the Platonist," and further declared in his *Enneads* translation that Plotinus should be read as Plato speaking in the person of his pupil . . . Similarly, Colet hailed Ficino as "the Platonist Marsilio," despite the fact that the Florentine's *Theologia Platonica* is so far removed from original Platonism that it goes wholly unmentioned in Professor Solmsen's authoritative work on the theology of the *Dialogues*.[13]

---

[11] Gilbert Highet, *The Classical Tradition* (London: Oxford University Press, 1949), p. 118.

[12] Feibleman, *Religious Platonism*, p. 209.

[13] Leland Miles, *John Colet and the Platonic-Tradition* (La Salle: Open Court, 1961), p. xiii-xiv. Historically the philosophy of Plato was either distorted or complemented, depending on one's point of view, in Platonism. Philip Merlan, *From Platonism to Neoplatonism*, (2nd ed.; The Hague: Martinus Nijhoff, 1960), p. 3, thinks that "the present tendency is towards bridging rather than widening the gap separating Platonism from Neoplatonism." According to C. J. de Vogel, "On the Neoplatonic Character of Platonism and the Platonic Character of Neoplatonism," *Mind*, 62 (1953), 54 Platonism ought to be understood in a Neoplatonic way since Neoplatonism is essentially legitimate Platonism. This view is not convincing because it depends on a mooted reconstruction of Plato's so-called "unwritten doctrines" from the writings of his disciples, especially Aristotle, as Harold Cherniss, *The Riddle of the Early Academy* (New York: Russell & Russell, 1962) has pointed out. (For a different evaluation see David Ross, *Plato's Theory of Ideas* (Oxford: Clarendon Press, 1951), p, 142-153). The doctrines, especially the mathematicals, developed by the disciples of Plato may have been suggested by Plato, but on the evidence presented in the *Dialogues* Plato did not hold them in the form which they took in Neoplatonism. Thus the Platonism which fused Plato, Aristotle, and the Stoa was not the Platonism of the *Dialogues*. The notion that Plato was a "Moses speaking Greek" or a "Christian before Christ" appealed one-sidedly to Plato's mystical view of love, his meditation on death, and his contempt for the body which could be taken as

It is true that during the Renaissance, students of Plato such as Pico, Ficino, and Colet were likely to interpret Plato in terms of Plotinus, Augustine, and Dionysius the Areopagite, and that Florentine philosophy, while indebted to Plato, was also greatly influenced by Aristotle, Aquinas, and the Arabic philosophy. Marsilio Ficino, whose *Theologia Platonica* represented the authoritative statement of Platonic philosophy to the Renaissance, desired to reconcile Plato and Aristotle and frequently used Aristotelian reasoning. Kristeller observes, "Historians of Western thought have often expressed the view that the Renaissance was basically an age of Plato, whereas the Middle Ages had been an age of Aristotle." He correctly asserts that this position can no longer be maintained. "Renaissance Platonism which many historians have been inclined to oppose to medieval Aristotelianism, was not as persistently anti-Aristotelian as we might expect."[14]

It is certainly true that in such "Platonic" figures as Plotinus and Ficino, Plato's doctrines are combined with Aristotle's, and under the sanction of the theology of Aquinas, the influence of Aristotle maintained a supremacy for much of Renaissance thought. Kristeller concludes,

> We must resign ourselves to the fact that in most cases the Platonist elements of thought are combined with doctrines of a different origin and character, and that even the professed Platonists did not express the thought of Plato in its purity, as modern scholars understand it, but combined it with more or less similar notions that had accrued to it in late antiquity, the Middle Ages, or more recent times. Yet if we understand Platonism with those qualifications and in a broad and flexible sense, it was a powerful intellectual force throughout the centuries, and we shall understand its nature best if we realize that until the rise of modern Plato scholarship, Plato appealed to his readers not only through the content of his inimitable dialogues, but also through the diverse and often complicated ideas which his commentators and followers down to the sixteenth and seventeenth centuries had associated with him.[15]

The Platonists of antiquity are not concerned with the historical

---

Christian themes. In short Plato's otherworldliness was emphasized and his this-worldliness was overlooked. Cf. Arthur O. Lovejoy, *The Great Chain of Being* (New York: Harper & Row, 1936), p. 24f.

[14] Kristeller, *The Classics and Renaissance Thought*, p. 24, 43. Cf. Raymond Klibansky, *The Continuity of the Platonic Tradition During The Middle Ages* (London: Warburg, 1939), p. 36.

[15] Kristeller, *The Classics and Renaissance Thought*, p. 69.

development of Plato's doctrines. Often as much under the spell of his genius as the force of his arguments, for them Plato is not merely a source, but the occasion for the presentation of ideas which may or may not accurately reflect the thought of Plato himself as modern scholars evaluate the *Dialogues*.

Nevertheless, Erasmus, Luther, Melanchthon, and Calvin recognize a difference between Plato and Aristotle and emphasize the close relation between Platonism and Christianity. The humanists regard Plato as their champion in the struggle against the Aristotelianism of scholasticism. Thus Erasmus complains that if classical learning is suspect why is such authority given to the pagan Aristotle.[16] Erasmus sees little connection between Christ and Aristotle.[17] He points out that Augustine prefers Plato and Pythagoras.[18] Erasmus writes to William Blount, Lord Mountjoy (Paris, June, 1500): "Now what has the world more eloquent than the speech of Plato or more divine than his philosophy."[19] And again "Of the philosophers, I should wish you to follow the Platonists, because both in very many sentences and their manner of speaking they came very near to the image of the prophets and the Gospel."[20] Luther says that "Aristotle poorly grasps and ridicules a philosophy better than his own—that of Platonic ideas" (Aristoteles male reprehendit ac ridet platonicarum idearum meliorem sua Philosophiam).[21] Melanchthon praises both Plato and Aristotle.[22] And Calvin views Plato not merely as one of the sounder class of philosophers,[23] but as the most religious and sober of the philosophers though he adds that Plato loses himself in his round globe.[24] While Augustine, whose conversion to Christianity and Platonism was almost simultaneous,

---

[16] *Opus Epistolarum Des. Erasmi Roterodami*, ed. by P. S. Allen II, (Oxford: Clarendon Press, 1910), 110.

[17] *Ibid.*, 101.

[18] Erasmus, *Enchiridion*, p. 107 (EO 5, 30 A).

[19] *Opus Epistolarum*, I, 291.

[20] Erasmus, *Enchiridion*, p. 51 (EO 5, 7 F).

[21] WA, I, 355, quoted in Spitz, *The Religious Renaissance of the German Humanists*, p. 238.

[22] Melanchthon, "De Platone" (1538), CR 11, 413-425.

[23] Com. Gen. 2 .18 (CO 23, 46).

[24] I. 5. 11 (OS III, 55, 27-28). The reference to the round globe (σφαιροειδής) comes from Plato, *Timaeus*, 33 b. *Cf. Phaedo*, 108 e. In *Phaedo*, 97 d Socrates questions whether the earth is flat or round. According to Justinian, Origen thinks that the resurrection body is spherical (σφαιροειδής). Henry Chadwick, "Origen, Celsus, and the Resurrection of the Body," *Harvard Theological Review*, 41, 2 (April, 1948), 94f.

is an enthusiastic Platonist, Calvin separates himself from Augustine on this point by criticizing Augustine as excessively Platonic.[25] Calvin insists that he is not Platonic or of some other sect opposed to Christ.[26] Calvin eschews Plato as a source of his theology, but he admits that Plato knows something about holiness.[27] It is not always possible, in specific instances, to ascertain whether Calvin's knowledge is derived from a direct reading of the philosopher cited or mediated to him through secondary sources,[28] but Calvin is certainly influenced by the various philosophical currents of his time, especially Platonism[29] and Stoicism.

On the relation between Calvin and Plato, Jean Boisset asserts that Calvin recognizes a master in the philosopher of the Academy. According to Boisset, "If Augustine is the theologian to whom Calvin refers most frequently, Plato is the philosopher most often cited and nearly always with favor. One can say that for Calvin Plato is, as a philosopher, what Augustine is as a theologian."[30] In a general way this statement is true, but it does not make clear how few times Calvin actually refers to Plato, and it suggests a more extensive Platonic influence than is warranted.

Boisset deals helpfully with the Platonism of Calvin's milieu, but the method by which he seeks to identify common themes in Plato is questionable. That is, there are Platonic themes which may be juxtaposed to Calvin's views, but Boisset does not demonstrate

---

[25] Com. Jn. 1. 3 (CO 47, 4).

[26] "Last Admonition to Joachim Westphal," *Calvin's Tracts*, II, 456 (CO 9, 222).

[27] Com. Lk. 1. 75 (CO 45, 50). Cf. Plato, *Protagoras*, 331 d.

[28] Calvin most likely read Plato in Ficino's Latin translation. Calvin's reference to philosophy as a meditation on death (CO I, 694; III. 3. 20; OS IV, 78, 9-11) may be derived from Ficino's translation of the *Phaedo*, 81 a which reads, "quod quidem nihil est aliud quam recte philosophari, mortemque reuera facile meditari, an non haec est meditatio mortis?" (p. 61) Plato's phrase μελέτη θανάτου means study or rehearsal or death rather than meditation. See A. E. Taylor, *Plato, The Man and His Work* (6th ed.; New York: The Humanities Press, 1952), p. 179, note 1. Calvin's reference to Plato's δαίμων as angelos may be derived from Ficino's introductory essay on the *Symposium* and Calvin's Latin quotation of the prayer in *Alcibiades* II, 143 a (CO I, 923; III. 20. 34; OS IV, 344, 17-23) is identical with Ficino's translation (p. 45) *Omnia Divini Platonis Opera*, trans. by Marsilli Ficini, ed. Simonis Grynaei (Basel: Froben, 1561). However it remains possible that Calvin's knowledge of the philosophers was derived from secondary sources. He apparently used Erasmus' *Adagia*. See note CO 42, 391.

[29] Joseph C. McClelland, "Calvin and Philosophy," *The Canadian Journal of Theology*, XI (Jan. 1965), 47.

[30] Jean Boisset, *Sagesse et Sainteté dans la Pensée de Jean Calvin*, (Paris: Université de France, 1959), pp. 284, 221.

that they are *Platonic themes in Calvin*. Boisset is on firm ground concerning the Platonic influence on Calvin's doctrine of soul since
Calvin cites Plato on the immortality of the soul, but, as we have
seen, Calvin's doctrine of the resurrection of the body also belongs to
his discussion. The other common themes which Boisset identifies such
as tranquillity, the two worlds, the contemplation of God, and the use
of the term "Academy" in Geneva are speculative if not fanciful.[31]

It is often enlightening to discuss intellectual parallels, but in
the absence of textual evidence the parallels may be in the mind
of the interpreter rather than in the sources. For example, Boisset
claims that the Platonic view of the sensible and intelligible realms
may be applied to Calvin's doctrine of the visible and invisible
church, and that Plato's doctrine of participation may be applied
to Calvin's doctrine of the church and sacraments.[32] This line of
interpretation is continued in Kilian McDonnell's study of Calvin's
view of the church and the Eucharist. McDonnell asserts, "Plato's
influence on Calvin cannot be limited merely to an atmosphere
vaguely Platonic. He was also *directly influenced* by Plato, and this
influence increased as the years passed."[33] Again he writes, "Since
Platonism is more a spirit than a system, it was a spirit and, in part,
a methodology which Calvin took over."[34] Further, "*Plato's concept
of participation* is to be seen *with even greater clarity* in Calvin's doctrine
of the sacraments."[35]

This assertion is worth considering in some detail as an example
of the tendency to find affinities between Calvin and Plato where
none seem to exist. Plato uses the concept of participation in an
attempt to bridge the gap between the theory of forms and the theory
of things. The forms are somehow immanent in things, and yet the
forms transcend things. The things participate in the forms, yet they
always fall short of perfectly exemplifying the forms. Cornford
rightly insists that "the much-vexed problem of 'participation'
(μέθεξις) Plato could never solve to his satisfaction."[36] In the *Phaedo*

---

[31] *Ibid.*, pp. 253ff.

[32] *Ibid.*, p. 267. See also Boisset's *Calvin et la Souveraineté de Dieu* (Paris: Editions Seghers, 1964), p. 117.

[33] Kilian McDonnell, *John Calvin, the Church, and the Eucharist* (Princeton:
Princeton University Press, 1967), p. 33. Emphasis added.

[34] *Ibid.*

[35] *Ibid.*, p. 35. Emphasis added.

[36] F. M. Cornford, *From Religion to Philosophy* (New York: Harper & Brothers,
1957), p. 254.

Plato says that nothing makes a thing beautiful but the presence (παρουσία) and participation (κοινωνία) of beauty.[37] Plato suggests that one may call the relation of form to sensible thing παρουσία (presence of a form) or κοινωνία (participation of a thing in the form) or whatever one pleases.[38] This indicates that Plato sometimes views the problem of the relation from the side of the forms and sometimes from the side of the things.[39]

Most of the time when Plato deals with participation from the side of the forms he uses παρουσία and related words. This is seen in *Lysis* where Socrates discussing the presence of good and evil in relationship to friendship, defines friendship as the love which the neither good nor evil has of the good on account of the presence of evil.[40] The same point of view of the presence of the idea is found in the *Euthydemus*. Socrates says that we should be happy if many goods were present to us.[41] Again in the *Gorgias* Socrates says that evil is evil because of the presence of evil. In the same way we would not call good things good unless good were present, or beautiful unless beauty were exhibited.[42] Plato is not saying that beauty is the cause of beautiful things, since the ideas are *not causes* but explanations. (If they were causes there would be no problem of participation!)[43] Rather Plato maintains that the presence of beauty is the explanation of a things being beautiful. The tendency of these references is to view the relation of forms and things from the side of the forms.

From the side of the things the relation to forms is κοινωνία (to take part in, communion) or μίμησις (mimic, imitate, represent) or μετέχω. In the *Gorgias* communion is one of the things that bind heaven and earth together. The man who takes part in justice is worthy to be a friend.[44] In *Phaedo* soul is fallen because it has com-

---

[37] *Phædo*, 100 c.

[38] *Ibid.*

[39] Cf. David Ross, *Plato's Theory of Ideas* (Oxford: Clarendon Press, 1951), p. 288 classifies the words which express the relation of forms and things by implying or suggesting immanence or transcendence of the forms.

[40] *Lysis*, 218 b.

[41] *Euthydemus*, 280 a.

[42] *Gorgias*, 498 d; 497 d.

[43] The ideas are not causes in the sense of having causal efficacy. They are the "because" of a thing being beautiful. See Gregory Vlastos, "Reasons and Causes in the *Phaedo*," *Plato*, ed. by Gregory Vlastos, I (Garden City: Anchor Books, 1971), 132-66.

[44] *Ibid.*, 507 e.

munion with body.[45] In the *Republic* Socrates points out that each of the ideas in itself is one and it is only by communion with actions and bodies that they appear multiple.[46] Thus κοινωνία appears in the context of an intermediary principle between ideas and things and refers to the ideas from the standpoint of the things. Most of the references containing forms of μίμησις refer to simple imitation, such as of good and worthy men.[47] However, Plato admits imitation into the world as a kind of making, but of images and not of real things.[48] As a doctrine concerned with the problem of the relation of the things and the forms, Plato deals with imitation in Book X of the *Republic*. The craftsman who makes a table fixes his eye on the form.[49] It could not be said that the craftsman makes the idea of the table, and it follows that the poet and painter, who imitate the craftsman are imitators thrice removed from the reality of the ideas. They imitate appearances, while the craftsman imitates reality.

Another of the attempts to relate the ideas and things is seen in the word μετέχω, which means to partake of, or to share in. This usage is seen in the *Protagoras*. Socrates thinks that pleasant things are called pleasant because they partake of pleasure.[50] In the *Gorgias* Socrates points out that things which in themselves are neither good nor bad can become good by participating or sharing in the good.[51] Sitting and walking are between (μεταξύ) good and evil, but they are done with the good in mind. In the *Lysis* discussion of beauty and friendship Socrates introduces the notion that there are three principles—the good, the bad, and that which is neither good nor bad.[52] This third principle "that which is neither good nor bad" is not developed in the *Lysis* but reappears in the *Gorgias*. Socrates believes that all things are either good or bad or indifferent. The intermediate things partake of the nature of good at times and at other times of the nature of evil. Nevertheless the indifferent (μεταξύ) is done for the sake of the good.[53]

It seems extremely wayward to assert that this discussion of Plato's

---

[45] *Phaedo*, 65 a.
[46] *Republic*, V, 476 a.
[47] *Ibid.*, III, 395 c.
[48] *Sophist*, 265 a.
[49] *Republic*, X, 596 b.
[50] *Protagoras*, 351 d.
[51] *Gorgias*, 468 a.
[52] *Lysis*, 216 d.
[53] *Gorgias*, 468 b.

regarding participation had any *direct* influence on Calvin's doctrine of the church and sacraments. The only similarity between Calvin and Plato on participation appears to be the word. No text is adduced to support the contention, and Plato's view is tied to his metaphysical theory. It would be equally erroneous to assert that this Platonic cluster of ideas may be applied to Calvin's view of the return (πα-ρουσία) of Christ, the imitation (μίμησις) of Christ, the fellowship (κοινωνία) of Christ or his view of indifferent things.

Undoubtedly Calvin is influenced by Plato not only directly, but through Cicero,[54] the early fathers,[55] Augustine and the Christian humanists as various writers have sought to demonstrate.[56] To the extent that all philosophy is a footnote to Plato or all men either Platonists or Aristotelians, then Calvin was a Platonist. It is likely correct, as Barth remarks, "From a philosophical point of view, Luther and Calvin were equally unmistakable Platonists; Luther more of a Neoplatonist, Calvin a classical Platonist."[57]

It is evident that Calvin uses certain Platonic insights and that he approves Plato's understanding of providence, partial though it is. Calvin writes,

---

[54] Cicero, *De Natura Deorum*, II. 12. 32 called "Plato, that divine philosopher" and said, *Tusculan Disputations*, I. 17. 39-40, "I prefer before heaven, to go astray with Plato . . . rather than hold true views with his opponents." In *De Legibus*, I. 5 Cicero's Atticus speaks of the "beloved Plato, whom you admire, revere above all others, and love above all others." Cf. John E. Rexine, *Religion in Plato and Cicero* (New York: Philosophical Library, 1954).

[55] R. Arnou, "Le Platonisme des Pères," in *Dictionnaire de Théologie Catholique*, XII, 2257-2392. Etienne Gilson, *History of Christian Philosophy in the Middle Ages*, p. 93 justly remarks, "It is important first of all to be forewarned against an almost inevitable error of perspective. The very attempt to discern the philosophical elements which theologians have used in their work throws these elements into an exaggerated relief with respect to the very theologies from which they are taken. For the Fathers of the Church, neither the truth of the faith, nor the dogma defining it, depended in any way on philosophy. In their minds, faith was the essential. The formula 'The Platonism of the Fathers' would lead to an absurd interpretation if it were meant to say that the Fathers were Platonists. They were essentially Christians, that is to say, teachers of a doctrine of salvation by faith in Jesus Christ, and not at all the disciples of a philosopher who conceived salvation as a natural reward for the philosophical exercise of reason."

[56] Studies which consider Platonic themes in Calvin include Martin Schulze, *Meditatio futurae vitae*; Battenhouse, "The Doctrine of Man in Calvin and in Renaissance Platonism," pp. 447-471; Bohatec's, *Budé und Calvin*, pp. 415-430; Heinrich Quistorp, *Calvin's Doctrine of the Last Things*, pp. 51-4, 72-3 and Boisset.

[57] Karl Barth, *Church Dogmatics*, trans. by G. T. Thomson and Harold Knight, I, 2 (Edinburgh: T. & T. Clark, 1956), 728. Cf. Barth's *Die Christliche Dogmatik* (Munich: Chr. Kaiser Verlag, 1927), p. 404.

We continue to live, so long as [God] sustains us by his power; but no sooner does he withdraw his lifegiving spirit than we die. Even Plato knew this, who so often teaches that, properly speaking, there is but one God, and that all things subsist, or have their being only in him. Nor do I doubt, that it is the will of God, by means of that heathen writer, to awaken all men to the knowledge that they derive their life from another source than themselves.[58]

Calvin and the Stoics

Stoic thought as a whole is an austere philosophical quest for salvation. In order to relate properly to the final goal of life, Stoicism posits a ground of being which is variously called God, Nature, Providence, Fate, or Necessity. Not consistent in terminology or conception, the Stoics hold that God is identical with nature, but they also maintain that God knows, governs, loves mankind, and desires our good. Theoretical reason concerning the nature of things issues in the conviction of a unity governed by fate (εἱμαρμένη) or necessity (ἀνάγκη) and ruled by mind (νοῦς) or reason (λόγος), but the primary Stoic emphasis is on practical reason, on virtue for virtue's sake and fulfilling the requirements of duty. In living according to nature, the Stoics renounce the world by adopting the role of apathy (ἀπάθεια) through which the wise man refuses to be diverted from following the course of wisdom and truth. According to the Stoics, man's only freedom is to be found in freely accepting the necessity of things.

Of all the classical philosophers the Stoics have the most developed consciousness of providence. As Bevan remarks, "It was for faith in providence above all else that the Stoic stood in the ancient world."[59] Since the Stoics believe that the universe is ruled by the providence of God,[60] they attack the Epicurean view as atheistic[61]

---

[58] Com. Ps. 104. 29 (CO 32, 95).

[59] Edwyn Bevan, *Stoics and Skeptics* (Cambridge: W. Heffer and Sons, 1913 (1965), p. 44.

[60] Cicero, *De Natura Deorum*, II, 29, 73f. Cf. Seneca, "De Providentia," In *Opera Omnia* (Leipzig: Tauchnitii, 1832). This work is chiefly concerned with theodicy. It is addressed to Lucilius who accepts providence but does not understand how so many misfortunes befall good men in a world governed by providence. According to Seneca the gods are more concerned with the whole than the individual (III. 1). And since fate assigns to each a lot at birth (V. 5), man must be resigned to destiny to which the founder (conditor) and governor (rector) is also bound (V. 6). Chrysippus argues, "There is absolutely nothing more foolish than those men who think that good could exist, if there were at the same time no evil". Aulus Gellius, *Noctes Atticae*, vol. II, Bk. VII, 1, 2-3.

[61] Cicero, *De Natura Deorum*, I, 44. 123.

and irreligious.[62] Cicero observes, "There are and have been philosophers who hold that the gods exercise no control over human affairs whatever. But if their opinion is the true one, how can piety, reverence or religion exist?"[63]

According to the Stoics the works of the gods are full of providence.[64] Therefore men should understand that the gods govern. The Stoics hold that deity expresses itself in the world process which follows a fixed law (λόγος) called fate or necessity (εἰμαρμένη) or providence (πρόνοια, Latin, providentia). Cicero has Quintus say,

> Reason compels us to admit that all things happen by Fate. Now by Fate I mean the same that the Greeks call εἰμαρμένη, that is, an orderly succession of causes, wherein cause is linked to cause and each cause of itself produces an effect.... Therefore nothing has happened which was not bound to happen, and, likewise, nothing is going to happen which will not find in nature every efficient cause of its happening. Consequently, we know that Fate is that which is called not ignorantly, but scientifically, "the eternal cause of things, the wherefore of things past, of things present, and of things to come".[65]

Stoic thought does not deny the force of Fortune and Chance,[66] but seeks to rise superior to it by the power of philosophy. "He who can bear Fortune, can also beware of Fortune."[67] Seneca writes,

> Perhaps someone will say: "How can philosophy help me, if Fate exists? Of what avail is philosophy, if God rules the universe? Of what avail is it, if Chance governs everything? For not only is it impossible to change things that are determined, but it is also impossible to plan beforehand against what is undetermined; either God has forestalled my plans, and decided what I am to do, or else Fortune gives no free play to my plans." Whether the truth, Lucilius, lies in one or in all of these views, we must be philosophers; whether Fate binds us down by an inexorable law, or whether God as arbiter of the universe has arranged everything, or whether Chance drives and tosses human affairs without method, philosophy ought to be our defence. She will encourage us to obey God cheerfully, but Fortune defiantly; she will teach us to follow God and endure Chance.[68]

---

[62] *Ibid.*, I, 43, 121. "Now when Epicurus robbed the immortal gods of their love for mankind and of their eagerness to minister to human needs, he removed from our souls every trace of religion."

[63] *De Natura Deorum*, I. 2. 3.

[64] Marcus Aurelius, *Meditations*, II. 3.

[65] *De Divinatione*, I. 55. 125.

[66] Cf. Seneca, *Epistulae Morales*, XCI, 8-10.

[67] *Ibid.*, XCVIII. 7.

[68] *Ibid.*, XCI. 5.

In his *De Fato* Cicero attacks the Epicurean position that events take place without a cause as intolerable. Again he says, "Surely nothing is so at variance with reason and stability as chance. Hence it seems to me that it is not in the power even of God himself to know what event is going to happen accidentally and by chance. For if he knows, then the event is certain to happen; but if it is certain to happen, chance does not exist. And yet chance does exist, therefore there is no foreknowledge of things that happen by chance."[69] The Stoics associate cause and reason and God.[70] Still there are problems. Cicero maintains that the necessity of fate is not to be understood as a series of causes which takes away free will because there is a difference between accidental and necessary causes. Every event has a cause but not an external cause. Fate means universal causation but does not deny volitional freedom since voluntary motion is within our power.[71] In trying to develop a doctrine of fate consistent with the providence of God and the free will of man, the author of "On Fate", which is attributed to Plutarch, considers fate to include everything which consequentially occurs but makes room for the possible, the contingent, choice, and chance which as antecedents follow their own nature in occurring.[72]

Epictetus suggests these possibilities:

> Concerning gods there are some who say that the divine does not so much as exist; and others, that it exists, indeed, but is inactive and indifferent, and takes forethought for nothing; and a third set, that it exists and takes forethought, though only for great and heavenly things and in no case for terrestrial things; and a fourth set, that it also takes forethought for things terrestrial and the affairs of men, but only in a general way, and not for the individual in particular; and a fifth set, to which Odysseus and Socrates belonged, who say: Nor when I move am I concealed from thee.[73]

---

[69] Cicero, *De Divinatione*, II. 7. 18.

[70] Seneca, *Epistulae Morales*, LXV. 2. 23.

[71] *De Fato*, IX. 18f. Cf. *De Finibus*. I. 6. 19. Aulus Gellius, *Noctes Atticae*, vol. II, Bk. VII, 2. I. wrote that Chrysippus defined fate as follows: "Fate is an eternal and unalterable series of circumstances, and a chain rolling and entangling itself through an unbroken series of consequences, from which it is fashioned and made up." If this is true, his critics argued, then men do not sin voluntarily and therefore may not be held responsible. Chrysippus answers that "the peculiar properties of our minds are subject to fate only according to their individuality and quality" (*Ibid.*, 7). Thus the evil man is fated to be evil, but somehow responsible for being evil. This position resembles Calvin's view that the reprobate is responsible for being evil.

[72] Plutarch, *Moralia*, vol. VII.

[73] *Discourses*, I. 12. 1-3. Against Chaldean astrologers, the philosopher Favorinus asked, "Are unimportant things more difficult to understand than the important?" Aulus Gellius, *Noctes Atticae*, vol. III, Bk. XIV. 1. 24.

If, in fact the world has no governor, Epictetus asks, "Yet how can it be that, while it is impossible for a city or a household to remain even a very short time without someone to govern and care for it, nevertheless this great and beautiful structure should be kept in such orderly arrangement by sheer accident and chance?"[74] The conclusion, according to Marcus Aurelius, is that

> There must either be a predestined Necessity and inviolable plan, or a gracious Providence, or a chaos without design or director. If then there be an inevitable Necessity, why kick against the pricks? If a Providence that is ready to be gracious, render thyself worthy of divine succor. But if a chaos without guide, congratulate thyself that amid such a surging sea thou hast in thyself a guiding Reason.[75]

Thus the Stoic doctrine of providence is derived from a reasoned consideration of the alternatives, and what Cochrane calls a "pathetic insistence upon the right to believe in an orderly world."[76]

In certain elements of Stoic thought early Christians find much to admire.[77] It was even once thought that Paul and Seneca were friends. For example, Clement's ideal of living superior to the vicissitudes of life like the impassible God is derived from the Stoics.[78] Further, Christian thought, especially in Justin Martyr and Clement, is also influenced by the Stoic doctrine of λόγος which could be related to John's use of the term in the Gospel. Likewise, Tertullian's view of the corporeality of soul is Stoic in origin. Moreover, Lactantius appeals to Cicero who "although he was a defender of the academic system, discussed at length and on many occasions respecting the providence which governs affairs, confirming the arguments of the Stoics, and himself adducing many new ones . . . ."[79] Lactantius considers Seneca "the keenest Stoic of the Romans"[80] and maintains, "If anyone considers the whole government of the

---

[74] *Ibid.*, II. 14. 26.

[75] *Meditations*, XII. 14.

[76] Charles N. Cochrane, *Christianity and Classical Culture* (New York: Oxford University Press, 1940), p. 166.

[77] Léontine Zanta, *La Renaissance du Stoicisme au XVIe Siècle* (Paris: Édouard Champion, 1914), p. 99f. treats Stoic themes in Lactantius, Augustine, Tertullian, Clement of Alexandria, and Origen.

[78] Clement of Alexandria, *Stromata*, ANF II, 437 (MPG VIII, 1356 d, 1360 c). Cf. *Pædagogus*, I, 2; ANF II, 210 (MPG VIII, 252 c) and Robert P. Casey, "Clement of Alexandria and the Beginnings of Christian Platonism," *Harvard Theological Review*, 18, 1 (Jan., 1925), 39-101.

[79] *Divine Institutes*, I, 2; ANF VIII, 11 (MPL VI, 121 a).

[80] *Ibid.*, I, 5 ANF VII, 14-5 (MPL VI, 135 a-136 b).

world, he will certainly understand how true is the opinion of the
Stoics, who say the world was made on our account."[81] Moreover,
Augustine cites Seneca with approval for attributing the order and
connection of causes to the will of God.[82]

The reformers also find congenial elements in Stoicism. Léontine
Zanta devotes a chapter in her *La Renaissance de Stoicisme au XVI*e
Siècle to Stoic themes in the Protestant Reformers: Luther, Zwingli,
Melanchthon, and Calvin. Zanta shows that the Reformers consciously define their positions with regard to certain Stoic doctrines.
For example, the relation of God and evil, reason and revelation,
man and nature, love and apathy, fate and predestination are developed with explicit recognition of the Stoic views.[83] Zanta also points
out that Calvin opposes the Stoic views of the equality of sin, pantheism, and apathy.

It is not surprising that Calvin approves of certain Stoic doctrines.
Calvin approves of the Stoic belief in the existence and sovereignty
of God, their praise of nature, and their view of man's rational and
social nature. According to an unsubstantiated tradition, Calvin
read through Cicero every year. Calvin's first book deals with Seneca,
and he continues to be interested in Seneca's ethics.[84]

The all-encompassing providence of God which Calvin teaches,
on the surface at least, resembles the Stoic doctrine. This similarity
was not lost on Calvin's critics. Calvin remarks, "Those who wish
to cast odium upon this doctrine defame it as the Stoics' dogma
of fate." This charge, he points out, was once hurled against Augustine.[85] Calvin, like Augustine, does not want to quarrel about words,
but he prefers not to use the word "fate". "We do not, with the
Stoics, contrive a necessity out of a perpetual connection and inti-
mately related series of causes, which is contained in nature; but

---

[81] *A Treatise on the Anger of God*, XIII; ANF VII, 269 (MPL VII, 115 a).

[82] *The City of God*, trans. by Marcus Dods (Chicago: Encyclopedia Britannica,
1952), V. 9 (MPL XLI, 148).

[83] Zanta, *La Renaissance du Stoicisme au XVI*e *Siècle*, pp. 47-71. See also Breen,
John Calvin: A Study in French Humanism, pp. 67-74 and E. F. Meylan, "The Stoic
Doctrine of Indifferent Things and the Conception of Christian Liberty in Cal-
vin's *Institutio Religionis Christianae*," *The Romanic Review*, 28 (1937), 135-45.

[84] For Calvin's continuing use of Seneca's ethics, see Ford Lewis Battles,
"Against Luxury and License in Geneva, A Forgotten Fragment of Calvin,"
Interpretation, 19 (April, 1965), 182-202.

[85] Cf. "Against Two Letters of the Pelagians" In *The Nicene and Post-Nicene
Fathers*, ed. by Philip Schaff (New York: The Christian Literature Co., 1887),
II. 5. 10-VI-12. (MPL 44, 577-9).

we make God the ruler and governor of all things...."[86] Calvin insists that fate and predestination are not the same thing. Fate is a term given by the Stoics to their doctrine of necessity while predestination is God's free counsel by which he governs all things by his incomprehensible wisdom and justice.[87]

According to Calvin not only heaven and earth and inanimate creatures but also the plans of men are governed by God's providence.[88] Thus the life and death of men and whatever else is ascribed to fate actually depends on the providence of God.[89] Calvin believes that his view is sufficiently differentiated from the Stoic view of fate by the fact that men deal directly with God as revealed in Jesus Christ rather than with God as merely a causative principle.

Still Calvin thinks that the Stoic doctrine which includes some belief in providence is superior to the Epicurean view which denies providence altogether. Thus in his commentary on Seneca's *De Clementia* (published April 4, 1532) Calvin affirms the resemblance between the Stoic and Christian view of the existence of a providence which excludes chance. The Stoics "who attribute the superintendence of human affairs to the gods, assert providence, and leave nothing to mere chance. The Epicureans, although they do not deny the existence of the gods, do the closest thing to it; they imagine the gods to be pleasure-loving, idle, not caring for mortals, lest anything detract from their pleasures; they deride Stoic providence as a prophesying old woman. They think everything happens by mere chance." Calvin summarizes by saying, "Our religion, too, has such a confession: *Power comes from God alone, and those that exist have been ordained by God* [Rom. 13.1].'[90]

Calvin's position is summed up in a long statement in the Commentary on Daniel which is worth quoting in its entirety.

> For we must of necessity adopt one or the other of these views, either that nature rules over human events, or else fortune turns about in every direction, things which ought to have an even course. As far as nature is concerned, its course would be even, unless God by

---

[86] I. 16. 8 (OS III, 198, 24-27). On Com. II Thes. 1. 5 (CO 52, 189) Calvin wrote that opposing blasphemers, we leave control to God.

[87] *Calumniae nebulonis cuiusdam quibus odio et invidia gravure conatus est doctrinam de occulta Dei providentia, et ad easdem responsio* (1558), CO 9, 287.

[88] I. 16. 8 (OS III, 199, 1-4).

[89] *Concerning the Eternal Predestination of God*, p. 164. (CO 8, 349).

[90] *Calvin's Commentary on Seneca's De Clementia*, pp. 28-31. Emphasis in translation.

his singular counsel, as we have seen, thus changes the course of the times. Yet those philosophers who assign the supreme authority to nature are much sounder than others who place fortune in the highest rank. For if we admit for a moment this latter opinion that fortune directs human affairs by a kind of blind impulse, whence comes this fortune? If you ask them for a definition, what answer will they make? They will surely be compelled to confess this, the word "fortune" explains nothing. But neither God nor nature will have any place in this vain and changeable government of the world, where all things throw themselves into distinct forms without the least order or connection and if this be granted, truly the doctrine of Epicurus will be received, because if God resigns the supreme government of the world, so that all things are rashly mingled together, he is no longer God. But in this variety he rather displays his hand in claiming for himself the empire over the world. In so many changes, then, which meet us on every side, and by which the whole face of things is renewed, we must remember that the providence of God shines forth; and things do not flow on in an even course, because then the peculiar property of God might with some show of reason be ascribed to nature . . . . we are compelled to acknowledge God's providence.[91]

Calvin does not claim that the Stoic view of providence is correct, but he asserts that it is preferable to the Epicurean. He seems to think the notion that fortune directs things is equivalent to saying that non-government governs or that human affairs are ordered by disorder. Fortune does not explain change because the doctrine of fortune is groundless and orderless. Calvin seems unwilling or unable to entertain the possibility that while men may, and must, bring some order to their experience—the world itself does not have an orderer nor exhibit order. Calvin's view is that God governs the world by his will and allows nothing to happen by chance or without his direction.[92]

Calvin's criticism of the Epicurean doctrine of chance and the Stoic doctrine of fate is not motivated by theoretical or speculative objections but by the concern that both views, in different ways, deny the providence of God revealed in Scripture as the Lord of history. The belief in the greatness and concern of God is the basis of what Bainton terms Calvin's "magnificent," "audacious," "almost roseate" view of history.[93] Thus Harbison is correct in pointing

---

[91] Com. Dan 2. 21 (CO 40, 576-8).

[92] *Ibid.*, 2. 20 (CO 40, 576-8).

[93] Roland H. Bainton, *Studies on the Reformation* (Boston: The Beacon Press, 1962), pp. 143-5.

out that "[h]umanist history, in fact, provided [Calvin] with the two false theories of history to which he developed his own theory of predestination. We sometimes forget that his doctrine of predestination was not simply an answer to free will, but a middle road, as it were, leading up and out of the dilemma posed by *two* wrong theories: the theory that history is the product of sheer chance (Fortune) and the theory that history is the result of inexorable determinism (Fate)."[94]

According to popular view, Calvin's doctrine of providence is basically Stoic. Calvin does indeed appreciate the Stoic conviction of God's all-encompassing providence, but he criticizes the Stoic view of causality which denies the freedom of God and the haughty pride which they inculcate in the wise man, as we see in the following comment:

> Although the Stoics said that the world is under the providence of God, yet they later spoiled that principle of their teaching with an absurd fiction or rather fantasy. For they did not acknowledge that God rules the world by his purpose, justice, and power, but they constructed a labyrinth out of a complex of causes, so that God himself was bound by the necessity of fate, and was violently carried along with the heavenly machine, just as the poets bind their Jupiter with golden fetters, because the fates govern, while he is doing something else. Although they placed the highest good in virtue, they did not grasp what true virtue was. And they inflated men with proud confidence so that they adorned themselves with the things they stripped off God. For although the grace of the Holy Spirit was made powerless by all, yet the boasting of no school was haughtier. Courage to them was nothing else than iron cruelty.[95]

---

[94] E. Harris Harbison, "Calvin's Sense of History," *Christianity and History* (Princeton: Princeton University Press, 1964), p. 280.

[95] Com. Acts 17. 28 (CO 48, 405-6). Karl Barth writes that the older Evangelical dogmaticians' "doctrine of gubernatio was aimed specifically against the two ancient systems of Stoicism on the one hand and Epicureanism on the other, both of which had come to life again as a result of the Renaissance. On the one hand they opposed the Stoic doctrine of fate, and on the other the Epicurean doctrine of chance. It is of a piece with the varying interests of the Reformed and Lutheran schools that the Lutherans broke the more expressly and sharply with the doctrine of fate and the Reformed with that of chance. But basically the same two enemies were engaged quite decisively on both fronts. There is therefore, no real point in concerning ourselves with the foreshortenings of perspective with which the Lutherans and Reformed view each other, leading the Lutherans to accuse and ridicule the Reformed as Stoics and the Reformed to accuse and ridicule the Lutherans as Epicureans." *Church Dogmatics*, trans. by G. W. Bromiley and R. J. Ehrlich (Edinburgh: T. & T. Clark, 1960), III, 3, 168.

Calvin disassociates his doctrine of providence from that of the Stoics by insisting on the free causality of the loving God revealed in Jesus Christ rather than on a God who is himself identical with the necessity of fate.

Calvin rejects the notion that God is responsible for man's evil because man's activity is fated. Man's behavior is entirely subject to God's control, but Calvin asserts that men are also responsible.[96] It is true that what God wills comes to pass of necessity,[97] but man sins not of necessity but voluntarily.[98] Thus Calvin writes:

> What God has determined must necessarily so take place, even though it is neither unconditionally, nor of its own peculiar nature, necessary. A familiar example presents itself in the bones of Christ. When he took upon himself a body like our own, no sane man will deny that his bones were fragile; yet it was impossible to break them. Whence again we see that distinction concerning relative necessity and absolute necessity, likewise of consequent and consequence, were not recklessly invented in schools, when God subjected to fragility, the bones of his Son, which he had exempted from being broken, and thus restricted to the necessity of his own plan what could have happened naturally.[99]

On the part of man Calvin's view of providence results in faith, love, and humility rather than in reason, apathy, and pride. Thus Calvin concludes:

> We are not Stoics who dream of fate according to an eternal connection of things, but we learn this much, that God presides over the world which he created; having not only the results of things in his providence, but he governs the hearts of men. He bends their wills by his will either here or there. He is the governor of actions so that nothing is produced except what he has decreed. Therefore what seems to be fortuitous in the highest degree, we learn is done by necessity, not by its own nature, but because the eternal and stable plan of God governs them.[100]

Those who search the history of ideas for similarities may indeed find parallels between Calvin's doctrine of providence and that of the Stoics, but it is extremely one-sided to appeal to the similarities

---

[96] I. 17. 3f. (OS III, 205, 20f)

[97] III. 23. 8 (OS IV, 402, 21).

[98] II. 5. 1 (OS III, 298, 24).

[99] I. 16. 9 (OS III, 201, 20-30).

[100] *Defensio sanae et orthodoxae doctrinae de servitute et Liberatione humani arbitrii Adversus Calumnias Alberti Pighii Campensis*, CO 6, 257.

as if the differences did not make any difference. Calvin states quite clearly that his view of providence is not Stoic because of his doctrine of God differs from theirs and it does not issue in passive and reasoned resignation but in responsible and loving service. These points should not be ignored nor dismissed.

CHAPTER NINE

CALVIN ON UNIVERSAL AND PARTICULAR PROVIDENCE

Plato teaches that men are the property (κτήματα) of the gods who are concerned about things both great and small.[1] However, Plato does not develop a doctrine of particular providence in any detail. Cicero seems to accept some kind of particular providence when he writes, "Nor is the care and providence of the immortal gods bestowed only upon the human race in its entirety, but it is also wont to be extended to individuals."[2] Still a few pages later he asserts, "The gods attend to great matters; they neglect small ones."[3] Like the philosophers Calvin affirms a universal providence, but his chief interest is to assert God's particular providence. Calvin's basic insight into God's care of his own and all things finds expression in both his doctrines of providence and predestination. Unlike the philosophers, Calvin's point of view is more concerned with the particularity of God's care rather than its universality, as this chapter seeks to demonstrate.

In the fourteenth chapter of the 1545 treatise, "Contre la secte phantastique et furieuse des Libertines qui se nomment spirituelz" Calvin says that we attribute to God an active power in all creatures. God created, governs, and maintains the world and disposes things as it seems good to him. To express this view Calvin considers God's work in the government of the world under three aspects. First, there is a universal operation by which God conducts all creatures according to the condition and properties which he gives to each of them when they are formed. This direction is called the order of nature. Still unbelievers who recognize the disposition of the world and the constitution of nature as a goddess who rules over all do not give praise to the will of God who alone rules over all things. When believers see the sun, the moon, and the stars moving in their courses, they know that the command of God is directing them. This universal providence is often mentioned in Scripture to the end that the glory of God may be apprehended in all his works.

---

[1] *Laws*, X, 902 b, 900 c.
[2] *De Natura Deorum*, II. 65. 164.
[3] *Ibid.*, II. 66. 167.

The second aspect of God's work in his creatures is that he extends his hand to help his servants and to punish the wicked. The pagans attribute to fortune what Christians assign to the providence of God—not alone to the universal providence—but to a special ordinance by which God directs all things as he sees it to be expedient. Thus prosperity and adversity, rain, wind, sleet, frost, fine weather, abundance, famine, war, and peace are works of the hand of God. The third aspect of the work of God consists in his governance of the faithful, living and reigning in them by his Holy Spirit. In spite of the fact that man's judgment is perverse, his will rebellious, and his nature vicious—God forms new hearts within them and by supernatural grace they are regenerated in a divine life.[4]

In his treatment of the same subject in *De aeterna Praedestinatione Dei* Calvin writes, "We mean by providence not an idle observation by God in heaven of what goes on in earth, but his rule of the world which he has made, for he is not the creator of the moment, but the perpetual governor. Thus the providence we ascribe to God belongs not only to his eyes but to his hands." The fact that the sun daily rises, the stars orbit, the seasons recur, and the earth produces is to be ascribed solely to God's directing hand. However the knowledge of God's universal providence, Calvin says, is confused unless it is understood that God cares for individual creatures. In this special providence it is convenient to recognize certain distinct grades. God governs the human race by his providence but with different grades of direction. To make God's providence clear Calvin asserts God's general government of the world, then his care of particular parts so that everything happens by God's will, then his particular care of the human race and finally his protection of the church.[5]

Étienne de Peyer thinks, "General Providence gives to human nature its plenitude and completion. Particular Providence directs the effects of this nature. Saving Providence brings to man the elements of a new nature or of nature restored...."[6] De Peyer believes that particular providence is identical with common grace.[7] Thus he outlines Calvin's doctrine of providence as (1) general providence;

---

[4] *Contre la secte phantastique et furieuse des Libertines qui se nomment spirituelz*, CO, 7, 186-90.

[5] *Concerning Eternal Predestination*, pp. 162-4 (CO 8, 348-9).

[6] Étienne de Peyer, "Calvin's Doctrine of Providence," *The Evangelical Quarterly*, X (1938), 37.

[7] *Ibid.*, p. 35.

(2) particular providence or common grace: and (3) special providence or saving grace.

Calvin does discuss general or universal providence and special or particular providence, also general or common grace and special grace, but Calvin does not work out the implications of the doctrines of providence and grace in the terms which de Peyer suggests. Krusche is correct in saying that Calvin's conceptualization of common grace is not uniform.[8] Calvin's basic distinction however is two-fold rather than tripartite. Thus common grace ought to be associated with universal providence and special grace with particular providence, though it should be noted that Calvin does not refer to common grace in the quotation above.

A great deal of attention has been given to the doctrine of common grace by some Calvin scholars.[9] They expand, schematize, and *distort* Calvin's cautious remarks on the closely related topics of natural or general revelation, universal providence, and common grace. Hermann Bavinck, for example, writes "[Calvin] found the will of God revealed not merely in Scripture, but also in the world, and he traced the connection and sought to restore the harmony between them."[10] Bavinck also remarks, "Though this gracious and omnipotent will

---

[8] Krusche, *Das Wirken des Heiligen Geistes nach Calvin*, p. 100, note 395. Krusche discusses gratia generalis, p. 95f.

[9] Abraham Kuyper, *De Gemeene Gratie*, 3 vols. (Pretoria: Hoveker and Wormser, 1902-4); Hermann Bavinck, *De Algemeene Genade* (Kampen: G. Ph. Zalsman, 1894); Herman Kuiper, *Calvin on Common Grace* (Grand Rapids: Smitter Book Co., 1928); Cornelius Van Til, *Common Grace* (Philadelphia: The Presbyterian and Reformed Publishing Company, 1947); H. Henry Meeter, *Calvinism: An Interpretation of its Basic Ideas* (Grand Rapids: Zondervan Publishing House, 1939), pp. 69-77. See also William Masselink, *General Revelation and Common Grace* (Grand Rapids: Wm. B. Eerdmans, 1953). Chapter 5 on Common Grace, Chapter 7 on Calvinistic Philosophy. See also the essay by A. Lecerf, "Le protestantisme et la philosophie," in *Études Calvinistes* (Paris: Delachaux et Niestle, 1949), pp. 107-113; and J. M. Spier, *What is Calvinistic Philosophy?* trans. by Fred. H. Klooster (Grand Rapids: Wm. B. Eerdmans Publishing Company, 1953) and William Young, *Toward a Reformed Philosophy* (Grand Rapids: Piet Hein Publishers, 1952).

[10] Hermann Bavinck, "Calvin and Common Grace," *Calvin and the Reformation* (New York: Fleming H. Revell Co., 1909), p. 128. Breen, *John Calvin: A study in French Humanism*, p. 165ff. adds a new chapter to his second edition defending the doctrine of common grace although his source, Kuiper, *Calvin on Common Grace*, pp. 177-8 professes to be able to find the term used by Calvin only four times: Com. Am. 9. 7 (CO 43, 164); Com. Col. 1. 20 (CO 52, 89); Com. Heb. 1. 5 (CO 55, 15); and Com. Rom. 5. 18 (CO 49, 101). These usages are not uniform nor technical and Calvin's comment in Romans makes the opposite point: "Paul makes grace common to all men, *not because it in fact extends to all*, but because it is offered to all." Emphasis added.

of God is made known in the gospel alone and experienced in faith only, nevertheless it does not stand isolated, but is encompassed, supported and reinforced by the operation of the same will in the world at large. Special grace is encircled by common grace...."[11]

In Bavinck's treatment common grace seems to be the presupposition of special grace. However Calvin does not make special grace depend on common grace nor special providence depend on universal providence. On the contrary, Calvin's main purpose is to insist that God does not sit idly in heaven but governs the world and that the doctrine of universal providence is only a partial understanding of God's providence. Therefore in discussing God's special providence, which he is chiefly concerned to emphasize, Calvin also treats common grace and universal providence. Calvin writes, "The sun discovers to our eyes the most beautiful theater of the earth and heaven and the whole order of nature, but God has visibly displayed the chief glory of his work in his Son."[12] According to Calvin the first of the distinct powers of the Son of God appears in the architecture of the world and in the order of nature and second in the renewal and restoration of fallen nature. Man lost the light of understanding by the fall, but he still sees and understands because what he naturally possessed from the grace of the Son of God is not entirely destroyed.[13]

The purpose of Calvin's discussion of universal providence is not to define a common ground or territory between the believer and the unbeliever, but to insist that the whole order of nature is the result of the special providence of God. God does not govern by chance or a general operation in nature but by his special providence. It is true that the whole order of nature serves the will of God,[14] but God can do more than nature,[15] and his command changes the order of nature.[16] In the Genesis Commentary, Calvin remarks that Joseph errs in binding the grace of God to the order of nature as if God does not often purposely change the law of nature in order to teach that what he freely confers upon man is entirely the result of his will.[17] It is God who withholds rain, then pours it down in

---

[11] Bavinck, "Calvin and Common Grace," p. 126.
[12] Com. Jn. 9 .5 (CO 47, 220).
[13] Com. Jn. 1. 5 (CO 47, 7).
[14] Com. II Pet. 3. 5 (CO 55, 473-4).
[15] As in the birth of John the Baptist, Com. Lk. 1. 18 (CO 45, 18f).
[16] Com. Zec. 10. 11 (CO 44, 298).
[17] Com. Gen. 48. 17 (CO 23, 586).

profusion, he burns the corn with heat, then he tempers the air; now he shows himself kindly toward men, now angry with them.[18] Thus God deals with his people both in an ordinary and common way and also in a wonderful and miraculous way.[19] It is true that God's daily and common ways are so many miracles, but they seem less wonderful because they are naturally comprehended.[20] When God fed the people, as recorded in Numbers 11, he raised a wind which was a miracle, but God did not cast aside the assistance of nature since he made use of the wind. God also took an herb which ascended to a great height and surpassed the usual course of nature in order to provide a covering for Jonah. The same thing applies to the preparation of the worm which did not happen by chance, but was governed by the hidden providence of God.[21]

Calvin admits that the carnal sense has some noetic value, but faith should not be content with a certain universal motion but understand God's particular providence [singulari quadam providentia],[22] and it is upon this particular providence that Calvin chiefly insists. Forstmann is correct in saying that in the section on providence Calvin approaches more nearly the tone of ecstacy than at any other point in the *Institutes*.[23] According to Calvin the knowledge of God's providence is the highest blessedness.[24] Since God's providence is a "rampart of defense",[25] Calvin objects to the idea of separating creation from providence and understanding providence as the provision of a kind of neutral context for life rather than as God's special care for all that he had created. God's care is experienced by his children and he provides for all things.[26] It is therefore only a partial understanding of providence to attribute to God a general governance of the beginning and origin of things without including specific direction of the individual creatures.

Calvin recognizes that in the sense of universal providence many acknowledge that all creatures are governed by God. They consider

---

[18] Com. Am. 4. 9 (CO 43, 62) refers to special providence not a general motion: Discamus ergo totum naturae ordinem referre ad specialem Dei providentiam.
[19] Com. Ps. 17. 7 (CO 31, 162): God deems the elect only worthy of special grace.
[20] Com. Hab. 3. 6 (CO 43, 572-3).
[21] Com. Jon. 4. 6-8 (CO 43, 275).
[22] I. 16. 1 (OS III, 187: 27-8, 188: 1-7).
[23] Forstmann, *Word and Spirit*, p. 98.
[24] I. 17. 11 (OS III, 216, 27-30).
[25] Com. Ps. 35. 22 (CO 31, 356).
[26] Com. Ps. 25. 9 (CO 31, 255); cf. Com. Ps. 28. 5 (CO 31, 283-4).

that man moves by his own free will because God continues the power which he once bestowed. "Their false explanation amounts to this, that the whole machinery of the world is upheld by the hand of God, but that his providence is not interposed to regulate particular movements." What they leave to God is hardly a thousandth part of the government he claims. "Justly, therefore, does Isaiah show that God presides over individual acts, as they call them, so as to move men, like rods, in whatever way he pleases, to guide their plans, to direct their efforts; and, in a word, to regulate their determinations, in order to inform us that everything depends on his providence, and not on the caprice of wicked man."[27]

Calvin could scarcely be more explicit on his view of the place of universal providence. Calvin says that he does not wholly repudiate the doctrine of universal providence provided it is granted that God rules the universe by watching over the order of nature and exercising special care over each of his works.[28] The doctrine of universal providence, Calvin thinks, could leave no place for God's mercy and judgment while the chief thing to believe is that God directs everything to his own end so that all things proceed from his plan and nothing happens by chance.[29] Whatever happens in the universe is governed by God's incomprehensible plans,[30] which the faithful understand from the experience of divine protection.[31]

Calvin believes that God's will is the cause of causes,[32] and that all things are directly governed by God's will which is the source of law and reason and the final appeal of justice.[33] This position is made abundantly clear in the *Institutes*. Calvin rejects

> the opinion of those who imagine a universal providence of God, which does not stoop to the especial care of any particular creature, yet first of all it is important that we recognize this special care toward us. Whence Christ, when he declared that not even a tiny sparrow of little worth falls to earth without the Father's will, immediately applies it in this way: that since we are of greater value than sparrows, we ought to realize that God watches over us with all the closer

[27] Com. Is. 10. 15 (CO 36, 222).

[28] I. 16. 4 (OS III, 194, 9-13).

[29] I. 16. 4 (OS III, 194, 27-9). Cf. Com. Jl. 2. 11 (CO 42, 540-541) and Com. Is. 7. 19 (CO 36, 161): nihil temere aut fortuito accidere, sed omnia regi manu Dei.

[30] I. 17. 2 (OS III, 204, 9-11).

[31] Com. Ps. 3. 6 (CO 31, 56).

[32] Com. Gen. 25. 29 (CO 23, 354); cf. Plato, *Epinomis*, 983 b, also Seneca, *Naturales Quaestiones*, I. 1. 13; III. 23. 8 (OS IV, 402, 19-20) quoting Augustine.

[33] Com. Dan. 4. 34 (CO 40, 685).

care; and he extends it so far that we may trust the hairs of our head are numbered. What else can we wish for ourselves, if not even one hair can fall from our head without his will? I speak not only concerning mankind; but, because God has chosen the church to be his dwelling place, there is no doubt that he shows by singular proofs his fatherly care in ruling it.[34]

Though Calvin left his major discussion of the church until Book Four of the *Institutes* he points out even in the first book that the providence of God is concerned to maintain the church. Thus the basic understanding of God's providence is not a neutral common grace, but the conviction that God has power to protect the faithful. This means that every success is to be regarded as God's blessing and every calamity as his curse, so that even the evils visited upon the faithful belong to God.[35] Calvin admits that this position was not without perplexity. To say that Judas was governed by God's providence and was yet guilty was offensive to human reason.[36] However since God is just, men should not debate with him.[37]

Calvin affirms a universal providence, but he does not seek to find in God's universal providence a common ground between believers and unbelievers. Calvin does not develop a "world view" in which the doctrine of universal providence could be isolated and treated as the presupposition of an anthropology, epistemology, or apologetics. It is true that Calvin thinks that unbelievers are without excuse for not worshiping God and that God's activity is not entirely curtailed by unbelief, but he does not use the doctrine of universal providence as a neutral beginning place for all men. God does indeed sustain all men through the power of his Spirit, but Calvin's doctrine of providence is based on God's direct care of the believers.

---

[34] I. 17. 6 (OS III, 209, 34-5, 210. 1-13).

[35] Calvin makes this point in I. 17. 7-8 (OS III, 210-212) and often in the Commentaries. For example, Com. Dan. 9. 14 (CO 41, 151): "In this passage we are taught to recognize God's providence in both prosperity and adversity, for the purpose of stirring us up to be grateful for his benefits, while his punishments ought to produce humility. For when any one explains these things by fortune or chance, he thereby proves his ignorance of the existence of God, or at least the kind of God we worship."

[36] Com. Mt. 26. 24 (CO 45, 702).

[37] See Serm. on Job 9. 1-6 (CO 33, 406-18). For a contemporary account of the same idea see George Dennis O'Brien, "Prolegomena to a Dissolution to the Problem of Suffering," *Harvard Theological Review*, 57, 4 (Oct., 1964), 301-23. O'Brien says, "The monarch cannot consider the formulation of a justification which goes beyond the assertion of his will without suggesting that there is some standard to which he appeals" (pp. 308-9).

Calvin not only makes a distinction between general and special providence, he also makes a distinction between general and special election. In commenting on Hosea 12. 3 Calvin says that Jacob was *specially* elect and his seed *generally* elect in that God offered his covenant to them. Nonetheless, they were not all regenerated since they were not given the spirit of adoption.[38] The stages of election are more fully expounded in the Commentary on Malachi. In the first place God was pleased to create us men rather than animals. In the second place, although the whole world was under his government, he chose the seed of Abraham. This election was not made on the basis of merit but on the gratuitous love of God. In the third place God selected only a part of the seed of Abraham. Thus God made a distinction between the sons of Abraham rejecting some and choosing others. The fourth stage is the acceptance of some of the sons of Jacob and the rejection of others. If it is asked why some are faithful and others are reprobate, the only answer is that it pleased God. Abraham was chosen by God in preference to all other nations, Isaac was preferred to Ishmael and Jacob to Esau.

Calvin admits that the Scriptural account may seem harsh—that God chooses some and not all, but to object is to attempt to restrain God's will by human judgment. Since the Scripture teaches that after the fall of Adam all are lost and that the election of God is prior to Adam's fall, then all who are saved are chosen in Christ before the creation of the world. God appoints Christ the head of the church so that those who are chosen might be saved in him.[39] Calvin maintains that it is not entirely unprofitable to be generally elect since this general election is intermediate between the rejection of mankind and the election of the godly.[40] Still, Calvin insists that God's free election is only fully explained when we come to individual persons to whom God not only offers salvation but also the certainty of salvation.[41] This certainty of faith does not result from the acuteness of the human mind but from the illumination of the Spirit. Predestination cannot be examined by the faculties of man, but a certain and clear knowledge is to be gained by the grace of the Holy Spirit.[42]

---

[38] Com. Hos. 12. 3 (CO 42, 454f.).
[39] Com. Mal. 1. 2-6 (CO 44, 401f.).
[40] III. 21. 7 (OS IV, 378, 9-10).
[41] III. 21. 7 (OS IV, 377, 21-22).
[42] Com. Rom. 11. 34 (CO 49, 231).

God's care for believers is the basis of both the doctrines of providence and predestination. However it is not easy to specify the relation between the doctrine of providence and of predestination in Calvin's theology. The problem is whether predestination is an aspect of the doctrine of providence or whether providence is a part of the doctrine of predestination or are they two similar but separate doctrines?

This topic has long been the subject of debate. Alexander Schweizer sees predestination as the central dogma of Reformed Christianity.[43] Against this view Albrecht Ritschl argues that while the doctrine of predestination is a very important appendage (Anhangsel) to Calvin's doctrine of redemption, it does not control Calvin's system. "It bears a near analogy to his basic doctrine (Stammlehre) of providence through the application to both areas of the causal omnipotence of God."[44] Bohatec observes that the doctrines of providence and predestination stand in closest connection and that most researchers grant that Calvin's doctrine of providence is the theological basis of his doctrine of predestination.[45] According to Doumergue, the three doctrines of providence, bondage of the will, and predestination are characteristic of the theology of the Reformation.[46] Doumergue argues that "the doctrine of predestination is a particular doctrine, inseparable from the general doctrine that of providence."[47] Seeberg agrees, "Thus the doctrine of predestination is most closely

---

[43] Alexander Schweizer, *Die Protestantischen Centraldogmen in ihrer Entwicklung innerhalb der Reformierten Kirche*, I (Zurich: Orell, Fuessli, 1854), 57. In like manner Otto Ritschl, *Dogmengeschichte des Protestantismus*, III (Göttingen: Vandenhoeck & Ruprecht, 1926), 156-198: believes that "the thought of predestination has overwhelming significance for the other doctrines of Christian dogmatics." A. M. Hunter, *The Teaching of Calvin*, says that providence is the experiential side of the divine decrees. Predestination is the metaphysical side of the divine decrees (p. 93). That is, providence is the activity of God by which he works out the predestinating decrees (p. 136).

[44] Albrecht Ritschl, "Geschichtliche Studien zur Christlichen Lehre von Gott," *Jahrbücher für Deutsche Theologie* (1868), 108.

[45] J. Bohatec, "Calvins Vorsehungslehre," *Calvinstudien* (Leipzig: Rudolf Haupt, 1909), p. 394. Jacobs, *Prädestination und Verantwortlichkeit bei Calvin*, p. 69 writes that "Predestination is a type of special providence and would be subordinate to formal providence." Hans Emil Weber, *Reformation, Orthodoxie und Rationalismus*, 1 (2nd ed.; Darmstadt: Wissenschaftliche Buchgesellschaft, 1966 (1937), 243 says that Calvin and Luther and Melanchthon regard predestination and providence together.

[46] Doumergue, *Jean Calvin*, IV, 155.

[47] *Ibid.*, 354. However Doumergue devotes only 7 pages (111-8) to providence and under the doctrine of God and 65 pages in a separate section to predestination (351-416).

connected with the concept of omnipotent providence for Calvin. Indeed, it is actually only a special case of the latter or its application to the empirical fact that there are sinners who believe and are saved and others who do not believe and are therefore lost."[48] Otten correctly states that "Calvin in his treatment of predestination never starts from the doctrine of God so that he would perhaps construct the gracious election from the idea of sovereignty and sole efficacy of God, but rather predestination is for him a part of soteriology."[49] Likewise, Dowey, in dealing with the two-fold knowledge of God as Creator and Redeemer, rightly insists on the importance of Calvin's location of the doctrine of predestination within his soteriology.[50] In the same direction, Werner Krusche writes

> The Holy Spirit is the author of providence and (since very special providence (providentia specialissima) equals predestination) the author of the doctrine of predestination. He is the first as the Spirit of the Eternal Son, the second as the Spirit of the Mediator Jesus Christ. The position of the doctrine of providence and predestination in the last edition of the *Institutes* shows this most clearly. Since it is the Spirit of the Eternal Word which brings the action of divine providence to fruition (Wirkung), the doctrine of providence can be developed in connection with the doctrine of the Trinity. Since it is the Spirit of the Mediator Jesus Christ, who makes the action of God's election efficacious, the doctrine of predestination must form the conclusion of Christology and Pneumatology.[51]

The obvious conclusion to be drawn from this discussion is that Calvin's understanding of God's government of the world and his care of his own are closely related to each other and crucial to his theology. The basic conviction of God's loving concern finds expression in both the doctrine of providence and predestination. However, although Calvin deals with both universal and special providence and general and individual election, his standpoint—unlike the philosophers—is the particularity of God's care. That is to say, Calvin treats the universal aspect of God's work, but his point

---

[48] Reinhold Seeberg, *Lehrbuch der Dogmengeschichte*, IV, 2 (5th. ed.; Basel: Benno Schwabe & Co., 1960), 580. Reviews of this discussion are found in Max Scheibe, *Calvins Prädestinationslehre* (Halle: Max Niemeyer, 1897), pp. 1-5; in Jacobs, *Prädestination und Verantwortlichkeit bei Calvin*, pp. 15-40; and Heinz Otten, *Calvins Theologische Anschauung von der Prädestination* (Munich: Chr. Kaiser Verlag, 1938), pp. 7-15.

[49] *Ibid.*, p. 87.

[50] Dowey, *The Knowledge of God in Calvin's Theology*, p. 222.

[51] Krusche, *Das Wirken des Heiligen Geistes nach Calvin*, p. 14.

of viewing is from God's particular work. This fact may be seen in the *development* of the doctrines of predestination and providence.

There are three discernible stages in Calvin's exposition of the doctrines of providence and predestination in the *Institutes*. In the first edition of 1536 providence is treated as part of the belief in God the Father Almighty, creator of heaven and earth. Calvin writes,

> By this we confess that we have all our trust fixed in God the Father, whom we acknowledge to be Creator of ourselves and of absolutely all things that have been created, which have been established by the Word, his eternal Wisdom (who is the Son) and by his Power (who is the Holy Spirit). And, as he once established, so now he sustains, nourishes, activates, preserves, by his goodness and power, apart from which all things would immediately collapse and fall into nothingness. But when we call him almighty and creator of all things, we must ponder such omnipotence of his whereby he works all things in all, and such providence whereby he regulates all things— not of the sort those Sophists fancy: empty, insensate, idle. By faith are we to be persuaded that whatever happens to us, happy or sad, prosperous or adverse, whether it pertains to the body or to the soul, comes to us from him (sin only being excepted, which is to be imputed to our own wickedness); also by his protection we are kept safe, defended, and preserved from any unfriendly force causing us harm. In short, nothing comes forth from him to us (since we receive all things from his hand) which is not conducive to our welfare, howsoever things may commonly seem at one time prosperous, at another adverse. Indeed all these things are done to us by him, not through any worth of ours, nor by any merit to which he owes this grace, not because we can force his beneficence to make any reciprocal payment. Rather it is through his fatherly kindness and mercy that he has to do with us, the sole cause of which is his goodness. For this reason, we must take care to give thanks for this very great goodness of his, to ponder it with our hearts, proclaim it with our tongue, and to render such praises as we are able. We should so reverence such a Father with grateful piety and burning love, as to devote ourselves wholly to his service, and honor him in all things. We should also so receive all adverse things with calm and peaceful hearts, as if from his hand, thinking that his providence so also looks after us and our salvation while it is afflicting and oppressing us. Therefore whatever may finally happen, we are never to doubt or lose faith that we have in him a propitious and benevolent Father, and no less are to await salvation from him.[52]

Calvin teaches here that God does not merely create, but sustains the created order in being by his providence. His omnipotence must

---

[52] John Calvin, *Institution of the Christian Religion* (1536), trans. and annotated by Ford Lewis Battles (Atlanta: John Knox, 1975), pp. 66-7. OS I, 75-6.

therefore be understood not as an empty power, but in such a way that the faithful acknowledge that whatever happens, good or bad, comes from God, who is good and is concerned for their welfare and salvation.

In the first edition, predestination or election is treated in connection with the doctrine of the church. Calvin says that "we believe the holy catholic church—that is, the whole number of the elect, whether angels or men . . . ." They are called "to be one church and society, and one people of God. Of it, Christ, our Lord is Leader and Ruler, and as it were Head of the one body; according as through divine goodness, they have been chosen in him before the foundation of the world, in order that all might be gathered into God's Kingdom." Calvin uses election and providence together in his comment that the church is holy "because as many as have been chosen [electus] by God's eternal providence to be adopted as members of the church —all these are made holy by the Lord."[53] However Calvin insists that it is not proper to judge those who are outside the church or to distinguish between the elect and the reprobate since this is the exclusive prerogative of God.[54] This is the first stage.

In his *Loci Communes* (1535) Melanchthon says that the topic of predestination is useless and confusing,[55] but Calvin in his edition of 1539 emphasizes the importance of the doctrines of predestination and providence by devoting a separate chapter to the subject. This is also the order used in the polemical situation which called forth *De aeterna Praedestinatione Dei* (1552), and Calvin is still treating providence and predestination together in *Calumniae nebulonis cuiusdam quibus odio et invidia gravure conatus est doctrinam de occulta Dei providentia, et ad easdem responsio* (1558). Calvin defends his doctrine of predestination at greater length than his doctrine of providence, although his conclusions on predestination are already contained in his view of particular providence. In the 1539 edition of the *Institutes* at the beginning of chapter seven on the similarities and differences between the Old and New Testaments, Calvin says that he has expounded the sum of Christian doctrine which consists in the knowledge of God and ourselves. Now he intends to add an article (vice appendix) to establish the truth of the doctrine taught, i.e. that those whom God

---

[53] *Ibid.*, pp. 78-9 (OS I, 86).
[54] *Ibid.*, pp. 82 (OS I, 88).
[55] Philip Melanchthon, *Loci Communes*, CR, 21, 452.

called before the foundation of the world into the company of his people attain a certain grace and are united to God.[56]

Calvin begins chapter eight on the predestination and providence of God by remarking that the covenant of life is not equally preached to all and where it is preached it is not equally received. The exterior preaching of the gospel is offered to all, but there is a special interior illumination of the Holy Spirit which the faithful receive. Some men accept the gospel and others reject it. This diversity of response is referred to God's good pleasure. The doctrine of predestination is a mystery of divine wisdom, but those who are predestined are illuminated to salvation. Calvin formally defines predestination as follows:

> Predestination we call the eternal decree of God by which he has determined in himself what he willed to become of each man. For all are not created on equal terms; rather eternal life is foreordained for some and eternal damnation for others. Therefore as any man has been created for one or the other of these ends, we speak of him as predestined to life or to death.[57]

This definition is not changed from 1539 to the final edition, but its purpose, according to Calvin, is not to drive men to despair or to curious speculations, but to exalt the grace of God and to deny the saving efficacy of merits. Predestination "builds up faith soundly, trains us to humility, elevates us to admiration of the immense goodness of God towards us, and excites us to praise this goodness."[58] In the *Congrégation sur L'Élection Éternelle de Dieu*, Calvin writes, "God has chosen us, that means not only before we knew him but before the world was created: and that he elected us by his gratuitous goodness, and that he has not sought any other cause; that he deliberated this proposal by itself, and it is necessary that we know that, in order that he be glorified by us as he deserves."[59] Thus the salvation of the faithful is founded on grace and not acquired by works. Jacob and Esau were equal except that God chose one and rejected the other. In the 1539 edition the doctrine of providence *follows* the discussion of predestination. Providence is defined as the order by which God governs the world and guides all things. Providence is not merely a matter of prescience, or a general government, but

---

[56] CO I, 801.
[57] CO I, 865. III. 21. 5 (OS IV, 374, 11-17).
[58] *Concerning Eternal Predestination*, p. 56 (CO 8, 260).
[59] *Congrégation sur L'Élection Éternelle de Dieu*, CO 8, 103.

God's determining what he will do by his wisdom and executing it by his power.

The third stage in the development of the doctrines of providence and predestination is reached in the final edition of the *Institutes*. Here the main exposition of providence *precedes* the treatment of predestination though Calvin does not explain why. Providence is placed in Book One as part of the doctrine of creation (returning to its location in the 1536 edition) while the doctrine of predestination is placed in Book Three (before the development of the doctrine of the church) as part of the perception of the grace of Christ.

On this arrangement Wendel comments, "Just as the doctrine of providence placed at the conclusion of the doctrine of God, might be said to complete the latter as the keystone finishes an arch, so also does the doctrine of predestination complete and illuminate the whole of the account of redemption."[60] However to be entirely accurate, the main exposition of providence concludes Book One of the *Institutes* which deals with the knowledge of God the Creator. Book Two deals with the knowledge of God the Redeemer (except for Chapters 1-5 which deal with sin), but it is important to recognize that the doctrine of predestination is found at the end of Book Three (except for the chapter on the resurrection of the body).

This location does not deny the centrality of the doctrine of Christ for the doctrine of election since predestination is now formally and materially part of the understanding of salvation, but it certainly indicates that predestination is not the basic doctrine from which Calvin deduces a theological system. As Victor Monod finely writes, "The Calvinistic predestination certainly did not come from an effort of logical and abstract systematization; it is for Calvin a point of arrival not a point of departure, a necessary hypothesis, not a principle of explication. The doctrine of election is the imperfect intellectual product of a humble and living faith."[61] The importance

---

[60] Wendel, *Calvin, The Origins and Development of his Religious Thought*, p. 268.

[61] Victor Monod, "La Prédestination Calviniste," *Foi et Vie*, (1909), 645. H. Bois disagrees. In "La prédestination d'après Calvin," *Études sur la Réforme* (Paris: Librairie Armand Colin, 1919), p. 674f., he argues that predestination is not a doctrine of experience, but a deduction from omnipotence. Providence and predestination are not based on the facts of experience but experience interpreted by certain principles such as (1) the negation of works, (2) the certainty of salvation and most especially (3) the sovereignty of God. (p. 678). Predestination is the dogmatic formulation of the idea of the sovereignty of God (p. 679). According to Calvetti, *La filosofia di Giovanni Calvino*, pp. 264-5 predestination is the inevitable logical consequence of the philosophic conception of the abso-

of the discussion of predestination *in* Book Three of the final edition of the *Institutes* should not be minimized, but neither should the close connection between special providence and predestination be forgotten.

In broad terms providence is concerned with God's work and will in creation, while predestination is concerned with God's work and will in redemption. As Otten observes, "The object of providence is accordingly man as creature and his world. The object of predestination is man as sinner and his eternal destination."[62] However, Calvin does not make a sharp distinction between providence and predestination.[63] The same God who elects by his providence also provides for his elect. Thus God, in his special or particular providence, takes care of the believers.[64] If God's particular providence for the believer is not identical with predestination, the doctrines are at least complementary since God is both Creator and Redeemer. Otten makes this point by saying that the unity of provi-

---

lute sovereignty of God which issues in an essentially irrationalistic pantheism. Maurice Neeser, *Le Dieu de Calvin* (Neuchâtel: Secrétariat de l'Université, 1956) in his highly critical treatment of Calvin's doctrine of providence and predestination (parts 2 and 3) does not deal with the philosophers and in exalting God as the absolute ignores the fact that Calvin rejected the scholastic notion of potentia absoluta (III. 23. 2 (OS IV, 396, 17) and considered God's providence and predestination primarily in terms of God's grace rather than his power. Neeser pictures Calvin as logically rigorous rather than trying to struggle to be faithful to the Scriptures. On the potentia absoluta see Wendel, *Calvin, the Origins and Development of his Religious Thought*, p. 127f. Doumergue, *Jean Calvin*, IV, 358 agrees with Monod that Calvin's doctrine of predestination is a posteriori and based on experience rather than a priori. Fullerton, "Calvinism and Capitalism," p. 172 repeats the ideas that for Calvin God is absolute will which issues in the intellectualized doctrine of the double decrees, in effect denying the roles of experience and emotion. "In other words, Calvinism as a system, though it starts from an irrational conception of God, is worked out in a thoroughly rationalistic way...." A sounder view is found in B. A. Gerrish," 'To the the Unknown God': Luther and Calvin on Hiddenness of God," *The Journal of Religion*, 53, 3 (July, 1973), 284 who remarks that "although talk about eternal decrees has the sound of rampant speculation, the doctrine of election is in fact woven into the fabric of human experience."

[62] Heinz Otten, *Calvins Theologische Anschauung von der Prädestination*, p. 111. S. Leigh Hunt, "Predestination in the 'Institutes of the Christian Religion,' 1536-1559," *Evangelical Quarterly*, IX (1937) 38-45 makes a distinction between general and particular predestination. Eternal predestination in the sense of government of the world is the same as eternal providence, "the execution of which is actual providence in time" (p. 39).

[63] In addition to the 1539 statement (note 57) see III. 23. 3 (OS IV, 397, 4-5); 5 (398, 26); 6 (400, 8); 8 (402, 38); 9 (403, 32).

[64] I. 17. 6 (OS III, 209, 21-24).

dence and predestination is analogous to the unity of God as Creator and Redeemer.[65] Therefore Calvin's doctrine of God's providence in creation cannot be fully expounded apart from God's providence in redemption. The philosophers understood something of the former, but nothing of the latter, as we have seen.

Although Calvin makes a distinction between universal and particular providence and general and special election, he does not work out a careful view of the relation between God's universal providence for all mankind and his general election of the fathers, or between God's particular providence for the Christian and his special election of them. Calvin affirms both a universal providence and a general election, but his chief interest is in particular providence or individual election.

In the final edition of the *Institutes* Calvin deals with providence as part of the understanding of creation, and predestination—not as part of the doctrine of God—but as part of the understanding of the benefits of Christ. However it must be admitted that Calvin does not distinguish between special providence and predestination. His insistence that election (which is a gift of God) precedes faith (which is also a gift of God) leaves the possibility open of re-locating the doctrine of predestination in the doctrine of God (as his followers do,[66]) rather than in the doctrine of salvation as part of the understanding of the gift of faith (as he himself does). Calvin says, "We see that faith proceeds from the sole election of God, that is to say, that God illumines those whom he had chosen by this gratuitous goodness before the creation of the world."[67] However, "we shall never understand this mystery here and a secret so high and so excellent except by having the meekness to say: Well, if we do not see the reason why God acts thusly, there is so much that it should be sufficient to us that he is just; and on that to profit always in the knowledge of his will."[68]

Calvin believes that his doctrine of predestination is Scriptural and Augustinian.[69] Thus he writes against Westphal that he does

---

[65] Otten, *Calvins Theologische Anschauung von der Prädestination*, p. 111.

[66] Weber, *Reformation, Orthodoxie, und Rationalismus*, p. 240 writes, "One may certainly not say that Calvin derived his theology out of his doctrine of predestination as it is done by the Calvinistic scholastics."

[67] *Congrégation sur L'Élection Éternelle de Dieu*, CO 8, 96.

[68] *Ibid.*, 106.

[69] Luchesius Smits, *Saint Augustin dans l'oeuvre de Calvin*, I (Assen: van Gorcum, 1957), 109 characterizes the 1559 edition as the *Institutes* of predestination. For

not begin with predestination but with the word,[70] and warns that in investigating predestination one must not go beyond the oracles of God.[71] The Scripture teaches that God chooses Jacob and rejects Esau. Jacob does not differ from Esau in terms of merit which demonstrates that God chooses on the basis of his mercy alone. Calvin remarks in a Sermon on Jacob and Esau that God does not choose on the basis of our beautiful eyes (quand Dieu elit, ce n'est pas pour nous beaux yeux).[72] Thus of two men, indistinguishable in merit, God chooses one and rejects the other. God's unmerited grace shows mercy where he wills and God's merited punishment judges where he wills. "The predestination of God is truly a labyrinth from which the mind of man is wholly incapable of extricating itself."[73] This fact does not mean the doctrine should be passed

Calvin's relation to Augustine see pp. 45f., 61f. and 104f. Reg. Garrigou-Lagrange, *La Prédestination des Saints et la Grace* (Paris: Declée de Brouwer et Cie, 1935), p. 136 believes that Calvin surpasses Luther and Zwingli in drawing logical conclusions and emphasizes the differences between Calvin and Thomas. J. B. Mozley, *A Treatise on the Augustinian Doctrine of Predestination* (2nd ed.; New York: E. P. Dutton and Co., 1878), p. 267 and note 21 p. 393f. sees no substantial difference between Augustine, Thomas, and Calvin on the doctrine of predestination. It is true that Calvin thought that he was correcting rather than changing the Christian doctrine of predestination. It is also true that these thinkers each deny that God is responsible for evil and affirms that man is responsible for sin. However Calvin criticized Thomas on his view of predestination to grace (III. 22. 9 (OS IV, 389, 31f) and went beyond Augustine in the clarity with which he dealt with reprobation. C. Friethoff, "Die Prädestinationslehre bei Thomas von Aquin und Calvin,". *Divus Thomas*, III, 4 (1926), 71-91, 195-206, 280- 302, 445-446; deals carefully with the similarities and differences between Thomas and Calvin. According to Friethoff there is a significant agreement between Thomas and Calvin concerning God's sovereignty that God's foreknowledge of the good works of man is not the cause or occasion of predestination to blessedness, but rather that predestination to blessedness is the cause of good works. However, there is an irreconcilable difference that according to Thomas, God arranged that men receive eternal salvation as the reward of merits which is earned by grace. Calvin denies the meritorious character of works and asserts that man comes into the possession of eternal life only through the stages of good works (p. 206). Calvin insists that reward to good works means that by these stages of his mercy God completes our salvation. That is, works are an order of sequence rather than a cause (III, 18. 1 (OS IV, 270, 21f)).

[70] "Second Defense against Westphal" *Calvin's Tracts*, II, 343 (CO 9, 118f.). G. Oorthuys, "La Prédestination dans la Dogmatique Calviniste", in *De l'Élection Éternelle de Dieu* (Genève: Editions Labor: 1936), p. 213 wrote, "Calvin refused to be a philosopher. He wanted to be a theologian, a teacher of the Holy Scripture, purveyor of the Good News, preacher of Christ, witness of the faith, nothing more."

[71] Com. Rom. 11. 34 (CO 49, 231).

[72] Sermon on Jacob and Esau, CO 58, 1-26.

[73] Com. Rom. 9. 14 (CO 49, 180).

over in silence since it is revealed in Scripture, but Calvin cautions that one should not seek to know more about the subject than the Scripture teaches. The salvation or destruction of men depends on God's free election. In the case of the elect one is invited to contemplate the gracious mercy of God and in the case of the reprobate to acknowledge his righteous judgment. God is not indebted to any man and his kindness is free to bestow where he pleases. Therefore no higher reason than God's will can be suggested to account for election.

Calvin insists that God's will to salvation is revealed in the Scripture and that he has expounded the doctrine with due humility. As an idea in itself, predestination cannot be considered. Men cannot satisfy their curious questions about it, but to acknowledge this fact will restrain men from speculative conclusions about election and help them to maintain a proper modesty and humility. The Scripture teaches that God chooses those whom he determined to save and also those whom he devotes to destruction.

Calvin's conception of the relationship of man and God is not based on reason, in fact it is offensive to reason, but it is, for Calvin, consonant with the experience of dealing with God in everything. This notion was already expressed in the 1536 edition of the *Institutes*. Calvin enlarged his treatment of the doctrines of providence and predestination in the 1539 edition, concentrating primarily on defending his view of predestination, although it is difficult, if not impossible, to separate Calvin's doctrine of predestination from his view of special providence. At least it is clear that Calvin's position is not primarily the logical result of a conception of the abstract sovereignty and power of God (though these elements are not entirely absent), but an insistence that everything depends on God. This absolute and direct dependence of man upon God causes problems in the doctrine of man, but the alternative conception of some kind of relative independence of man from God causes problems for a doctrine of God's providence. Calvin could not believe that God, like a bird, anxious and uncertain, awaits the decisions of man.[74] However Calvin recognizes, at least most of the time, that his position is not a conclusion of reason based on God's sovereignty, but a confession of faith. This is made evident in the location of the doctrine of predestination in Calvin's soteriology following faith, regeneration, and justification.

---

[74] *Concerning Eternal Predestination*, p. 67 (CO 8, 294).

This intent was not followed by others. On Zanchi, Otto Gründler writes, "Thus it appears that for Zanchi the doctrine of predestination, from his first formulation of it until his last works, remained an integral part of the doctrine of God's essence."[75] Gründler concludes, "It is of no small significance that Zanchi should choose to discuss both providence and predestination as part and conclusion of his doctrine of God, thereby following the example of Thomas[76] rather than that of Calvin's final edition of the *Institutes*."[77]

It must be admitted that Calvin's doctrine of God's particular providence for the believer, and his view that election precedes faith raises the question, which Calvin did not, and perhaps could not, solve between supra- and infra-lapsarian points of view. H. Bois thinks that Calvin vacillates between a metaphysical point of view which was supralapsarian and an ethical view for which infra-lapsarianism would be sufficient.[78] The terms infra- and supra-lapsarianism were developed in the Arminian controversy. The infralapsarians hold that the sin of man results in the decree of reprobation. The supralapsarians maintain that the decree of reprobation, through God's permission, results in the sin of man. Calvin is usually claimed as supralapsarian and there is evidence to support this view.[79] However Calvin taught that sin was *positively* decreed (with the supralapsarians) when he was dealing with the doctrine of God; and *permissively* decreed (with the infralapsarians) when he was dealing with the doctrine of man. However neither position solves the problem of sin. The supralapsarian view logically requires that God is the author of sin, but both they, and Calvin, deny this result. The infralapsarian view of a *permissive* decree denies God's sovereignty if the emphasis is placed on permission while if the emphasis is placed on decree leads back to the supralapsarian position. Calvin can be claimed in some senses for both sides.

---

[75] Otto Gründler, *Die Gotteslehre Girolami Zanchis und ihre Bedeuting für seine Lehre von der Prädestination* (Neukirchen: Neukirchener Verlag des Erziehungs-vereins, 1965), p. 23. Hereafter cited as *Die Gotteslehre Zanchis*.

[76] In the *Summa Theologica* Thomas discusses providence (I[a], qu. 22) and predestination (I[a], qu. 23) in the doctrine of the unity of God, but also deals with predestination in III[a], qu. 24). See also *Summa Contra Gentiles*, III, chapters 64-113.

[77] Gründler, *Die Gotteslehre Zanchis*, p. 97. I have cited the German pagination, but used the original English text of Gründler's Princeton Th. D. dissertation.

[78] Bois, "La prédestination d'aprés Calvin," p. 670ff.

[79] Dowey, *The Knowledge of God in Calvin's Theology*, p. 213. Cf. Friethoff, "Die Prädestinationslehre bei Thomas von Aquin und Calvin," p. 448ff.

Calvin is not concerned with an abstract defense of the notion of the sovereignty of God and therefore not with a theoretical construction of its extent or its application. Calvin teaches a universal providence, but his exposition is focused on God's intensely loving care of his own. In this context his agreement with the philosophers' view of providence is more apparent than real. Further, Calvin does not move from a theological doctrine of universal providence to develop a view of special providence. Rather he begins with the particularity of God's providence which is clearly seen in his doctrine of eternal election, but also finds expression in his exposition of providence. The doctrine of predestination is the focus of a good deal of Calvin's attention and debates not because of its logicality but because of its practicality. That is, Calvin is not trying to create a system which a neutral observer would recognize as logical but to expound the Christian faith in God's providential care. The immediacy and singularity of this care leads Calvin to confess, "If our faith is not founded on the eternal election of God, it is certain that our faith would be ravaged by Satan at every moment."[80]

---

[80] Sermon on Eph. 1. 3-4 (CO 51, 265).

CONCLUSION

This study has undertaken to demonstrate that John Calvin belongs to that part of the Christian tradition which affirms philosophical achievements (Part One); that the way in which Calvin uses philosophical insights is instructive (Part Two); and that while Calvin sees distinctions among the classical philosophers, he is not an uncritical admirer of those whom he prefers (Part Three). Without doubt Calvin's knowledge of classical philosophy influences his thinking. It would be a mistake, therefore, to dismiss Calvin's references to philosophy as an inconsequential residue of his early humanistic training. It would be no less a mistake to think that Calvin provides a definitive synthesis of classical and Christian philosophy.

Calvin does, however, offer a model for dealing with philosophy. Calvin's remarks on Cicero and Seneca are certainly and his comments on Plato and Aristotle are almost certainly, derived from a first-hand acquaintance with their writings. But it is important to recognize that Calvin's use of philosophy is *historical* rather than *systematic!* Thus Calvin looks to philosophy for illustration of the truth rather than as a guide to it. By implication, Calvin answers the question, "What has Athens to do with Jerusalem?" by suggesting that Athens is valuable for the purpose of "in-Sight-seeing". Calvin may be less enthusiastic about philosophy than Erasmus, Zwingli, and Melanchthon, but he is also less hostile than Luther and Colet. Calvin is convinced that "None will ever be a good minister of the word of God except that he be a first-rate scholar."[1] As a first-rate scholar, Calvin refers to philosophic insights when it occurs to him to do so. Calvin does not attempt to deal with all the concerns of philosophy but rather with those which he thinks will illuminate his discussion of the Christian faith.

It has been said that Reformed theology consists of "the Bible, the whole Bible, and nothing but the Bible." Of course, Calvin affirms the centrality of the Scripture, but, by his example, he suggests that one who knows only the Bible does not even know the Bible. Calvin has a sound respect for the values of the theological tradition.

---

[1] CO 26, 406.

Moreover, he states that it is ungrateful to ignore the philosophers entirely or to despise the insights which God has granted to them. "[I]t is superstitious to refuse to make any use of secular authors. For since all truth is of God, if any ungodly man has said anything true, we should not reject it, for it also has come from God."[2]

---

[2] Com. Tit. 1. 12 (CO 52, 414-5).

BIBLIOGRAPHY

CALVIN SOURCES

Ioannis Calvini opera quae supersunt omnia. ed. by G. Baum, E. Cunitz, and E. Reuss, 59 vols. Brunsvigae: C. A. Schwetschke, 1863-1900.

Calvini opera selecta. ed. by P. Barth and W. Niesel, vols. I, III, IV, V. Monachii: Kaiser, 1926-1936.

Institution de la religion chrestienne. ed. by Jaques Pannier, Paris: Société les belles lettres, 1936 (1541 edition).

Predigten über das 2. Buch Samuelis. ed. by Hanns Rückert, Neukirchen Kr. Moers: Neukirchen Verlag des Erziehungsvereins, 1961.

CALVIN TRANSLATIONS

Calvin, John. "Academic Discourse." trans. and annotated by Dale Cooper and Ford Lewis Battles. *Hartford Quarterly.* 6 (Fall, 1965), 76-85.

——. *Institution of the Christian Religion* (1536). trans. and annotated by Ford Lewis Battles. Atlanta: John Knox Press, 1975.

Concerning the Eternal Predestination of God. trans. by J. K. S. Reid: London: James Clarke and Co., 1961.

Commentaries of John Calvin. various translators, 46 vols.; Edinburgh: The Calvin Translation Society, 1843-1855.

Calvin's New Testament Commentaries. ed. by David W. Torrance and Thomas F. Torrance, various translators, 12 vols.; Grand Rapids; William B. Eerdmans, 1959-1972.

Calvin's Commentary on Seneca's De Clementia. ed. and trans. by Ford Lewis Battles and André Malan Hugo, Leiden: E. J. Brill, 1969.

Institutes of the Christian Religion, ed. by John T. McNeill, trans. by Ford Lewis Battles, 2 vols. Philadelphia: The Westminster Press, 1960.

Letters of John Calvin. ed. by Jules Bonnet, trans. by David Constable, 2 vols. Edinburgh: Thomas Constable & Co., 1855.

Calvin: Theological Treatises. trans. by J. K. S. Reid, Philadelphia: The Westminster Press, 1954.

Tracts Relating to the Reformation. trans. by Henry Beveridge, 3 vols. Edinburgh: Calvin Translation Society, 1844-1851.

LITERATURE

Adams, James. *The Religious Teachers of Greece.* Edinburgh: T. & T. Clark, 1908.

Atwater, Lyman H. "Calvinism in Doctrine and Life." *Presbyterian Quarterly and Princeton Review,* 4 (Jan., 1875), 73-106.

Arnim, H. von. *Stoicorum Veterum Fragmenta.* Vol. III, Leipzig: B. C. Teubner, 1903.

Armstrong, Brian G. *Calvinism and the Amyraut Heresy: Protestant Scholasticism and Humanism in Seventeenth Century France.* Madison: University of Wisconsin Press, 1969.

Arnou, R. "Le Platonisme des Pères." in *Dictionnaire de Théologie Catholique,* XII, 2257-2392.

Augustine. "Against Julian." trans. by Matthew A. Schumacher, vol. 35, New York: Fathers of the Church, 1957.

——. "Against Two Letters of the Pelagians." *The Nicene and Post-Nicene Fathers.*

ed. by Philip Schaff, New York: The Christian Literature Company, 1887.
——. *Basic Writings of Saint Augustine.* ed. by Whitney J. Oates, trans. by G. C. Leckie, New York: Random House, 1948.
——. *The City of God.* trans. by Marcus Dods, Chicago: William Benton, 1952.
——. *On Christian Doctrine.* trans. by J. F. Shaw, Chicago: William Benton, 1952.
Autin, Albert. *L'Institution Chrétienne de Calvin.* Paris: Edgar Malfère, 1929.
Bailey, Cyril. *The Greek Atomists and Epicurus.* New York: Russell and Russell, 1928. reprinted 1964.
Bainton, Roland H. *Erasmus of Christendom.* New York: Charles Scribner's Sons, 1969.
——. *Studies on the Reformation.* Boston: The Beacon Press, 1962.
Barnikol, Hermann. *Die Lehre Calvins vom unfreien Willen und ihr Verhältnis zur Lehre der übrigen Reformatoren und Augustins.* Neuwied a. Rh.: Heusersche Buchdruckerei (J. Meincke), 1927.
Barth, Peter. *Das Problem der Natürlichen Theologie, Theologische Existenz Heute.* No. 18, Munich: Chr. Kaiser Verlag, 1927.
Battenhouse, Roy W. "The Doctrine of Man in Calvin and in Renaissance Platonism." *Journal of the History of Ideas,* IX (1948), 447-471.
Battles, Ford Lewis. "Against Luxury and License in Geneva, A Forgotten Fragment of Calvin." *Interpretation.* 19 (April, 1965), 182-202.
——. "The Sources of Calvin's Seneca Commentary." *Courtenay Studies in Reformation Theology,* I John Calvin, ed. by G. E. Duffield, Appleford: The Sutton Courtenay Press, 1966, pp. 38-66.
Bauke, Hermann. *Die Probleme der Theologie Calvins.* Leipzig: J. C. Hinrich'schen, 1922.
Bavinck, Hermann. *De Algemeene Genade.* Kampen: C. Ph. Zalman, 1894.
——. "Calvin and Common Grace." *Calvin and the Reformation,* ed. by W. P. Armstrong, New York: Fleming H. Revell Co., 1909.
——. "The Future of Calvinism." trans. by G. Vos, *Presbyterian and Reformed Review,* 5, 17 (Jan., 1894), 1-24.
Beard, Charles. *The Reformation of the Sixteenth Century in its Relation to Modern Thought and Knowledge* (The Hibbert Lectures of 1883). 5th ed. London: William and Norgate, 1907.
Beck, C. "Ueber die Prädestination, Die augustinische, calvinische, und lutherische." *Theologische Studien und Kritiken,* (1847). 70-128, 331-368.
Béné, Charles. *Érasme et Saint Augustin, ou l'Influence de Saint Augustin sur l'Humanisme d'Érasme.* Geneva: Librairie Droz, 1969.
Benoit, Jean Daniel. *Jean Calvin, la vie, l'homme, la pensée.* 2nd ed. n.p.: La Cause, 1948.
Berger, H. *Calvins Geschichtsauffassung.* Zurich: Zwingli-Verlag, 1955.
Bevan, Edwyn. *Stoics and Sceptics.* Cambridge: W. Heffer and Sons, 1913, reprinted 1965.
Beyerhaus, Gisbert. *Studien zur Staatsanschauung Calvins.* Berlin: Trowitzsche, 1910.
Bigg, C. *The Christian Platonists of Alexandria.* 2nd ed. Oxford: Clarendon Press, 1913.
Boas, George. *Rationalism in Greek Philosophy.* Baltimore: The Johns Hopkins Press, 1961.
Boettner, Lorraine. *The Reformed Doctrine of Predestination.* Grand Rapids: Wm. B. Eerdmans Publishing Company, 1932.
Bohatec, Josef. *Budé und Calvin: Studien zur Gedankenwelt des französischen Frühhumanismus.* Graz: Hermann Bohlaus, 1950.
——. *Calvin und das Recht.* Feudigen: Buchdruckerei u. Verlagsanstalt, 1934.
——. "Calvins Vorsehungslehre." *Calvinstudien: Festschrift zum 400 Geburts-*

tage Johann Calvin, ed. by J. Bohatec, Leipzig: Rudolf Haupt, 1909, pp. 409-425.

Bois, Henri. *La Philosophie de Calvin*. Paris: Librairie Générale et Protestante, 1919.

———. "La Prédestination d'après Calvin." *Études sur la Réforme*. Paris: Librairie Armand Colin, 1919, pp. 669-705.

Boisset, Jean. *Calvin et la Souveraineté de Dieu*. Paris: Editions Seghers, 1964.

———. *Sagesse et Sainteté dans la Pensée de Jean Calvin*. Paris: Université de France, 1959.

Bourrilly, E. "Humanisme et Réforme, La Formation de Jean Calvin." *Calvin et la Réforme en France*, Aix-en-Provence: Faculté Libre de Théologie Protestante, n.d. pp. 2-22.

Bray, John S. Theodore Beza's Doctrine of Predestination. Nieuwkoop: De Graff, 1975.

Breen, Quirinus. *Christianity and Humanism*. Grand Rapids: William B. Eerdmans, 1968.

———. *John Calvin: A Study in French Humanism*. 2nd ed. Hamden, Conn.: Archon Books, 1968.

Bréhier, Émile. "Y a-t-il une philosophie chrétienne?" *Revue de metaphysique et de Moralle*, 38 (1931), 133-62.

Budé, Eugène de. *Vie de Guillaume Budé*. Paris: Librairie Academique Didies, 1884.

Büsser, Fritz. *Calvins Urteil über sich selbst*. Zurich: Zwingli-Verlag, 1950.

Cadix, Marcel. "Le Calvinisme et l'expérience religieuse." *Études sur Calvin et la Calvinisme*, Paris: Exposition à la Bibliothèque Nationale à l'occasion du IVe Centenaire de *l'Instituion chrétienne*, 1935, pp. 173-187.

Caird, Edward. *The Evolution of Theology in the Greek Philosophers*. 2 vols. Glasgow: James MacLehose and Sons, 1904.

Calvetti, Carla. *La filosofia di Giovanni Calvino*. Milan: Società editrice vita e pensiero, 1955.

Casey, Robert P. "Clement of Alexandria and the Beginnings of Christian Platonism." *Harvard Theological Review*, 18, 1 (January, 1925), 39-101.

Chadwick, Henry. "Origen, Celsus, and the Resurrection of the Body." *Harvard Theological Review*, 41, 2 (April, 1948), 83-102.

Cherniss, Harold. *The Riddle of the Early Academy*. New York: Russell & Russell, 1962.

Clavier, Henri. *Études sur la Calvinisme*. Paris: Librairie Fischbacher, 1936.

Cochrane, Charles N. *Christianity and Classical Culture*. New York: Oxford University Press, 1940.

Cocker, B. F. *Christianity and Greek Philosophy*. New York: Harper and Bros., 1872.

Cornford, F. M. "The Division of the Soul." *The Hibbert Journal*, XXVIII, (Oct. 1929-July 1930), 206-219.

———. *From Religion to Philosophy*. New York: Harper and Bros., 1957.

———. *Plato's Theory of Knowledge*. London: Routledge and Kegan Paul, 1935.

Cullmann, Oscar. *Immortatality of the Soul or Resurrection of the Dead*. London: The Epworth Press, 1958.

Dakin, A. *Calvinism*. London: Duckworth, 1940.

Diès, A. *Platon*. Paris: Les Grands Cœurs, 1930.

———. *Autour de Platon*. Paris: Gabriel Beauchesne, 1927.

Demos, Raphael. *The Philosophy of Plato*. New York: Charles Scribner's Sons, 1939.

Dominicé, Max. *L'Humanité de Jésus d'après Calvin*. Paris: Je Sers, 1933.

Donnelly, John Patrick, "Calvinist Thomism." *Viator*, 7 (1976), 441-55.
——, "Italian Influences on the Development of Calvinist Scholasticism." *The Sixteenth Century Journal*, VII, 1 (April, 1976), 81-101.
Dooyeweerd, Herman. *In the Twilight of Western Thought*. Nutley, N. J.: The Craig Press, 1960.
Dörries, Hermann. "Calvin und Lefèvre." *Zeitschrift für Kirchengeschichte*, 44 (1925), 554-81.
Doumergue, Emile. "Calvin, Le Prédicateur de Genève." Address delivered at the 400th anniversary of Calvin's birth, July 2, 1909.
——. *Le Caractère de Calvin*. 2nd. ed. Neuilly: La Cause, 1931.
——. *Jean Calvin, Les Hommes et les choses de son temps*. 7 vols. Lausanne: G. Bridel et Cie, 1897-1927.
Dowey, Edward A. Jr. *The Knowledge of God in Calvin's Theology*. 2nd ed. New York: Columbia University Press, 1965.

Edelstein, Ludwig. *The Meaning of Stoicism*. Cambridge: Harvard University Press, 1966.
Edwards, D. Miall. *Christianity and Philosophy*. Edinburgh: T. & T. Clark, 1932.
Erasmus. *The Enchiridion of Erasmus*. ed. and trans. by Raymond Himelick, Bloomington, Ind.: Indiana University Press, 1963.
——. *Opera Omnia*. ed. by Jean Leclerc, 10 vols. Leiden: Petri vander Aa, 1703-6.

Feibleman, James K. *Religious Platonism*. London: George Allen and Unwin, 1959.
Ferguson, W. K. *The Renaissance in Historical Thought*. Boston: Houghton Mifflin Company, 1948.
Festugière, A. J. *Epicurus and His Gods*. trans. by C. W. Chilton, Cambridge: Harvard University Press, 1956.
Foster, Herbert Darling. "Liberal Calvinism; The Remonstrants at the Synod of Dort in 1618." *Harvard Theological Review*, 16, 1 (Jan., 1923), 1-37.
Forstmann, H. J. *Word and Spirit*. Stanford: Stanford University Press, 1962.
Friedländer, Paul. *Plato*. trans. by Hans Meyerhoff, New York: Pantheon Books, 1958.
Friethoff, C. "Die Prädestinationslehre bei Thomas Aquin und Calvin." *Divus Thomas*, III, 4 (1926), 71-91, 195-206, 280-302, 445-466.
Fuhrmann, Paul T. "Philosophical Elements in Early Reformed Theology." *Columbia Theological Seminary Bulletin*, 57, 3 (July, 1964), 46-61.
Fullerton, Kemper. "Calvinism and Capitalism." *Harvard Theological Review*, 21, 3 (July, 1928), 163-195.

Ganoczy, Alexandre. *Le Jeune Calvin: Genèse et Évolution de sa Vocation Réformatrice*. Wiesbaden: Franz Steiner Verlag, 1966.
——. *Calvin, Théologien de l'Église et du Ministère*. Paris: Unam Sanctam 48, 1964.
Garrigou-Lagrange, Reg. *La Prédestination des Saints et la Grace*. Paris: Desclée de Brouwer et Cie, 1935.
Gelder, H. A. Enno van. *The Two Reformations in the Sixteenth Century; A study of the Religious Aspects and Consequences of Renaissance and Humanism*. trans. by J. F. Finlay, The Hague: Martinus Nijhoff, 1961.
Gerber, Henri. La Doctrine Calvinienne de la Providence (Étude des chapitres XVI à XVIII du Ier Livre de l'*Institution chrétienne*. Unpublished dissertation, University of Neuchâtel. 1940.
Gerrish, B. A. *Grace and Reason*. Oxford: Clarendon Press, 1962.
——. " 'To the Unknown God': Luther and Calvin on the Hiddenness of God." *The Journal of Religion*, 53, 3 (July, 1973), 263-92.
Gilson, Etienne. *Christianity and Philosophy*. trans. by Ralph MacDonald, New York: Sheed and Ward, 1939.

——. *History of Christian Philosophy in the Middle Ages.* New York: Random House, 1955.

——. *Reason and Revelation in the Middle Ages.* New York: Charles Scribner's Sons, 1938.

——. *The Spirit of Medieval Philosophy.* trans. by A. H. C. Downes, New York: Charles Scribner's Sons, 1936.

Gloede, Günter. *Theologia Naturalis bei Calvin.* Stuttgart: Kohlhammer, 1935.

Göhler, Alfred. *Calvins Lehre von der Heiligung.* Munich: Chr. Kaiser Verlag, 1934.

Goldschmidt, Victor. *La Religion de Platon.* Paris: Presses Universitaires de France, 1949.

Goumaz, Louis. *La Doctrine du Salut d'après les Commentaires de Jean Calvin sur Le Nouveau Testament.* Paris: Librairie Fischbacher, 1917.

Grislis, Egil. "Calvin's use of Cicero in the *Institutes* I: 1-5—A Case Study in Theological Method." *Archiv für Reformationsgeschichte,* 62 (1971), 5-37.

Gründler, Otto. *Die Gotteslehre Girolami Zanchis und ihre Bedeutung für seine Lehre von der Prädestination.* Neukirchen: Neukirchener Verlag des Erziehungsvereins, 1965.

Guthrie, W. K. C. *The Greeks and Their Gods.* London: Methuen and Co., 1950.

Hall, Basil. *John Calvin, Humanist and Theologian.* London: The Historical Association, 1956.

Harbison, E. Harris. "Calvin's Sense of History." *Christianity and History.* Princeton: Princeton University Press, 1964, pp. 270-88.

——. *The Christian Scholar in the Age of the Reformation.* New York: Charles Scribner's Sons, 1965.

Harkness, Georgia. *John Calvin: The Man and His Ethics.* New York: Henry Holt and Company, 1931.

Hauck, Wilhelm-Albert. *Calvin und die Rechtfertigung.* Gütersloh: C. Bertelsmann, 1938.

——. *Die Erwählten, Prädestination und Heilsgewissheit nach Calvin.* Gütersloh: C. Bertelsmann, 1950.

——. *Vorsehung und Freiheit nach Calvin.* Gütersloh: C. Bertelsmann, 1947.

Heidtmann, Günter. "Die Philosophia Christi des Erasmus." *Evangelische Theologie,* 12 (1952-3), 187-198.

Heim, Karl. *Das Gewissheitsproblem in der systematischen Theologie bis zu Schleiermacher.* Leipzig: Hinrichs'schen, 1911.

Hendry, G. S. "Election and Vocation." *De l'Élection éternelle de Dieu,* Geneva: Éditions Labor, 1936, pp. 75-93.

Hessen, Johannes. *Platonismus und Prophetismus.* Munich: Ernst Reinhardt Verlag, 1955.

Hicks, R. D. *Stoic and Epicurean.* New York: Russell and Russell, 1910, reprinted 1962.

Highet, Gilbert. *The Classical Tradition.* London: Oxford University Press, 1949.

Higman, Francis M. *The Style of John Calvin in his French Polemical Treatises.* London: Oxford University Press, 1967.

Hoffman, Ernst. *Platonismus und Christliche Philosophie.* Zurich: Artemis-Verlag, 1960.

Hoyland, John S. *The Great Forerunner, Studies in the Inter-relation of Platonism and Christianity.* London: Constable and Co., 1928.

Hugo, André Malan. *Calvin en Seneca.* Groningen: J. B. Wolters, 1957.

Hunt, S. Leigh. "Predestination in the 'Institutes of the Christian Religion' 1536-1559." *Evangelical Quarterly,* IX (1937), 38-45.

Hunter, A. M. "The Education of Calvin." *Evangelical Quarterly,* IX (1937), 20-33.

——. "The Erudition of John Calvin." *Evangelical Quarterly,* XVIII (1946), 199-208.

——. *The Teaching of Calvin.* 2nd. ed. London: James Clarke and Company, 1950.

Ivánka, Endre V. *Plato Christianus.* Einsiedeln: Johannes Verlag, 1964.

Jacobs, Paul. *Prädestination und Verantwortlichkeit bei Calvin.* Neukirchen Kr. Moers: Buchhandlung des Erziehungsvereins, 1937.

Jaeger, Werner. *Aristotle, Fundamentals of the History of his Development.* trans. by Richard Robinson, 2nd ed., Oxford: Clarendon Press, 1948.

——. *Paideia: The Ideals of Greek Culture.* trans. by Gilbert Highet, 3 vols. New York: Oxford University Press, 1944.

——. "The Greek Ideas of Immortality." *Harvard Theological Review*, 52, 3 (July, 1959), 135-147.

——. *The Theology of the Early Greek Philosophers.* trans. by Edward S. Robinson, Oxford: Clarendon Press, 1947.

Jansen, John Frederick. *Calvin's Doctrine of the Work of Christ.* London: James Clarke and Co., 1956.

Jayne, Sears. *John Colet and Marsilio Ficino.* Aberdeen: Oxford University Press, 1963.

Kampschulte, F. W. *Johann Calvin: seine Kirche und sein Staat in Genf,* 2 vols. Vol. I, Leipzig: Duncker and Humblot, 1869. Vol. II, ed. by W. Goetz, Leipzig: Duncker und Humblot, 1899.

Klibansky, Raymond. *The Continuity of the Platonic Tradition during The Middle Ages.* London: Warburg, 1939.

Kohls, Ernst-Wilhelm. *Die Theologie des Erasmus.* 2 vols. Basel: Friedrich Reinhardt Verlag, 1966.

Kolfhaus, W. *Christusgemeinschaft bei Johannes Calvin.* Neukirchen: Kr. Moers: Buchhandlungen des Erziehungsvereins, 1939.

——. *Vom Christlichen Leben nach Johannes Calvin.* Neukirchen: Kr. Moers: Buchhandlungen des Erziehungsvereins, 1949.

Koopmans, Jan. *Das Altkirchliche Dogma in der Reformation.* trans. by H. Quistorp, Munich: C. Kaiser, 1938, tr. 1955.

Köstlin, J. "Calvins Institutio nach Form und Inhalt in ihrer geschichtlichen Entwicklung." *Theologische Studien und Kritiken,* (1868), 6-62, 410-486.

Kristeller, Paul Oskar. *The Classics and Renaissance Thought.* Cambridge: Harvard University Press, 1953.

Kroner, Richard. *Speculation in Pre-Christian Philosophy.* Philadelphia: The Westminster Press, 1956.

Krusche, Werner. *Das Wirken des Heiligen Geistes nach Calvin.* Göttingen: Vandenhoeck & Ruprecht, 1957.

Kuiper, Herman. *Calvin on Common Grace.* Grand Rapids: Smitter Book Company, 1928.

Kuyper, A. "Calvinism and Confessional Revision." trans. by G. Vos, *Presbyterian and Reformed Review*, 2, 71 (July, 1891), 369-99.

——. *De Gemeene Gratie.* 3 vols. Pretoria: Hoveker and Wormser, 1902-1904.

Lactantius. *The Divine Institutes. The Ante-Nicene Fathers.* ed. by Alexander Roberts and James Donaldson, VII, Buffalo: The Christian Literature Company, 1886.

Lecerf, A. *Études Calvinistes.* Paris: Delachaux et Niestle, 1949.

Leclerq, J. "Pour l'histoire de l'expression Philosophie chrétienne." *Mélanges de sciences religieuses,* IX (1952), 221-226.

Le Coq, John P. "Was Calvin a Philosopher?" *The Personalist,* XXIX (July, 1948), 252-260.

Lefranc, Abel. *Calvin et l'éloquence française.* Paris: Librairie Fischbacher, 1934.

——. *La Jeunesse de Calvin.* Paris: Librairie Fischbacher, 1888.

Levi, Anthony. "Humanist Reform in Sixteenth Century France." *Heythrop Journal*, 6 (1965), 447-64.

Linder, Robert D. "Calvinism and Humanism: The First Generation." *Church History*, 44, 2 (July, 1975), 167-181.

Little, David. "Calvin and the Prospects for a Christian Theory of Natural Law." *Norm and Context in Christian Ethics*. ed. by Gene H. Outka and Paul Ramsey, New York: Charles Scribner's Sons, 1968, pp. 175-97.

Lobstein, Paul. "La Connaissance Religieuse d'après Calvin." *Revue de Théologie et Philosophie*, Paris: Librairie Fischbacher, 1909.

Lovejoy, Arthur O. *The Great Chain of Being*. New York: Harper and Row, 1936.

Luther, Martin. *D. Martin Luthers Werke*, Kritische Gesammtausgabe. ed. by J. K. F. Knaake, G. Kawerau, E. Thiele, et. al. Weimar: H. Böhlau, 1883-

Lüttge, Willy. *Die Rechtfertigungslehre Calvins*. Berlin: Reuter und Reichard, 1909.

Lütgert, Wilhelm. "Calvins Lehre vom Schöpfer." *Zeitschrift für systematische Theologie*, 9 (1932), 421-440.

McClelland, Joseph C. "Calvin and Philosophy." *The Canadian Journal of Theology*, XI (Jan., 1965), 45-53.

———. "The Reformed Doctrine of Predestination, According to Peter Martyr." *Scottish Journal of Theology*, 8, 3 (Sept., 1955), 255-71.

McDonnell, Kilian. *John Calvin, the Church, and the Eucharist*. Princeton: Princeton University Press, 1967.

McNeill, John T. "Natural Law in the Theology of the Reformers." *Journal of Religion*, XXVI (July, 1946), 168-182.

Maier, Heinrich. *An der Grenze der Philosophie*. Tübingen: J. C. B. Mohr (Paul Siebeck), 1909.

Mann, Margaret. *Érasme et les Débuts de la Réforme Française*. Paris: Honoré Champion, 1934.

Marmelstein, J. W. *Étude comparative des textes latins et français de l'Institution de la Religion Chrétienne de Calvin*. Groningen: J. B. Wolters, 1921.

Masselink, William. *General Revelation and Common Grace*. Grand Rapids: Wm. B. Eerdmans, 1953.

Meeter, H. Henry. *Calvinism: An Interpretation of its Basic Ideas*. Grand Rapids: Zondervan Publishing House, 1939.

Merlan, Philip. *From Platonism to Neoplatonism*. 2nd. ed. The Hague: Martinus Nijhoff, 1960.

Meylan, E, F. "The Stoic Doctrine of Indifferent Things and the Conception of Christian Liberty in Calvin's *Institutio Religionis Christianae*." *The Romanic Review*, 28 (1937), 135-145.

Miles, Leland. *John Colet and the Platonic Tradition*. La Salle: Open Court, 1961.

Monod, Victor. "La Prédestination Calviniste." *Foi et Vie* (1909), 643-647.

More, Paul Elmer. *The Religion of Plato*. Princeton: Princeton University Press, 1921.

Mozley, J. B. *A Treatise on the Augustinian Doctrine of Predestination*. 2nd ed. New York: E. P. Dutton and Co., 1878.

Neeser, Maurice. *Le Dieu de Calvin*. Neuchâtel: Secrétariat de l'Université, 1956.

Neuenhaus, Johaness. "Calvin als Humanist." *Calvinstudien: Festschrift zum 400 Geburtstage Johann Calvin*, ed. by J. Bohatec, Leipzig: Rudolf Haupt, 1909, pp. 1-26.

Neuser, Wilhelm H. *Der Ansatz der Theologie Philipp Melanchthons*. Neukirchen: Verlag der Buchhandlung des Erziehungsvereins, 1957.

Niesel, Wilhelm. "Calvin wider Osianders Rechtfertigungslehre." *Zeitschrift für Kirchengeschichte*, 46, 3 (1927), 410-30.

——. *Die Theologie Calvins.* 2nd ed. Munich: Chr. Kaiser Verlag, 1957.

Nygren, Anders. *Agape and Eros.* trans. by Philip S. Watson, Philadelphia: The Westminster Press, 1953.

Obendiek, H. "Die Erfahrung in ihrem Verhältnis zum Worte Gottes bei Calvin." *Aus Theologie und Geschichte der Reformierten Kirche: Festgabe für E. F. Karl Müller.* Neukirchen: Buchhandlung des Erziehungsvereins Neukirchen, 1933, pp. 180-211.

Oberman, Heiko A. " 'Iustitia Christi' and 'Iustitia Dei': Luther and the Scholastic Doctrines of Justification." *Harvard Theological Review*, 59, 1 (Jan., 1961), 1-26.

——. "The 'Extra' Dimension in the Theology of Calvin." *Journal of Ecclesiastical History*, 21, 1 (Jan., 1970), 43-64.

O'Brien, George Dennis. "Prolegomena to a Dissolution to the Problem of Suffering." *Harvard Theological Review*, 57, 4 (Oct., 1964), 301-23.

Ong, Walter J. *Ramus, Method and Decay of Dialogue.* Cambridge: Harvard University Press, 1958.

Oorthuys, G. "La Prédestination dans la Dogmatique Calviniste." *De L'Élection Éternelle de Dieu*, Geneva: Éditions Labor, 1936, pp. 207-241.

Otten, Heinz. *Calvins Theologische Anschauung von der Prädestination.* Munich: Chr. Kaiser Verlag, 1938.

Pannier, Jaques. *Recherches sur la formation intellectuelle de Calvin.* Paris: Librairie Alcan, 1931.

Parker, T. H. L. *Calvin's Doctrine of the Knowledge of God.* Grand Rapids: Wm. B. Eerdmans, 1959.

Partee, Charles. "Calvin and Determinism." *Christian Scholar's Review*, 5, 2 (1975), 123-8.

——. "Calvin and Experience." *Scottish Journal of Theology*, 26, 2 (May, 1973), 169-181.

——. "The Revitalization of the Concept of 'Christian Philosophy' in Renaissance Humanism." *Christian Scholar's Review*, 3, 4 (1974), 360-9.

——. "The Soul in Plato, Platonism, and Calvin." *Scottish Journal of Theology*, 22, 3 (September, 1969), 278-295.

Pater, Walter. *Plato and Platonism.* New York: Macmillan and Company, 1893.

Patrologiae cursus completus, series Graeca, ed. by J. P. Migne, 167 vols. Paris: Garnier, 1857-1912.

Patrologiae cursus completus, series Latina. ed. by J. P. Migne, 221 vols. Paris: Garnier, 1878-1890.

Peyer, Étienne de. "Calvin's Doctrine of Providence." *Evangelical Quarterly*, X (1938), 30-44.

Potgieter, Frederick J. M. *Die Verhouding Tussen die Teologie en die Filosofie bij Calvijn.* Amsterdam: N.V. Noord-Hollandsche Uitgevers Maatschappij, 1939.

Quistorp, Hans. *Calvin's Doctrine of the Last Things.* trans. by Harold Knight, Richmond: John Knox Press, 1955.

Reardon, P. H. "Calvin on Providence: The Development of an Insight." *Scottish Journal of Theology*, 28, 6 (1975), 517-33.

Renaudet, Augustin. *Préréforme et Humanisme à Paris pendant les premières guerres d'Italie.* 2nd ed. Paris: Librairie D'Argences, 1953.

Reuter, Karl. *Das Grundverständnis der Theologie Calvins.* Neukirchen: Neukirchener Verlag des Erziehungsvereins, 1963.

Reverdin, Olivier. *La Religion de la Cité Platonicienne.* Paris: E. de Boccard, 1945.

Rice, Eugene F. Jr. "John Colet and the Annihilation of the Natural." *Harvard Theological Review*, 52, 3 (July, 1959), 135-147.

——. "The Humanist Idea of Christian Antiquity: Lefèvre d'Étaples and his Circle." *Studies in the Renaissance*, 9 (1962), 126-160.

Rich, Arthur, *Die Anfänge der Theologie Huldrych Zwinglis*. Zurich: Zwingli-Verlag, 1949.

Rist, Gilbert. "Modernité de la Méthode Théologique de Calvin." *Revue de Théologie et de Philosophie*. 3, 18 (1968), 19-33.

Ritschl, Albrecht. "Geschichtliche Studien zur Christlichen Lehre von Gott." *Jahrbücher für Deutsche Theologie*, (1868), 67-133.

Ritschl, Otto. *Dogmengeschichte des Protestantismus*. Vol. III. Göttingen: Vandenhoeck and Ruprecht, 1926.

Robin, Léon. *Platon*. Paris: Felix Alcan, 1935.

Rohde, Edwin. *Psyche*. trans. by W. B. Ellis, New York: Harcourt, Brace, and Company, 1925.

Ross, David. *Plato's Theory of Ideas*. Oxford: Clarendon Press, 1951.

Ross, W. D. *Aristotle*. 5th. ed. New York: Barnes and Noble, 1949.

Rutenber, Culbert Gerow. *The Doctrine of Imitation of God in Plato*. Morningside Heights, N.Y.: Kings Crown Press, 1946.

Santayana, George. *Platonism and the Spiritual Life*. New York: Charles Scribner's Sons, 1927.

Santmire, H. Paul. "Justification in Calvin's 1540 Romans Commentary." *Church History*, 33 (Sept., 1964), 294-313.

Schaerer, René. *Dieu, L'Homme et la Vie d'après Platon*. Neuchâtel: Editions de la Baconniere, 1944.

Schaff, Philip. "Calvin's Life and Labors." *Presbyterian Quarterly and Princeton Review*, 4 (April, 1875), 254-72.

Scheibe, Max. *Calvins Prädestinationslehre*. Halle: Max Niemeyer, 1897.

Schulze, Martin. *Calvins Jenseitschristentum in seinem Verhältnisse zu religiosen Schriften des Erasmus*. Gorlitz: Rudolf Dulfer, 1902.

——. *Meditatio futurae vitae*. Leipzig: Dieterich'sche, 1901.

Schweizer, Alexander. *Die Protestantischen Centraldogmen in ihrer Entwicklung innerhalb der Reformierten Kirche*. 2 vols. Zurich: Orell, Fuessli, 1854.

Seeberg, Reinhold. *Lehrbuch der Dogmengeschichte*. 5th ed. Basel: Benno Schwabe, 1960, IV, 2.

Shorey, Paul. *Platonism, Ancient and Modern*. Berkeley: University of California Press, 1938.

Seigel, Jerrold E. *Rhetoric and Philosophy in Renaissance Humanism*. Princeton: Princeton University Press, 1968.

Skemp, J. B. *The Theory of Motion in Plato's Later Dialogues*. Cambridge: Cambridge University, 1942.

Smith, John E. *The Analogy of Experience*. New York: Harper and Row, 1973.

——. *Experience and God*. London: Oxford University Press, 1968.

——. "The Permanent Truth in the Idea of Natural Religion." *Harvard Theological Review*, 54, 1 (Jan., 1961), 1-19.

Smith, Preserved. *Erasmus*. New York: Frederick Ungar Publishing Co., 1923, reprinted 1962.

Smits, Luchesius. *Saint Augustin dans l'œuvre de Calvin*. 2 vols. Assen: Van Gorcum, 1957.

Solmsen, Friedrich. *Plato's Theology*. Ithaca: Cornell University Press, 1942.

Souilhé, Joseph. *La Notion Platonicienne d'Intermédiaire dans la Philosophie des Dialogues*. Paris: Librairie Felix Alcan, 1919.

Spier, J. M. *What is Calvinistic Philosophy?* trans. by Fred H. Klooster, Grand Rapids: Wm. B. Eerdmans, 1953.

Spitz, Lewis W. *The Religious Renaissance of the German Humanists*. Cambridge: Harvard University Press, 1963.

Stauffer, Richard. *The Humanness of John Calvin*. trans. by George H. Shriver. Nashville: Abingdon Press, 1971.

Stocks, J. L. "Plato and the Tripartite Soul." *Mind*, XXIX (1915), 207-221.

The Stoic and Epicurean Philosophers. trans. by Cyril Bailey, ed. by Whitney J. Oates, New York: The Modern Library, 1940.

Strohl, Henri. "La Pensée de Calvin sur la Providence divine au temps où il était réfugie à Strasbourg." *Revue d'Histoire et de Philosophie Religieuses*, 22, 2-3 (1942), 154-69.

——. *La Pensée de la Réforme*. Paris: Delachaux et Niestle, 1951.

Taylor, Alfred Edward. *Platonism and its Influence*. New York: Longmans, Green and Co., 1927.

Temple, William. *Plato and Christianity*. London: Macmillan and Co., 1916.

Torrance, T. F. *Calvin's Doctrine of Man*. London: Lutterworth Press, 1949.

——. "Knowledge of God and Speech About Him according to John Calvin." *Regards Contemporains sur Jean Calvin*: Actes du Colloque Calvin, Strassbourg, 1964. Paris: Presses Universitaires de France, 1965, pp. 140-60.

Trinkhaus, C. "Renaissance Problems in Calvin's Theology." *Studies in the Renaissance*, III (1954), 59-80.

Van Til, Cornelius. *Common Grace*. Philadelphia: The Presbyterian and Reformed Publishing Company, 1947.

Vlastos, Gregory. "Reasons and Causes in the *Phaedo*." in *Plato* I. ed. by Gregory Vlastos, Garden City: Anchor Books, 1972, pp. 132-166.

Vogel, C. J. de. "On the Neoplatonic Character of Platonism and the Platonic Character of Neoplatonism." *Mind*, 62 (1953), 43-64.

Wallace, Ronald S. *Calvin's Doctrine of the Christian Life*. Grand Rapids: Wm. B. Eerdmans, 1959.

Warfield, B. B. *Calvin and Calvinism*. New York: Oxford University Press, 1931.

——. "Predestination in the Reformed Confessions." *Presbyterian and Reformed Review*, 12 (Jan., 1901), 49-128.

Webb, Clement C. J. *Studies in the History of Natural Theology*. Oxford, Clarendon Press, 1915.

Weber, Hans Emil. *Reformation, Orthodoxie und Rationalismus*. 2nd ed. Darmstadt: Wissenschaftliche Buchgesellschaft, 1937 (1966).

Wencelius, Léon. "Le Classicisme de Calvin." *Humanisme et Renaissance*, V (1938), 231-246.

Wendel, François. *Calvin, the Origins and Development of his Religious Thought*. trans. by Phillip Mairet, New York: Harper and Row, 1963.

Wernle, Paul. *Der Evangelische Glaube nach den Hauptschriften der Reformatoren*. Vol. III. Tübingen: J. C. B. Mohr (Paul Siebeck), 1919.

——. *Die Renaissance des Christentums im 16. Jahrhundert*. Tübingen: J. C. B. Mohr (Paul Siebeck), 1904.

Wesley, John. "Predestination Calmly Considered." *John Wesley: A Library of Protestant Thought*, ed. by Albert C. Outler, New York: Oxford University Press, 1964, 425-472.

Willis, E. David. *Calvin's Catholic Christology*. Leiden: E. J. Brill, 1966.

——. "Notes on A. Ganoczy's *Calvin Theologien de l'Église et du Ministère*." *Bibliothèque d'Humanisme et Renaissance*, XXX (1968), 185-198.

——. "Rhetoric and Responsibility in Calvin's Theology." in *The Context of Contemporary Theology: Essays in Honor of Paul Lehmann*. ed. by Alexander

J. McKelway and E. Davis Willis. Atlanta: John Knox Press, 1974, pp. 43-63.

Wolf, Hans Heinrich. *Die Einheit des Bundes: das Verhältnis von Altem und Neuem Testament bei Calvin.* Neukirchen: Kr. Moers, 1958.

Young, William. *Towards a Reformed Philosophy.* Grand Rapids: Piet Hein, 1952.

Zanta, Léontine. *Le Renaissance du Stoicisme au XVIe Siècle.* Paris: Édouard Champion, 1914.

Zeller, E. *Aristotle and the Earlier Peripatetics.* trans. by B. F. C. Costelloe and J. H. Muirhead, II, London: Longmans, Green and Co., 1897.

——. *Outlines of the History of Greek Philosophy.* trans. by L. R. Palmer, rev. by Wilhelm Nestle, 13th ed. London: Routledge and Kegan Paul, 1958.

——. *The Stoics, Epicureans and Skeptics.* trans. by Oswald J. Reichel, New York: Russell and Russell, 1962.

Zweig, Stefan. *The Right to Heresy* (German: *Castellio gegen Calvin*). trans. by Eden and Ceder Paul, New York: The Viking Press, 1936.

Zwingli, Huldreich. *Huldreich Zwinglis sämmtliche Werke (Corpus Reformatorum,* vols. 88-101). ed. by Emil Egli and Georg Finsler, Berlin: Hensius, 1905-59.

INDEX OF NAMES

INDEX OF SUBJECTS

Printed in the United Kingdom
by Lightning Source UK Ltd.
104956UKS00003B/226-270